OXFORD **READERS**

Class

Edited by Patrick Joyce

Oxford · New York

OXFORD UNIVERSITY PRESS

Oxford University Press, Walton Street, Oxford OX2 6DP

Oxford New York
Athens Auckland Bangkok Bogota Bombay
Buenos Aires Calcutta Cape Town Dar es Salaam
Delhi Florence Hong Kong Istanbul Karachi
Kuala Lumpur Madras Madrid Melbourne
Mexico City Nairobi Paris Singapore
Taipei Tokyo Toronto

and associated companies in
Berlin Ibadan

Oxford is a trade mark of Oxford University Press

British Library Cataloguing in Publication Data
Data available

Library of Congress Cataloging in Publication Data
Data available
ISBN 0-19-289252-5

10 9 8 7 6 5 4 3 2

Printed in Great Britain
on acid-free paper by
Bookcraft (Bath) Ltd
Midsomer Norton
Avon

OXFORD READERS WITHDRAWN

Class

Patrick Joyce is a lecturer in History at the University of Manchester. His most recent publications include *Visions of the People: Industrial England and the Question of Class 1840–1914* (CUP, 1991), and *Democratic Subjects: The Self and the Social in Nineteenth-Century England* (CUP, 1994).

before

For Tom Cleary

Acknowledgements

Conversations with the following of my colleagues at Manchester University helped shape the form of this reader, though the outcome is something none of them is responsible for: Huw Beynon, John Breuilly, Penny Harvey, Peter McMylor, Nicos Papastergiadis, Iorwerth Prothero, Wes Sharrock, and Rod Watson. I wish to thank all of these, and Nikolas Rose of Goldsmiths' College, University of London. I would also like to thank the Economic and Social Research Council of Great Britain for research support during the period when this book was being compiled.

Contents

Class

Introduction

In recent years the concept of class has come under increasing scrutiny as a means of explaining both the present and the past. The reasons for this lie in the profound economic, political, and intellectual changes marking our time. Class is seen by some to be unequal to the task of explaining our present reality. And this view has been of great effect among historians too: if class fails to interpret the present, perhaps it has not given an adequate account of our past either? The first purpose of this introduction is to describe these changes which have led to the questioning of class. Of course, there are many—and perhaps, indeed, the majority—for whom the utility of class has not come in question. For many of these the degree of social change in the present is seen to be exaggerated. There is, therefore, considerable debate (as well as a good deal of people talking past one another). This reader aims to reflect this debate, but also to add to it by bringing different positions together, and suggesting some new ways of proceeding.

Before turning to this, the changes that underlie this ferment can first be noted in terms of the economic. The restructuring of the western economies away from the manual and industrial sectors has meant the dwindling of the old manual 'working class', and the coming of what has been called 'post-industrial' society. Within industry itself, so-called 'post-Fordist' forms of production, and new forms of industrial management, have restructured the labour force in ways that have broken up traditional hierarchies and outlooks. Not least of these changes, particularly in Britain, has been the expansion of work, chiefly part-time, for women. There has been a corresponding rise of new sorts of employment of a non-manual kind, in the service sector chiefly. There has also been much under- and unemployment. The result has been not only a numerical decline of the manual working class, but the declining significance of manual work, and work in general, certainly of work as a fairly stable, uniform, lifelong experience.

These changes cannot be without considerable effect on people's sense of collective and personal identity. The shift in employment and investment from production to consumption industries has been paralleled by the rise of consumption itself as an arena in which people's desires and hopes are centred. The result, and it is one much argued about, is a movement from production to consumption as the new basis of structural divisions and unities in society, as well as of people's conceptions of themselves and the social order. All these changes, in turn, have become aspects of what some term the 'postmodern' condition of contemporary society: the extracts from Zygmunt Bauman and Alain Touraine that follow describe this conception of society. It is one marked by the 'de-centring' of power and authority of all sorts. Former centres are held to be in a process of disintegration, as a globalized economy and culture displace previous centres of power, above all the national state, its political institutions, its cultural norms and associations, and its integrated, autonomous economy.

Profoundly important changes in communication, especially in computer technology, produce standardization on the one hand, but, on the other, increasing capacities for the decentralization of power, for self-monitoring, and the 'reflexivity' of subjects. Authority is in this process repositioned on a subject who is now fated to be free. In advanced liberal capitalism the self is now the subject *and* the object of rule: we rule ourselves, the argument goes, and have real authority over our condition, but this rule is inseparable from the numerous other technologies of rule, built on the self, in which authority is shared with many authorities beyond ourselves. The self is a condition of both freedom and rule. Something of the prehistory and character of this condition of society, which need not of course be termed 'postmodern', is given in Rose's account below. The implications for how we describe social distinctions and social identities are clear, and greatly important. Old sources of identity, among which class has been greatly significant, have given place to radically new ones.

Much of this is reflected in the intellectual changes that have marked the challenge to class, and which have developed in very complex ways with these economic and social changes. Theoretical conceptions of identity as 'de-centred', mobile, and conflictual have developed alongside the idea that this is how identity actually is in the contemporary world. Economic and intellectual change in turn is paralleled in the political sphere. There the rise of the right and of neo-liberalism over the past decade and more, have brought with them ideologies in which the solidarities of class, with its communitarian sentiments, have retreated before the rhetoric of privacy, choice, freedom, and the individual (though, ironically, the submergence of class has frequently been accomplished by means of an unashamed appeal to the instincts and prejudices of class). Though a matter of some debate, the ideology of Thatcherism in the UK, just as of Reaganism in the USA, bit deeply into older sorts of class loyalty, themselves already loosened by change from other quarters. Of equal weight with neo-liberalism has been the rise of 'movement' or 'identity' politics, for instance the politics of environmentalism and consumerism, and of gender and ethnic groups. The identity that has not been registered in this 'identity' politics is class.

This absence is also evident in much new left thinking, particularly the vein of post-Marxism, where classes are seen to have been completely transformed by the combination of conditions described here. An 'objective' class interest is deemed illusory, and with it a politics based on class. The need to appeal to different sources of power and different social constituencies is apparent (indeed politics is now seen to involve the creation of such constituencies, not the reflection of them). What may loosely be termed French post-Marxism has had the greatest intellectual impact in bringing about the rethinking of class. In Baudrillard, for example, an analysis based on the production of goods gives way to one based on the exposure and critique of the production of meaning, for instance the 'simulation' and 'hyperreality' that characterize sustaining fictions of the 'real' within modern culture.[1] In Foucault power is theorized as omnipresent and de-centred, dispersed in all social relations and contexts. Thus conceived, it is cut off from a clear-cut social base, from which it is deemed to originate. Classes have formed the bases of power in the traditional sorts of analysis this approach so radically questions. The selections from Baudrillard, Foucault, and Castoriadis given here indicate this current, and Crompton provides a description of post-Marxism. Meiksins Wood offers a restatement of the traditional Marxist position. The most epochal change of all has been the collapse of world communism. With this has gone the retreat of intellectual Marxism, a retreat already under way under the impact of the corrosive critique of post-Marxism.

Politics and theoretical influences have overlapped here, and they have also done so in feminism. Feminism has offered as great a challenge as any to the sovereignty of class in social theory, sociology, and history. Feminist theory—and feminist political practice—has offered a new subject for analysis, and new conceptions of identity for our understanding, in the shape of gender. More than simply offering a new category—either competing with or complementing the old ones, such as class—feminist theory has problematized the whole question of what identity is. Gender identities are seen as historically and culturally formed. They are not the product of an external 'referent' which confers meaning on them, in this case a biologically given 'woman' which is a foundation for identity. Identity is seen as a product of conflicting cultural forces, and viewed as relational, composed of systems of difference. The debt here is to post-structuralist theory, and its conception of language not as the mirror of a world external to it, but as a conventional and arbitrary structure of relations and differences, the eventual shape of which is produced through cultural and power relations. This takes us directly into the area of the theoretical currents dissolving the earlier certainties of class, and it is worth dwelling briefly on some of the implications involved.[2]

[1] Jean Baudrillard, *The Mirror of Production*, trans. Mark Foster (Telos Press, St Louis, 1975).

[2] For readers in post-structuralist and postmodernist theory, and their implications, see Thomas Docherty (ed.), *Postmodernism: A Reader* (Harvester Press, Hemel Hempstead, 1993); Antony Easthope and Kate McGowan (eds.), *A Critical and Cultural Theory Reader* (Open University Press, Buckingham, 1992); *The Polity Reader in Social Theory* (Polity Press, Cambridge, 1994); Nicholas B. Dirks, Geoff Eley, Sherry B. Ortner (eds.), *Culture/Power/History: A Reader in Contemporary Social Theory* (Princeton University Press, 1994); Steven Seidman and David G. Wagner (eds.), *Postmodernism and Social Theory: The Debate over General Theory* (Basil Blackwell, Oxford, 1992).

The implications arising from feminist theory will already be apparent: if gender cannot be related to an external 'referent' which is its foundation, then the same would follow for class. It too cannot be referred to an external 'social' referent which is its foundation, origin, or cause. Post-structuralist, and what may loosely be called postmodernist, currents of thought question in a radical way the often unproblematically conceived relationship between the observer and his or her object of study, in which the 'reality' of that object is simply recuperated. In the model of much natural science, there is believed to be a clear distinction between the observer and the observed. Taking language as the model of culture in the ways indicated above this is seen not to be the case. In this model the purely formal nature of the relationship between words and things conceives of language not as passive and reflective, but as active and constitutive. Language does not correspond to a social referent outside it. The questions then become, 'How have the links between language and its object—the wrongly assumed social referent—become established, and how have the conventional operations of discourse been produced?'

These, eminently historical, questions produce a rather different agenda from more orthodox understandings of class. If the relation between the sign 'class' and its object is conventional how have these conventions been established? The search now is for how meanings have been historically produced by relations of power, rather than for 'external', or 'objective', class 'structures'. The further challenge to orthodox accounts—those in what I term the 'classical tradition' in this reader—concerns the central problem of structure and agency, or structure and action (as we shall see, there are many terms for a dualism that has been a central concern of sociology and history). If these new accounts are right it becomes very difficult to conceive of a structure of class relationships, or a structure of any set of 'social' variables (occupation, income, etc.), as lying objectively outside the agent or observer. This goes for the historical agent in the past, or the sociological one in the present, *and* for the observer who is employing a concept of structure in order to explain how society is organized or how people feel or behave. Agents in these accounts might usefully be seen as involved in creating or reproducing structure; observers as implicated in producing the knowledge they purport to be simply reporting on. Part B in this reader takes up some of the difficulties and possibilities in this knotty but quite crucial area of social theory, one full of significance for understanding class.

The third sort of challenge thrown up by this newer sort of theory concerns the nature of identity, touched upon in the consideration of feminist theory. If identity is composed through the relations of systems of difference, then it would seem to follow that it is marked by conflict, and is plural, diverse, and what was earlier termed 'mobile'. If identity is structured by a series of differences, which are in fact a series of exclusions (in order to be X, a concept of not-X is required), then what is excluded is in a sense present, if suppressed, in the identity in question. 'Deconstruction' is the name of the technique used to discern these suppressions. This view of identity is of something volatile and complex, one in which, in fact, many 'identities' press in and conflict with one another (we are men and women, parents and children, members of classes and nations, modernists and postmodernists, and so on). It is a view rather at odds with many accounts of class where class is seen as a relatively stable and coherent identity (the very notion of a class having an identity or conscious- ness involves a very strong emphasis on these characteristics). Class is regular- ly stacked up with similarly stable and coherent identities (race, gender, nation, and so on). Out of these rough-hewn blocks sociologies and histories continue to be made. Perhaps it is time for a more credible notion of identity in which competing possibilities press in and merge, and we are led to ask how these possibilities are composed into unities, fragile and conditional as these unities may sometimes be. This is a notion found to operate in some of the more recent historical writing on class considered in Parts C and F below, 'Class and the Historians' and 'The Language of Class'.

These ideas of identity involve notions of the human subject itself. Instead of a human subject conceived as the centre and organizing principle of multiple identities, human subjectivity is itself a historical creation. As Fou- cault has argued, the idea of a 'centred', controlling human subject is a product of the 'classical age', particularly the eighteenth century, when the emergence of 'man' in his true grandeur becomes evident. In this argument the western subject has been constructed as an 'individual'. Inseparable from this creation, and simultaneous with it, was the construction of 'the social'. The individual's rights, obligations, and conduct were measured in terms of a 'social' that both guaranteed their integrity and policed their excesses. Strategies for the im- plementation of the individual—such as the constitution of the 'private sphere'—were inseparable from strategies implementing the social—such as the constitution of the 'public sphere' and 'civil society'. Thus it is the case that the radical questioning of identity and subjectivity indicated here poses further fundamental problems for the concept of class: that concept is one of the consequences of the implementation of 'the social' considered here. 'Society' is the ground upon which the figures of class have been placed, figures that in some readings of class have become not only social 'facts' but collective actors on the historical stage. It is necessary to go back and look at the history of this ground if the figures that are its consequence are to be understood. This is something that is pursued in the part below called 'The History of the Social'. It is necessary to understand the historical forces at work composing the differences that in fact comprise the reality of the human subject. It is also necessary to inquire into the origins of that subject, origins that are inseparable from the coming of 'the social' and of 'social class'.

The implementation of the human subject and of society some have seen as the implementation of 'modernity'. From this point of view 'modernity' describes a subject and a society which, while eminently real in their consequences, are in fact themselves elements in a project. The project of modernity disguises the fact that 'individual' and 'society' are not real, 'object-ive' entities, but historical and normative creations, designed to handle the exigencies of political power and social order. This perspective on modernity, one of critique, can be understood as the perspective of postmodernity, though many of those involved in the critique would not describe themselves thus. From a postmodern viewpoint, 'class', alongside categories like 'society' and 'economy', but also 'reason', 'experience', 'the self', 'the body', indeed 'men' and 'women' themselves, are all seen as exemplifications of a modernity that takes them to be the 'foundations' of knowledge. Modernity has 'essentialized' these, reifying them as having an existence beyond their discursive and histor-ical creation. Modernism is also conceived as writing the 'grand narratives' of history in which these various essences play leading roles, for instance the narratives of science and progress, and of liberalism, socialism, and conser-vatism. From a modernist perspective these foundations and narratives confer power because they provide knowledge. In a postmodernist view power creates knowledge, not knowledge power.

This reader explains and reflects what is described here as the challenge to the concept of class. As indicated earlier, it also aims to bring different positions together, and to suggest new ways of proceeding. This active as well as passive role is necessary given that there is a tendency in history and sociology to maintain entrenched positions. While debate in some areas has been very vigorous, large areas of both disciplines have simply ignored the challenge of the new (this challenge in some manifestations has of course ignored the achievements of traditional approaches). In social history, for instance, the basic repertoire of concepts is still essentially Marxist. The discipline is eclectic in origin and development, but Marxism provided its common sense in its heyday, from the 1960s to the 1980s, when the British Marxist historians were dominant. However 'culturalist' this social history became, and Gramsci's culturalist Marxism was influential, the basic idea remained that class, power, and politics were rooted in the realities of material life, and that these realities could be uncovered by research. In turn, classes were seen to determine the fundamental shape of culture and 'consciousness'. These assumptions in-volved conceiving of society as a system, or totality. The ambition of social history was to be 'total history', a history truly reflecting the reality of society's totality. Of course, totalizing narratives like Marxism were best placed to prosecute this history of totalities. Knowledge in this dispensation was also about the possibility of transforming its object (classes, women, the op-pressed). The political aim was clear. The clearly different idea of the relation-ship between knowledge and its object in 'postmodernism', and its critique of the 'foundationalism' of materialism, and of society as a totality, has posed a profound challenge to traditional social (and labour) history. Despite this, *middle + bourgeoisie differences.*

much academic life continues in the old groove. Much the same might be said for considerable areas of sociology, where the critique of the 'modernist' project of sociology presented by Bauman and Touraine below falls on deaf ears. This critique involves an attack upon the concept of 'society' itself, particularly society viewed as a system and a totality (an idea still powerful in sociology as well as social history).

The challenges to class, however, are not only theoretical in character, and it is necessary to say something about historiographical developments before describing the general shape of this reader. I shall take the British case, though similar observations may be made about other instances of industrialization. The burden of much research on the 'Industrial Revolution' over the last decade or two presents a much more nuanced picture of change than previously obtained. The resulting notion of industrialization goes some way to removing two of the central pillars of the class interpretation of history. The notions of the hegemony of the industrial bourgeoisie and of the 'proletarianization' of the worker both come under scrutiny. The latter raises particularly difficult problems.

For some time the existence of marked differences within the English middle classes has been apparent. One analysis of these divisions has drawn attention to the considerable educational, religious, political, and economic differences between the industrial north of England and the south, centred upon London. The basic cleavage is held to be one between industrial and commercial–financial capital. The northern, industrial bourgeoisie are in fact seen to be the 'poor relations' of the class structure, deficient in both capital and power.[1] Though overdrawn,[2] this account has been influential, and has contributed to a sort of cultural analogue of this picture of structural differentiation. In this the middle class, especially the industrial and commercial sectors, are held to have been subordinated to gentry and aristocratic values from the mid-nineteenth century onwards. Britain is therefore characterized by the 'failed revolution' of the bourgeoisie, and this is the cause of its failure to modernize its institutions and economy. Martin J. Wiener's articulation of this position is considered below, an interpretation, curiously enough, that has received enthusiastic support from the extremes of right and left.[3] As the readings presented here indicate, differences within the 'middle class' were marked not only within the nation, but even within particular cities. This picture of differentiation has been complemented by a recognition of the

[1] W. D. Rubinstein, 'Wealth, Élites and the Class Structure of Modern Britain', *Past and Present*, 76 (Aug. 1977).

[2] S. Gunn, 'The "Failure" of the Victorian Middle Class: A Critique', in J. Wolff and J. Seed (eds.), *The Culture of Capital: Art, Power and the Nineteenth-Century Middle Class* (Manchester University Press, 1988).

[3] P. Anderson, 'Origins of the Present Crisis', *New Left Review*, 23 (Jan.–Feb. 1964); also *New Left Review*, 35 (Jan.–Feb. 1966); See also E. P. Thompson, 'The Peculiarities of the English', *The Socialist Register* (1965).

importance of non-industrial, indeed 'gentlemanly', capital, in industrialization;[1] also by an awareness of the nineteenth-century British state as markedly
neutral in negotiating the claims of labour and capital, and the competing
politics of class interest that emerged from time to time.

The notion of working-class formation in many accounts has turned upon
the idea of the progressive proletarianization of the workforce. In this process
ownership and control over production are held to have been lost, and the
worker is understood to be subject to the disciplines of waged labour. Workers
are subject to contract rather than to extra-economic compulsions and traditions. There is an attendant homogenization of the condition, and eventually
the outlook, of waged labour. This account of proletarianization is invariably
presented as the 'material' substratum upon which the emergence of the
working class in the nineteenth century is based. However, recent work on
eighteenth-century France suggests that many of the characteristics of proletarianization obtained much earlier.[2] Therefore, their advent can hardly be said
to mark what was in fact the much later development of class. Conversely, the
picture for nineteenth-century Britain reveals the 'combined and uneven'
development of different forms of production. This entailed the incorporation
of earlier forms of production, not their supersession. In supposedly 'modern'
forms of production, the 'archaism' of much organization is evident. Change
was not centred upon the factory and a factory proletariat. It did not involve a
linear process of the de-skilling of workers, but complex situations involving
the interdependence of labour and capital, and the independence as well as
dependence of labour. The worker had often more to lose than his, or her,
chains. Explanations of capital reveal a similar complexity. What stands revealed is a very diverse and fragmented labour force, and one to which the
term 'proletariat' does scant justice. Socio-economic 'class position' or situation emerges as so diverse and ambiguous from this account of proletarianization that the term 'working class' is exceedingly tenuous as an adequate
description of the supposedly resulting social formation. It can be defended
only with much qualification.[3]

Despite such knocks the category of class still continues to do sterling service
within historical writing. This is no less the case outside Marxism and the
social-historical paradigm described above. In liberal as well as right historiography class is still a central term. When its Marxist framework is challenged it
none the less remains unscathed as part of professional common sense. In fact
the more the notion is questioned the more it appears to become entrenched

[1] e.g. M. Daunton, ' "Gentlemanly Capitalism" and British Industry, 1820–1914', *Past and
Present*, 122 (Feb. 1989).

[2] Michael Sonenscher, *Work and Wages: Natural Law, Politics, and the Eighteenth-Century French
Trades* (Cambridge University Press, 1989).

[3] For a full discussion, Patrick Joyce, 'Work' in F. M. L. Thompson (ed.), *The Cambridge Social
History of Great Britain 1750–1950*, ii (Cambridge 1990), esp. 148–69; also P. Joyce, *Visions of the
People: Industrial England and the Question of Class* (Cambridge University Press, 1991), ch. 1.

in this common sense. Numerous textbooks and monographs continue to be written in which classes are still historical actors, albeit without their Marxist roles. As an adjective, 'class' sends millions marching up and down the pages of history, complete with 'working-class' values, 'middle-class' politics, and so on. As a narrative principle it gives these actors their various parts in the resulting stories of past and present. Perhaps it is time to look for new actors and new narratives?

The opening part of the reader concerns the classical inheritance and its development. Marx and Weber have been the outstanding figures in the theory of class, and Toennies's understanding of the difference between classes and estates has also been highly influential. The legacy of Marx and Weber is amply evident in the contemporary sociology of class, especially in Britain. Crompton provides an account of this legacy. The extracts from Marx reveal what has been perhaps the central problem in class theory since his time, namely the relationship between 'structure' and 'action', or between the 'objective' and 'subjective' aspects of class. In Marx this is the famous distinction between 'class-in-itself' and 'class-for-itself'. The former is apparent in the social relations a class enters into; the latter is realized, in terms of politics and struggle, as the consciousness a class comes to have of itself and other classes. Marx raises the problem of how the two are related but, as the quotation from the *Critique of Political Economy* shows, the difficulty tends to be resolved in favour of the priority of material life and production, of 'structure' in short. Consciousness is ultimately seen as a product of the conflict of 'the social forces of production' and 'the relations of production'. For Weber classes are not communities, and represent only possible, if frequent, bases for communal action. They are not conceived as collective actors, world-historical forces, in the sense of Marx. A contingent and not a necessary relation between structure and action or consciousness is indicated. None the less, the market is seen as determining the life chances around which classes may or may not arise. As in Marx, if seen differently, the structure of the economy comes to have a central role.

   Crompton's account makes plain just how significant the dualism of structure and action has been in contemporary debates on class. Arguments around these dualisms operate not only between different schools, but within them as well, for instance within Marxism. And they go to the heart of what society and sociology are. This part ends with contemporary restatements of traditional accounts. Crompton ends by questioning whether the terms of nineteenth-century sociology are really satisfactory in describing the nature of twentieth- and twenty-first-century society. This suggests the possibility of a radical rethinking of the founding propositions of sociology, and social theory more generally, 'society' and 'class' amongst them. Her account does not pursue this possibility, which is taken up in the second part here. There is a further, and equally searching, question to be asked of nineteenth-century sociology: if it does not describe contemporary reality can we be so sure it describes the reality of the times in which it grew up? And, just as the problem of structure and action is central to the debate on class, so it is central to this more general question of the categories of sociology and of thought about the nature of the social itself, which has of course been much wider in scope than sociology alone.

So much becomes evident in the second part, 'An Inheritance in Question'. The contributions of Bauman and Touraine offer categories of analysis which they regard as better able to interpret present reality than existing ones, class among them. Aiming to describe a world moving beyond the modern phase of society, they find the tools of a 'modernist' sociology inadequate. The new tools they offer involve the attempt to transcend the old dualism of structure and agency. However, it is distinctly possible that such tools may help us understand the past as well as the present, especially as the old ones—among them class—are indeed seen to be part of a normative, historically situated 'project', the project of modernity. Both see the ideas of sociology, and the idea of society, to be modelled on the nation state, and in this mode conceived of as a system or a totality. The notion of society is also seen to be related to the problem of how political order might be secured in a period of what was held to be unparalleled change (a period in fact marked by 'progress', or the more neutral term, 'modern'). Classes were integral to this understanding of 'society' as a structure: they were the content of which it was the form, or—conceived more actively—they were the motors by which this structure was changed. This is not to say that the terms of classical sociology did not sometimes, indeed often, well describe the society that produced them, but the point, precisely, is that they were a historical product and not a neutral analytic.

The same need to historicize the categories of the social employed in sociology is evident in the wider history of the social too, from which in fact sociology arose. This history extends far beyond the history of 'thought' alone, as Part D makes plain below. It was ultimately related to questions of politics, power, and economy. It can be traced in many ways, for instance through the history of the language of class itself, as in the final part of this reader. The history of the social also describes 'ideologies' of the social in their many forms: in the readings that follow the 'positions' outlined by Bauman and Touraine, the contributions of Baudrillard and Haraway indicate how the ideology of the social has been thought, and may be rethought.

What becomes evident in this second part therefore are new kinds of social category ('sociality' instead of 'society' for instance, or 'habitat' instead of 'class') which interpret the reality under consideration, including structure, as processual rather than static. The contributions of Giddens, Bourdieu, Castoriadis, and the ethnomethodologists point in this direction, as well as Bauman and Touraine: the general aim is to dissolve the old dualisms which have haunted our understanding of the past no less than the present. The conceptual understandings of these new sociologies are of great value for historical as well as sociological work. For instance, the refusal of Castoriadis to reduce the level of the symbolic to the structural and the functional emphasizes the creative activity of what he calls the 'social imaginary'. In order for 'social referents' to be thought of in the first place the social imaginary has to come into play. If this is so, it means that the 'reality' of fantasy and the unconscious must be insisted upon: in the past, and the present, those many forms of the symbolic, such as religion, which have been seen as epiphenomenal or secondary, now become fundamental to understanding how society has been conceived.

This kind of approach emphasizes the creative role of the symbolic and the agents who implement it. In these new sociologies in general the strong emphasis on process, on how 'societies' and the 'social' are put together in the first place by agents, tends to highlight 'sociation', rather than 'society'. What are the processes by which people are involved in, and create, the interpersonal and the inter-subjective, and what are the outcomes of this activity of 'sociation'? The phenomenological approach outlined by Sharruck and Watson in this second part opens up these matters: as well as histories and ideologies of the social one has something akin to an anthropology of the social (which of course some would itself call an ideology). What are the codes by which we give our being in the world with others meaning, and how have these codes become available to us? What are the categories in which these codes of 'sociation' deal? This second part thus introduces the whole question of how people *interpret* the social, and it serves as a context for Part E, called 'The Hermeneutics of the Social: Codes and Categories'.

The third part of the reader, 'Class and the Historians', begins to pursue more systematically the lines of inquiry opened up in the first two. The structure/agency question is raised directly in Thompson's writing, and in Katznelson's attempts to marry structural and cultural models of class. Dissatisfaction with the social-historical orthodoxy reflected in both historians' attempts to handle these matters is apparent in the other historians cited in this part. Their work has sometimes been described as an example of the 'linguistic turn' in history. The real problem in orthodox accounts is held to be accounting for how class actually becomes available as a basis for people's cognition and their action. The insights of the 'linguistic turn', evident in this introduction, are held to mark a powerful way forward here. This is apparent is Stedman Jones's discussion of the idea of 'experience', which, as he says, has been fundamental to traditional accounts of how structure and action are linked. In his account it is not structures of inequality, and the 'experience' that is held to reflect them, that produce politics. Rather, politics produces 'consciousness' and 'experience'. Rather than reflecting class experience and action politics actually makes class available as a principle for both. The historically situated discursive forms of politics ('language') articulate 'experience' and not vice versa. 'Language' is also to be understood as constituting terms analogous to 'experience', such as 'class interest'. 'Interests' do not pre-exist their discursive articulation.

However, the concept of 'language' itself raises many questions. Some of these are pursued in the contribution of Joan W. Scott, who wants to employ a much wider conception of language, and of politics, than Stedman Jones. It is the sort of wider understanding urged in this introduction. A concern with what is to be understood as 'language' is involved in Joyce's contribution too, as is the desire to work out some of the implications for historical work of the complex view of identity described above. Once the idea of 'class consciousness' as a unitary, coherent form of identity is questioned, then the matter of multiple identities and the relationships between them becomes apparent (alongside class we have 'people', gender, and so on). The social and labour history of France has been as much a source of innovation as that of Britain, and this is reflected in the contributions of Rancière and Sewell.

The fourth part, 'The History of the Social', first offers two possible models of how such a history might be written, those of Habermas and Foucault. Habermas retains a fairly traditional understanding of class, in which the bourgeoisie are seen as the principal historical agents of the late eighteenth-century 'public sphere'. Foucault's theorization of power breaks the link to a clear socio-economic 'centre' of power, as in a bourgeois class. He also 'decentres' the state as the agent of power, viewing it as dispersed in a 'micro-physics' of power evident everywhere, particularly in 'everyday life'. Though differing theoretically, they offer models for a history of the social that can both be drawn upon. The Foucauldian notion of 'governmentality' links the operation of rule at its many levels, especially in the form of the governmentality of liberalism in the west, from the late eighteenth century. This perspective enables 'society' and 'the social' to be understood in a particular, and revealing, way. The readings in this part show this, and the place of 'class' and 'classes' within the resulting understanding of the social.

The less protean understanding of power in Habermas produces a different angle from which to view class. Though near to traditional accounts in many ways, the Habermasian view opens up the whole question of the practical and discursive ways in which explanations and justifications for power and inequality have operated: to complement a history of class we need a history that deals with the 'public sphere' and 'civil society'. It was against the background of these that the figures of class, and of other social identities, took their meaning: 'class', 'people', 'citizenry', 'the public' (in its manifold forms), and 'public opinion' were only conceivable in terms of the legitimacy and explanation offered by these versions of the social. 'Class', 'people', and 'democracy', for instance, were the collective subjects made possible by notions of civil society. The question became, in whose name should society and the public speak and be organized. 'Classes' and 'peoples' were two of the answers forthcoming.

As suggested, the categories of the social were at once practical *and* discursive, legitimation and explanation always being prosecuted in terms of action (in the schoolroom of Foucauldian explanations, for example, or in the ideology and practice of the 'public sphere' evident in the history of the newspaper, say). It is necessary to emphasize this link to practice in the light of some portrayals of the views described here as purely 'discursive' or 'linguistic'. The inseparability of practice and discourse, and of the material and the symbolic, are also apparent in the penultimate part on the hermeneutics of the social. The readings here concern, broadly, the meanings brought to 'everyday life', and a heuristic distinction between these and those of the public and political spheres may be drawn (though, as has been seen, this distinction can only be a useful fiction, given the dispersal of the state into daily life). The distinction helps us think further about how 'everyday' codes and categories are related to more public sorts of discourse, for instance the 'language of class' as reflected in the final part of this reader. How did collective identities centred around classes, and other identities of a public sort, articulate with, or simply pass beyond, these less public codes? This problem is also taken up in the part on class and the historians.

These 'everyday' codes, this 'anthropology of the social', does not of course represent a bedrock of 'experience' upon which politics and class discourse could be based. Such codes are themselves the results of overlapping 'languages' and systems of value, which are articulated one with another in the same way as class and political appeals are articulated with all of them. There is a danger, not absent in the readings for this part, of making those many codes into something too coherent. None the less, what is striking here is how seemingly diverse and unconnected aspects of life can come together in meaningful patterns, and patterns that confer meanings. This is to say something about how people interpret their worlds. There is also the question of how observers interpret these acts of interpretation. The contributions on Germany and France in this section partly concern themselves with these hermeneutic operations of the observer: how are the writings and other traces of the past to be read? How can we get beyond the many layers of interpretation that overlie the original account, and, assuming we have done this, how do we locate that account as itself an active intervention in, and construction of, its own world?

Finally, 'The Language of Class' traces some episodes in the development of the terms of class themselves, terms that began to be used with greatly increasing frequency from the early nineteenth century. The meaning and contexts of class language are considered: the early nineteenth-century co-incidence of class language and rapid industrialization has tended to produce interpretations of class discourse which centre exclusively upon the economy and production. However, political and cultural contexts were perhaps more important at the time. Certainly, the meanings of class discourse have varied greatly over time, similarities of terminology masking these variations. A close and patient attention to these meanings can in fact be a very productive way forward: it reveals how understandings of class we have taken to be products of 'modern', industrial society in the nineteenth century may in fact be of relatively recent origin. Understandings that are the product of relatively recent times have mistakenly been imaged back upon the past, so distorting it. The very fact that these views of class have had such enormous influence is itself testimony to the practical and intellectual power of the discourse of class. Once they are themselves revealed to be in fact part of a long history of class discourse, and not an objective report on the past, it may at last be possible to move beyond them to new understandings.

The Classical Inheritance and its Development

I n *The Eighteenth Brumaire of Louis Bonaparte* Marx describes how the French peasantry, though showing similar conditions, do not enter into social relations with each other, and hence cannot form a class-in-itself. Workers, on the other hand, do experience a common set of social relations, though they may not yet evince the class-for-itself that eventuates from struggle and politics. Marx's *Poverty of Philosophy* describes the condition of the worker, while the *Manifesto* sets the world-historical scene in which the then present situation of the revolutionary 1840s may be understood: the various processes of class formation evident in the other three readings are seen in the *Manifesto* to be on the verge of a complete and revolutionary transformation of society. For Weber, on the other hand, classes may play a very significant role in modern society, but they are not the principles of historical transformation evident in Marx. Instead, not only is the inevitability of class denied, but class may often take second place to status. Status, associated with honour and prestige, may be uppermost, and may be in conflict with the demands of the market.

Toennies describes 'estates societies' in which status predominated. These societies are held to cohere around honour and status, whereas modern, 'class', societies cohere around contract, status tending to follow the market, rather than distinctions of honour evident in law, custom, and politics. The distinction is also viewed in terms of dualisms which have been of fundamental effect on social thought, especially sociology, those between *Gemeinschaft* and *Gesellschaft*, 'community' and 'society', 'traditional' and 'modern'. In Toennies estates tend to be seen as consensual and static, whereas class societies are marked by change, the 'organic' solidarities of tradition giving way to the more 'mechanical' social relations of modern societies. As the reading from Peter Burke in Part F reveals, this idealizes the nature of estates, taking them very much on their own valuations, the valuations very often of those wishing to justify existing relations of power. As Burke also argues, rather like E. P. Thompson in Part C, estates societies do not necessarily preclude class identities and conflict.

Crompton describes the seminal influence of Marx and Weber on the contemporary sociology of class. She describes 'class structure' approaches, but also approaches where structure and action are seen to be related. Instances of the latter are Gidden's explanation of how 'economic' relationships are 'translated' into 'non-economic' social structure, and Lockwood's view of particular societal images that 'correspond' to particular structural locations. In these and other examples where structure and action are seen as 'indivisible', it is arguable that traditional views of their separability are in fact not so absent as is assumed. The logic of 'translation' and 'correspondence', as in the two examples above, is, after all, one of the distinctiveness and separability of two elements, the elements of structure and action, or culture. The claim that they are 'indivisible' still seems to entail the conception they are none the less separate entities. Crompton's account does not enter into the more radical and sceptical questioning of traditional categories and dualisms evident in Part B. She rightly notes towards the end of her chapter that the debate on class is ultimately about the nature of social reality itself, but her account does not engage with this.

Nor do the two restatements of existing positions. The 'questionnaire' method of exploring identity apparent in Newby, *et al.*, exists on almost a different plane from the conceptions of identity-formation revealed in Part B (conceptions also described in the Introduction). This is a good example of approaches completely talking past one another. The challenges to class offered in the following part are perhaps somewhat stiffer than the opponents Newby, *et al.*, choose in the second half of this account, the 'liberal' view of Daniel Bell and the 'Marxist' one of Harry Braverman. Again, different traditions are not in communication with one another. As for the substantive findings of this Weberian approach, it may be a case of the same glass being half full from one viewpoint, and half empty from another. On their account, class structure and identity in Britain have been reconfigured in such a way as to make class a good deal less salient than previously. Finally, Meiksins Wood restates what she conceives of as an essential Marx against the depredations of 'New True Socialists'.[1] The 'working class' has an objective 'interest', which is 'by nature' opposed to capitalist exploitation. History is a 'determinate process', in which the 'collective actor' of the working class enacts its given historical role. Identities and interests are in this account given by the script of history. 'Discursive' interpretations of class, emphasizing that identities and interests are *not* pre-constituted, are dismissed as 'idealism'.

[1] This term is explained in the reading from Crompton that follows.

1 on Class

A spectre is haunting Europe—the spectre of communism. All the powers of old Europe have entered into a holy alliance to exorcise this spectre: Pope and Czar, Metternich and Guizot, French radicals and German police spies.

Where is the party in opposition that has not been decried as communistic by its opponents in power? Where the opposition that has not hurled back the branding reproach of communism against the more advanced opposition parties, as well as against its reactionary adversaries?

Two things result from this fact:

I. Communism is already acknowledged by all European powers to be itself a power.

II. It is high time that communists should openly, in the face of the whole world, publish their views, their aims, their tendencies, and meet this nursery tale of the spectre of communism with a Manifesto of the party itself.

To this end, communists of various nationalities have assembled in London and sketched the following Manifesto, to be published in the English, French, German, Italian, Flemish, and Danish languages.

1. Bourgeois and Proletarians[1]

The history of all hitherto existing society[2] is the history of class struggles.

Freeman and slave, patrician and plebeian, lord and serf, guild master[3] and journeyman, in a word, oppressor and oppressed, stood in constant opposition to one another, carried on an uninterrupted, now hidden, now open fight, a

[1] By 'bourgeoisie' is meant the class of modern capitalists, owners of the means of social production and employers of wage labour. By proletariat, the class of modern wage labourers who, having no means of production of their own, are reduced to selling their labour power in order to live. [Note by Engels to the English edition of 1888]

[2] That is, all *written* history. In 1847 the pre-history of society, the social organisation existing previous to recorded history, was all but unknown. Since then Haxthausen discovered common ownership of land in Russia, Maurer proved it to be the social foundation from which all Teutonic races started in history, and by and by village communities were found to be, or to have been, the primitive form of society everywhere from India to Ireland. The inner organisation of this primitive communistic society was laid bare, in its typical form, by Morgan's crowning discovery of the true nature of the *gens* and its relation to the *tribe*. With the dissolution of these primeval communities society begins to be differentiated into separate and finally antagonistic classes. I have attempted to retrace this process of dissolution in *Der Ursprung der Familie, des Privateigenthums und des Staats* [*The Origin of the Family, Private Property and the State*], second edition, Stuttgart, 1886 [Note by Engels to the English edition of 1888]

[3] Guild master, that is, a full member of a guild, a master within, not a head of a guild. [Note by Engels to the English edition of 1888]

fight that each time ended either in a revolutionary reconstitution of society at large or in the common ruin of the contending classes.

In the earlier epochs of history we find almost everywhere a complicated arrangement of society into various orders, a manifold gradation of social rank. In ancient Rome we have patricians, knights, plebeians, slaves; in the Middle Ages, feudal lords, vassals, guild masters, journeymen, apprentices, serfs; in almost all of these classes, again, subordinate gradations.

The modern bourgeois society that has sprouted from the ruins of feudal society has not done away with class antagonisms. It has but established new classes, new conditions of oppression, new forms of struggle in place of the old ones.

Our epoch, the epoch of the bourgeoisie, possesses, however, this distinctive feature: it has simplified the class antagonisms. Society as a whole is more and more splitting up into two great hostile camps, into two great classes directly facing each other: bourgeoisie and proletariat.

From the serfs of the Middle Ages sprang the chartered burghers of the earliest towns. From these burgesses the first elements of the bourgeoisie were developed.

The discovery of America, the rounding of the Cape opened up fresh ground for the rising bourgeoisie. The East Indian and Chinese markets, the colonisation of America, trade with the colonies, the increase in the means of exchange and in commodities generally, gave to commerce, to navigation, to industry an impulse never before known, and thereby, to the revolutionary element in the tottering feudal society, a rapid development.

The feudal system of industry, under which industrial production was monopolised by closed guilds, now no longer sufficed for the growing wants of the new markets. The manufacturing system took its place. The guild masters were pushed on one side by the manufacturing middle class; division of labour between the different corporate guilds vanished in the face of division of labour in each single workshop.

Meantime the markets kept ever growing, the demand ever rising. Even manufacture no longer sufficed. Thereupon steam and machinery revolutionised industrial production. The place of manufacture was taken by the giant, modern industry, the place of the industrial middle class by industrial millionaires, the leaders of whole industrial armies, the modern bourgeois.

Modern industry has established the world market, for which the discovery of America paved the way. This market has given an immense development to commerce, to navigation, to communication by land. This development has, in its turn, reacted on the extension of industry; and in proportion as industry, commerce, navigation, railways extended, in the same proportion the bourgeoisie developed, increased its capital, and pushed into the background every class handed down from the Middle Ages.

We see, therefore, how the modern bourgeoisie is itself the product of a long course of development, of a series of revolutions in the modes of production and of exchange.

Each step in the development of the bourgeoisie was accompanied by a corresponding political advance of that class. An oppressed class under the sway of the feudal nobility, an armed and self-governing association in the medieval commune;[1] here independent urban republic (as in Italy and Germany), there taxable 'third estate' of the monarchy (as in France), afterwards, in the period of manufacture proper, serving either the semi-feudal or the absolute monarchy as a counterpoise against the nobility, and, in fact, cornerstone of the great monarchies in general, the bourgeoisie has at last, since the establishment of modern industry and of the world market, conquered for itself, in the modern representative state, exclusive political sway. The executive of the modern state is but a committee for managing the common affairs of the whole bourgeoisie.

The bourgeoisie, historically, has played a most revolutionary part.

The bourgeoisie, wherever it has got the upper hand, has put an end to all feudal, patriarchal, idyllic relations. It has pitilessly torn asunder the motley feudal ties that bound man to his 'natural superiors', and has left remaining no other nexus between man and man than naked self-interest, than callous 'cash payment'. It has drowned the most heavenly ecstasies of religious fervour, of chivalrous enthusiasm, of Philistine sentimentalism in the icy water of egotistical calculation. It has resolved personal worth into exchange value and, in place of the numberless indefeasible chartered freedoms, has set up that single, unconscionable freedom—freetrade. In one word, for exploitation, veiled by religious and political illusions, it has substituted naked, shameless, direct, brutal exploitation.

The bourgeoisie has stripped of its halo every occupation hitherto honoured and looked up to with reverent awe. It has converted the physician, the lawyer, the priest, the poet, the man of science into its paid wage labourers.

The bourgeoisie has torn away from the family its sentimental veil, and has reduced the family relation to a mere money relation. [. . .]

We see then: the means of production and of exchange, on whose foundation the bourgeoisie built itself up, were generated in feudal society. At a certain stage in the development of these means of production and of exchange, the conditions under which feudal society produced and exchanged, the feudal organisation of agriculture and manufacturing industry, in one word, the feudal relations of property, became no longer compatible with the

---

[1] 'Commune' was the name taken, in France, by the nascent towns even before they had conquered from their feudal lords and masters local self-government and political rights as the 'third estate'. Generally speaking, for the economic development of the bourgeoisie, England is here taken as the typical country; for its political development, France. [Note by Engels to the English edition of 1888]

already developed productive forces; they became so many fetters. They had to be burst asunder; they were burst asunder.

Into their place stepped free competition, accompanied by a social and political constitution adapted to it, and by the economic and political sway of the bourgeois class.

A similar movement is going on before our own eyes. Modern bourgeois society with its relations of production, of exchange, and of property, a society that has conjured up such gigantic means of production and of exchange, is like the sorcerer who is no longer able to control the powers of the nether world whom he has called up by his spells. For many a decade past, the history of industry and commerce is but the history of the revolt of modern productive forces against modern conditions of production, against the property relations that are the conditions for the existence of the bourgeoisie and of its rule. It is enough to mention the commercial crises that by their periodic return put on its trial, each time more threateningly, the existence of the entire bourgeois society. In these crises a great part not only of the existing products but also of the previously created productive forces are periodically destroyed. In these crises there breaks out an epidemic that in all earlier epochs would have seemed an absurdity—the epidemic of overproduction. Society suddenly finds itself put back into a state of momentary barbarism; it appears as if a famine, a universal war of devastation had cut off the supply of every means of subsistence; industry and commerce seem to be destroyed; and why? Because there is too much civilisation, too much means of subsistence, too much industry, too much commerce. The productive forces at the disposal of society no longer tend to further the development of the conditions of bourgeois property; on the contrary, they have become too powerful for these conditions, by which they are fettered, and as soon as they overcome these fetters they bring disorder into the whole of bourgeois society, endanger the existence of bourgeois property. The conditions of bourgeois society are too narrow to comprise the wealth created by them. And how does the bourgeoisie get over these crises? On the one hand, by enforced destruction of a mass of productive forces; on the other, by the conquest of new markets, and by the more thorough exploitation of the old ones. That is to say, by paving the way for more extensive and more destructive crises, and by diminishing the means whereby crises are prevented.

The weapons with which the bourgeoisie felled feudalism to the ground are now turned against the bourgeoisie itself.

But not only has the bourgeoisie forged the weapons that bring death to itself; it has also called into existence the men who are to wield those weapons—the modern working class—the proletarians.

In proportion as the bourgeoisie, i.e., capital, is developed, in the same proportion is the proletariat, the modern working class, developed—a class of labourers, who live only so long as they find work, and who find work only so long as their labour increases capital. These labourers, who must sell themselves piecemeal, are a commodity, like every other article of commerce, and are consequently exposed to all the vicissitudes of competition, to all the fluctuations of the market. [. . .]

The lower strata of the middle class—the small tradespeople, shopkeepers, and retired tradesmen generally, the handicraftsmen and peasants—all these sink gradually into the proletariat, partly because their diminutive capital does not suffice for the scale on which modern industry is carried on, and is swamped in the competition with the large capitalists, partly because their specialised skill is rendered worthless by new methods of production. Thus the proletariat is recruited from all classes of the population. [. . .]

But with the development of industry the proletariat not only increases in number; it becomes concentrated in greater masses, its strength grows, and it feels that strength more. The various interests and conditions of life within the ranks of the proletariat are more and more equalised, in proportion as machinery obliterates all distinctions of labour and nearly everywhere reduces wages to the same low level. The growing competition among the bourgeois and the resulting commercial crises make the wages of the workers ever more fluctuating. The unceasing improvement of machinery, ever more rapidly developing, makes their livelihood more and more precarious; the collisions between individual workmen and individual bourgeois take more and more the character of collisions between two classes. Thereupon the workers begin to form combinations (trade unions) against the bourgeois; they club together in order to keep up the rate of wages; they found permanent associations in order to make provision beforehand for these occasional revolts. Here and there the contest breaks out into riots.

Now and then the workers are victorious, but only for a time. The real fruit of their battles lies not in the immediate result, but in the ever expanding union of the workers. This union is helped on by the improved means of communication that are created by modern industry and that place the workers of different localities in contact with one another. It was just this contact that was needed to centralise the numerous local struggles, all of the same character, into one national struggle between classes. But every class struggle is a political struggle. And that union, to attain which the burghers of the Middle Ages, with their miserable highways, required centuries, the modern proletarians, thanks to railways, achieve in a few years.

This organisation of the proletarians into a class, and consequently into a political party, is continually being upset again by the competition between the workers themselves. But it ever rises up again, stronger, firmer, mightier. It compels legislative recognition of particular interests of the workers by taking advantage of the divisions among the bourgeoisie itself. Thus the ten-hour bill in England was carried.

Altogether collisions between the classes of the old society further, in many ways, the course of development of the proletariat. The bourgeoisie finds itself involved in a constant battle. At first with the aristocracy; later on, with those portions of the bourgeoisie itself whose interests have become antagonistic to the progress of industry; at all times, with the bourgeoisie of foreign countries. In all these battles it sees itself compelled to appeal to the proletariat, to ask for its help, and thus to drag it into the political arena. The bourgeoisie itself, therefore, supplies the proletariat with its own elements of political and general education: in other words, it furnishes the proletariat with weapons for fighting the bourgeoisie.

Further, as we have already seen, entire sections of the ruling classes are, by the advance of industry, precipitated into the proletariat, or are at least threatened in their conditions of existence. These also supply the proletariat with fresh elements of enlightenment and progress.

Finally, in times when the class struggle nears the decisive hour, the process of dissolution going on within the ruling class, in fact within the whole range of old society, assumes such a violent, glaring character that a small section of the ruling class cuts itself adrift and joins the revolutionary class, the class that holds the future in its hands. Just as, therefore, at an earlier period, a section of the nobility went over to the bourgeoisie, so now a portion of the bourgeoisie goes over to the proletariat, and in particular a portion of the bourgeois ideologists, who have raised themselves to the level of comprehending theoretically the historical movement as a whole.

Of all the classes that stand face to face with the bourgeoisie today, the proletariat alone is a really revolutionary class. The other classes decay and finally disappear in the face of modern industry; the proletariat is its special and essential product.

The lower-middle class, the small manufacturer, the shopkeeper, the artisan, the peasant, all these fight against the bourgeoisie, to save from extinction their existence as fractions of the middle class. They are therefore not revolutionary, but conservative. Nay, more, they are reactionary, for they try to roll back the wheel of history. If by chance they are revolutionary they are so only in view of their impending transfer into the proletariat; they thus defend not their present but their future interests, they desert their own standpoint to place themselves at that of the proletariat.

The 'dangerous class', the social scum, that passively rotting mass thrown off by the lowest layers of old society, may, here and there, be swept into the movement by a proletarian revolution; its conditions of life, however, prepare it far more for the part of a bribed tool of reactionary intrigue.

In the conditions of the proletariat those of old society at large are already virtually swamped. The proletarian is without property; his relation to his wife and children has no longer anything in common with the bourgeois family relations; modern industrial labour, modern subjection to capital, the same in

England as in France, in America as in Germany, has stripped him of every trace of national character. Law, morality, religion are to him so many bourgeois prejudices, behind which lurk in ambush just as many bourgeois interests.

All the preceding classes that got the upper hand sought to fortify their already acquired status by subjecting society at large to their conditions of appropriation. The proletarians cannot become masters of the productive forces of society, except by abolishing their own previous mode of appropriation, and thereby also every other previous mode of appropriation. They have nothing of their own to secure and to fortify; their mission is to destroy all previous securities for, and insurances of, individual property.

All previous historical movements were movements of minorities, or in the interest of minorities. The proletarian movement is the self-conscious, independent movement of the immense majority, in the interests of the immense majority. The proletariat, the lowest stratum of our present society, cannot stir, cannot raise itself up, without the whole superincumbent strata of official society being sprung into the air.

Though not in substance, yet in form, the struggle of the proletariat with the bourgeoisie is at first a national struggle. The proletariat of each country must, of course, first of all settle matters with its own bourgeoisie.

In depicting the most general phases of the development of the proletariat, we traced the more or less veiled civil war, raging within existing society, up to the point where that war breaks out into open revolution, and where the violent overthrow of the bourgeoisie lays the foundation for the sway of the proletariat.

Hitherto every form of society has been based, as we have already seen, on the antagonism of oppressing and oppressed classes. But in order to oppress a class certain conditions must be assured to it under which it can, at least, continue its slavish existence. The serf, in the period of serfdom, raised himself to membership in the commune, just as the petty bourgeois, under the yoke of feudal absolutism, managed to develop into a bourgeois. The modern labourer, on the contrary, instead of rising with the progress of industry, sinks deeper and deeper below the conditions of existence of his own class. He becomes a pauper, and pauperism develops more rapidly than population and wealth. And here it becomes evident that the bourgeoisie is unfit any longer to be the ruling class in society, and to impose its conditions of existence upon society as an overriding law. It is unfit to rule because it is incompetent to assure an existence to its slave within his slavery, because it cannot help letting him sink into such a state that it has to feed him instead of being fed by him. Society can no longer live under the bourgeoisie: in other words, its existence is no longer compatible with society.

The essential condition for the existence, and for the sway of the bourgeois class, is the formation and augmentation of capital; the condition for capital is wage labour. Wage labour rests exclusively on competition between the labourers. The advance of industry, whose involuntary promoter is the bourgeoisie, replaces the isolation of the labourers, due to competition, by their revolutionary combination, due to association. The development of modern industry, therefore, cuts from under its feet the very foundation on which the bourgeoisie produces and appropriates products. What the bourgeoisie, therefore, produces, above all, is its own gravediggers. Its fall and the victory of the proletariat are equally inevitable.

* * * * * *

The small-holding peasants form a vast mass, the members of which live in similar conditions but without entering into manifold relations with one another. Their mode of production isolates them from one another instead of bringing them into mutual intercourse. The isolation is increased by France's bad means of communication and by the poverty of the peasants. Their field of production, the small holding, admits of no division of labour in its cultivation, no application of science, and, therefore, no diversity of development, no variety of talent, no wealth of social relationships. Each individual peasant family is almost self-sufficient; it itself directly produces the major part of its consumption, and thus acquires its means of life more through exchange with nature than in intercourse with society. A small holding, a peasant and his family; alongside them another small holding, another peasant and another family. A few score of these make up a village, and a few score of villages make up a Department. In this way the great mass of the French nation is formed by simple addition of homologous magnitudes, much as potatoes in a sack form a sack of potatoes. In so far as millions of families live under economic conditions of existence that separate their mode of life, their interests, and their culture from those of the other classes and put them in hostile opposition to the latter, they form a class. In so far as there is merely a local interconnection among these small-holding peasants and the identity of their interests begets no community, no national bond, and no political organisation among them, they do not form a class. They are consequently incapable of enforcing their class interest in their own name, whether through a parliament or through a convention. They cannot represent themselves, they must be represented. Their representative must at the same time appear as their master, as an authority over them, as an unlimited government power that protects them against the other classes and sends them rain and sunshine from above. The political influence of the small-holding peasants, therefore, finds its final expression in the executive power subordinating society to itself.

* * * * * *

The first attempts of workers to *associate* among themselves always take place in the form of combinations.

Large-scale industry concentrates in one place a crowd of people unknown to one another. Competition divides their interests. But the maintenance of wages, this common interest which they have against their boss, unites them in a common thought of resistance—*combination*. Thus combination always has a double aim, that of stopping competition among the workers, so that they can carry on general competition with the capitalist. If the first aim of resistance was merely the maintenance of wages, combinations, at first isolated, constitute themselves into groups as the capitalists in their turn unite for the purpose of repression, and in face of always united capital, the maintenance of the association becomes more necessary to them than that of wages. This is so true that English economists are amazed to see the workers sacrifice a good part of their wages in favour of associations, which, in the eyes of these economists, are established solely in favour of wages. In this struggle—a veritable civil war—all the elements necessary for a coming battle unite and develop. Once it has reached this point, association takes on a political character.

Economic conditions had first transformed the mass of the people of the country into workers. The combination of capital has created for this mass a common situation, common interests. This mass is thus already a class as against capital, but not yet for itself. In the struggle, of which we have noted only a few phases, this mass becomes united, and constitutes itself as a class for itself. The interests it defends become class interests. But the struggle of class against class is a political struggle.

In the bourgeoisie we have two phases to distinguish: that in which it constituted itself as a class under the regime of feudalism and absolute monarchy, and that in which, already constituted as a class, it overthrew feudalism and monarchy to make society into a bourgeois society. The first of these phases was the longer and necessitated the greater efforts. This too began by partial combinations against the feudal lords.

* * * * * *

[. . .] The general conclusion at which I arrived and which, once reached, became the guiding principle of my studies can be summarised as follows. In the social production of their existence, men inevitably enter into definite relations, which are independent of their will, namely relations of production appropriate to a given stage in the development of their material forces of production. The totality of these relations of production constitutes the economic structure of society, the real foundation, on which arises a legal and political superstructure and to which correspond definite forms of social consciousness. The mode of production of material life conditions the general process of social, political and intellectual life. It is not the consciousness of men that determines their existence, but their social existence that determines their consciousness. At a certain stage of development, the material productive forces of society come into conflict with the existing relations of production or—this merely expresses the same thing in legal terms—with the property relations within the framework of which they have operated hitherto. From forms of development of the productive forces these relations turn into their fetters. Then begins an era of social revolution. The changes in the economic foundation lead sooner or later to the transformation of the whole immense superstructure. In studying such transformations it is always necessary to distinguish between the material transformation of the economic conditions of production, which can be determined with the precision of natural science, and the legal, political, religious, artistic or philosophic—in short, ideological forms in which men become conscious of this conflict and fight it out. Just as one does not judge an individual by what he thinks about himself, so one cannot judge such a period of transformation by its consciousness, but, on the contrary, this consciousness must be explained from the contradictions of material life, from the conflict existing between the social forces of production and the relations of production. No social order is ever destroyed before all the productive forces for which it is sufficient have been developed, and new superior relations of production never replace older ones before the material conditions for their existence have matured within the framework of the old society. Mankind thus inevitably sets itself only such tasks as it is able to solve, since closer examination will always show that the problem itself arises only when the material conditions for its solution are already present or at least in the course of formation. In broad outline, the Asiatic, ancient, feudal and modern bourgeois modes of production may be designated as epochs marking progress in the economic development of society. The bourgeois mode of production is the last antagonistic form of the social process of production—antagonistic not in the sense of individual antagonism but of an antagonism that emanates from the individuals' social conditions of existence—but the productive forces developing within bourgeois society create also the material conditions for a solution of this antagonism. The prehistory of human society accordingly closes with this social formation.

[Karl Marx and Friedrich Engels, *The Manifesto of the Communist Party* (English edn.; London, 1888), selections from first section; Karl Marx, *The Eighteenth Brumaire of Louis Bonaparte*, in Marx and Engels, *Selected Works* (3 vols.; Progress Publishers, Moscow, 1969), 478–9; Karl Marx, *The Poverty of Philosophy* (International Publishers, New York, 1963), 172–3; Karl Marx, *A Contribution to the Critique of Political Economy*, trans. S. W. Ryazanskya, ed. M. Dobb (Lawrence and Wishart, London, 1971), 20–2.]

The Distribution of Power: Class, Status, Party

ECONOMICALLY DETERMINED POWER AND THE STATUS ORDER

The structure of every legal order directly influences the distribution of power, economic or otherwise, within its respective community. This is true of all legal orders and not only that of the state. In general, we understand by 'power' the chance of a man or a number of men to realize their own will in a social action even against the resistance of others who are participating in the action.

'Economically conditioned' power is not, of course, identical with 'power' as such. On the contrary, the emergence of economic power may be the consequence of power existing on other grounds. Man does not strive for power only in order to enrich himself economically. Power, including economic power, may be valued for its own sake. Very frequently the striving for power is also conditioned by the social honor it entails. Not all power, however, entails social honor: The typical American Boss, as well as the typical big speculator, deliberately relinquishes social honor. Quite generally, 'mere economic' power, and especially 'naked' money power, is by no means a recognized basis of social honor. Nor is power the only basis of social honor. Indeed, social honor, or prestige, may even be the basis of economic power, and very frequently has been. Power, as well as honor, may be guaranteed by the legal order, but, at least normally, it is not their primary source. The legal order is rather an additional factor that enhances the chance to hold power or honor; but it cannot always secure them.

The way in which social honor is distributed in a community between typical groups participating in this distribution we call the 'status order'. The social order and the economic order are related in a similar manner to the legal order. However, the economic order merely defines the way in which economic goods and services are distributed and used. Of course, the status order is strongly influenced by it, and in turn reacts upon it.

Now: 'classes', 'status groups', and 'parties' are phenomena of the distribution of power within a community.

DETERMINATION OF CLASS SITUATION BY MARKET SITUATION

In our terminology, 'classes' are not communities; they merely represent possible, and frequent, bases for social action. We may speak of a 'class' when (1) a number of people have in common a specific causal component of their life chances, insofar as (2) this component is represented exclusively by economic interests in the possession of goods and opportunities for income, and (3) is represented under the conditions of the commodity or labor markets. This is 'class situation'.

It is the most elemental economic fact that the way in which the disposition over material property is distributed among a plurality of people, meeting competitively in the market for the purpose of exchange, in itself creates specific life chances. The mode of distribution, in accord with the law of marginal utility, excludes the non-wealthy from competing for highly valued goods; it favors the owners and, in fact, gives to them a monopoly to acquire such goods. Other things being equal, the mode of distribution monopolizes the opportunities for profitable deals for all those who, provided with goods, do not necessarily have to exchange them. It increases, at least generally, their power in the price struggle with those who, being propertyless, have nothing to offer but their labor or the resulting products, and who are compelled to get rid of these products in order to subsist at all. The mode of distribution gives to the propertied a monopoly on the possibility of transferring property from the sphere of use as 'wealth' to the sphere of 'capital', that is, it gives them the entrepreneurial function and all chances to share directly or indirectly in returns on capital. All this holds true within the area in which pure market conditions prevail. 'Property' and 'lack of property' are, therefore, the basic categories of all class situations. It does not matter whether these two categories become effective in the competitive struggles of the consumers or of the producers.

Within these categories, however, class situations are further differentiated: on the one hand, according to the kind of property that is usable for returns; and, on the other hand, according to the kind of services that can be offered in the market. Ownership of dwellings; workshops; warehouses; stores; agricul- turally usable land in large or small holdings—a quantitative difference with possibly qualitative consequences; ownership of mines; cattle; men (slaves); disposition over mobile instruments of production, or capital goods of all sorts, especially money or objects that can easily be exchanged for money; disposi- tion over products of one's own labor or of others' labor differing according to their various distances from consumability; disposition over transferable mo- nopolies of any kind—all these distinctions differentiate the class situations of the propertied just as does the 'meaning' which they can give to the use of property, especially to property which has money equivalence. Accordingly, the propertied, for instance, may belong to the class of rentiers or to the class of entrepreneurs.

Those who have no property but who offer services are differentiated just as much according to their kinds of services as according to the way in which they make use of these services, in a continuous or discontinuous relation to a recipient. But always this is the generic connotation of the concept of class: that the kind of chance in the *market* is the decisive moment which presents a common condition for the individual's fate. Class situation is, in this sense, ultimately market situation. The effect of naked possession *per se*, which among cattle breeders gives the non-owning slave or serf into the power of the cattle owner, is only a fore-runner of real 'class' formation. However, in the cattle loan and in the naked severity of the law of debts in such communities for the first time mere 'possession' as such emerges as decisive for the fate of the individual; this is much in contrast to crop-raising communities, which are based on labor. The creditor-debtor relation becomes the basis of 'class situations' first in the cities, where a 'credit market', however primitive, with rates of interest increasing according to the extent of dearth and factual monopolization of lending in the hands of a plutocracy could develop. Therewith 'class struggles' begin.

Those men whose fate is not determined by the chance of using goods or services for themselves on the market, e.g., slaves, are not, however, a class in the technical sense of the term. They are, rather, a status group.

SOCIAL ACTION FLOWING FROM CLASS INTEREST

According to our terminology, the factor that creates 'class' is unambiguously economic interest, and indeed, only those interests involved in the existence of the market. Nevertheless, the concept of class-interest is an ambiguous one: even as an empirical concept it is ambiguous as soon as one understands by it something other than the factual direction of interests following with a certain probability from the class situation for a certain average of those people subjected to the class situation. The class situation and other circumstances remaining the same, the direction in which the individual worker, for instance, is likely to pursue his interests may vary widely, according to whether he is constitutionally qualified for the task at hand to a high, to an average, or to a low degree. In the same way, the direction of interests may vary according to whether or not social action of a larger or smaller portion of those commonly affected by the class situation, or even an association among them, e.g., a trade union, has grown out of the class situation, from which the individual may expect promising results for himself. The emergence of an association or even of mere social action from a common class situation is by no means a universal phenomenon.

The class situation may be restricted in its efforts to the generation of essentially *similar* reactions, that is to say, within our terminology, of 'mass behavior'. However, it may not even have this result. Furthermore, often merely amorphous social action emerges. For example, the 'grumbling' of workers known in ancient Oriental ethics: the moral disapproval of the work-master's conduct, which in its practical significance was probably equivalent to an increasingly typical phenomenon of precisely the latest industrial development, namely, the slowdown of laborers by virtue of tacit agreement. The degree in which 'social action' and possibly associations emerge from the mass behavior of the members of a class is linked to general cultural conditions, especially to those of an intellectual sort. It is also linked to the extent of the contrasts that have already evolved, and is especially linked to the transparency of the connections between the causes and the consequences of the class situation. For however different life chances may be, this fact in itself, according to all experience, by no means gives birth to 'class action' (social action by the members of a class). For that, the real conditions and the results of the class situation must be distinctly recognizable. For only then the contrast of life chances can be felt not as an absolutely given fact to be accepted, but as a resultant from either (1) the given distribution of property, or (2) the structure of the concrete economic order. It is only then that people may react against the class structure not only through acts of intermittent and irrational protest, but in the form of rational association. There have been 'class situations' of the first category (1), of a specifically naked and transparent sort, in the urban centers of Antiquity and during the Middle Ages; especially then when great fortunes were accumulated by factually monopolized trading in local industrial products or in foodstuffs; furthermore, under certain conditions, in the rural economy of the most diverse periods, when agriculture was increasingly exploited in a profit-making manner. The most important historical example of the second category (2) is the class situation of the modern proletariat.

TYPES OF CLASS STRUGGLES

Thus every class may be the carrier of any one of the innumerable possible forms of class action, but this is not necessarily so. In any case, a class does not in itself constitute a group (*Gemeinschaft*). To treat 'class' conceptually as being equivalent to 'group' leads to distortion. That men in the same class situation regularly react in mass actions to such tangible situations as economic ones in the direction of those interests that are most adequate to their average number is an important and after all simple fact for the understanding of historical events. However, this fact must not lead to that kind of pseudo-scientific operation with the concepts of class and class interests which is so frequent these days and which has found its most classic expression in the statement of a talented author, that the individual may be in error concerning his interests but that the class is infallible about its interests.

If classes as such are not groups, nevertheless class situations emerge only on the basis of social action. However, social action that brings forth class situations is not basically action among members of the identical class; it is an action among members of different classes. Social actions that directly determine the class situation of the worker and the entrepreneur are: the labor market, the commodities market, and the capitalistic enterprise. But, in its turn, the existence of a capitalistic enterprise presupposes that a very specific kind of social action exists to protect the possession of goods *per se* and especially the power of individuals to dispose, in principle freely, over the means of production: a certain kind of legal order. Each kind of class situation, and above all when it rests upon the power of property *per se*, will become most clearly efficacious when all other determinants of reciprocal relations are, as far as possible, eliminated in their significance. It is in this way that the use of the power of property in the market obtains its most sovereign importance.

Now status groups hinder the strict carrying through of the sheer market principle. In the present context they are of interest only from this one point of view. Before we briefly consider them, note that not much of a general nature can be said about the more specific kinds of antagonism between classes (in our meaning of the term). The great shift, which has been going on continously in the past, and up to our times, may be summarized, although at a cost of some precision: the struggle in which class situations are effective has progressively shifted from consumption credit toward, first, competitive struggles in the commodity market and then toward wage disputes on the labor market. The class struggles of Antiquity—to the extent that they were genuine class struggles and not struggles between status groups—were initially carried on by peasants and perhaps also artisans threatened by debt bondage and struggling against urban creditors. For debt bondage is the normal result of the differentia-tion of wealth in commercial cities, especially in seaport cities. A similar situ-ation has existed among cattle breeders. Debt relationships as such produced class action up to the days of Catilina. Along with this, and with an increase in provision of grain for the city by transporting it from the outside, the struggle over the means of sustenance emerged. It centered in the first place around the provision of bread and determination of the price of bread. It lasted throughout Antiquity and the entire Middle Ages. The propertyless flocked together against those who actually and supposedly were interested in the dearth of bread. This fight spread until it involved all those commodities essential to the way of life and to handicraft production. There were only incipient discussions of wage disputes in Antiquity and in the Middle Ages. But they have been slowly increas-ing up into modern times. In the earlier periods they were completely second-ary to slave rebellions as well as to conflicts in the commodity market.

The propertyless of Antiquity and of the Middle Ages protested against monopolies, pre-emption, forestalling, and the withholding of goods from the market in order to raise prices. Today the central issue is the determination of the price of labor. The transition is represented by the fight for access to the market and for the determination of the price of products. Such fights went on between merchants and workers in the putting-out system of domestic handi-craft during the transition to modern times. Since it is quite a general phe-nomenon we must mention here that the class antagonisms that are conditioned through the market situations are usually most bitter between those who actually and directly participate as opponents in price wars. It is not the rentier, the share-holder, and the banker who suffer the ill will of the worker, but almost exclusively the manufacturer and the business executives who are the direct opponents of workers in wage conflicts. This is so in spite of the fact that it is precisely the cash boxes of the rentier, the share-holder, and the banker into which the more or less unearned gains flow, rather than into the pockets of the manufacturers or of the business executives. This simple state of affairs has very frequently been decisive for the role the class situation has played in the formation of political parties. For example, it has made possible the varieties of patriarchal socialism and the frequent attempts—formerly, at least—of threatened status groups to form alliances with the proletariat against the bourgeoisie.

STATUS HONOR

In contrast to classes, *Stände* (*status groups*) are normally groups. They are, however, often of an amorphous kind. In contrast to the purely economically determined 'class situation', we wish to designate as *status situation* every typical component of the life of men that is determined by a specific, positive or negative, social estimation of *honor*. This honor may be connected with any quality shared by a plurality, and, of course, it can be knit to a class situation: class distinctions are linked in the most varied ways with status distinctions. Property as such is not always recognized as a status qualification, but in the long run it is, and with extraordinary regularity. In the subsistence economy of neighborhood associations, it is often simply the richest who is the 'chieftain'. However, this often is only an honorific preference. For example, in the so-called pure modern democracy, that is, one devoid of any expressly ordered status privileges for individuals, it may be that only the families coming under approximately the same tax class dance with one another. This example is reported of certain smaller Swiss cities. But status honor need not necessarily be linked with a class situation. On the contrary, it normally stands in sharp opposition to the pretensions of sheer property.

Both propertied and propertyless people can belong to the same status group, and frequently they do with very tangible consequences. This equality of social esteem may, however, in the long run become quite precarious. The equality of status among American gentlemen, for instance, is expressed by the fact that outside the subordination determined by the different functions of business, it would be considered strictly repugnant—wherever the old tradition still prevails—if even the richest boss, while playing billiards or cards in his club would not treat his clerk as in every sense fully his equal in birthright, but would bestow upon him the condescending status-conscious 'benevolence' which the German boss can never dissever from his attitude. This is one of the most important reasons why in America the German clubs have never been able to attain the attraction that the American clubs have.

In content, status honor is normally expressed by the fact that above all else a specific *style of life* is expected from all those who wish to belong to the circle. Linked with this expectation are restrictions on social intercourse (that is, intercourse which is not subservient to economic or any other purposes). These restrictions may confine normal marriages to within the status circle and may lead to complete endogamous closure. Whenever this is not a mere individual and socially irrelevant imitation of another style of life, but consensual action of this closing character, the status development is under way. . . .

ETHNIC SEGREGATION AND CASTE

Where the consequences have been realized to their full extent, the status group evolves into a closed caste. Status distinctions are then guaranteed not merely by conventions and laws, but also by religious sanctions. This occurs in such a way that every physical contact with a member of any caste that is considered to be lower by the members of a higher caste is considered as making for a ritualistic impurity and a stigma which must be expiated by a religious act. In addition, individual castes develop quite distinct cults and gods.

In general, however, the status structure reaches such extreme consequences only where there are underlying differences which are held to be 'ethnic'. The caste is, indeed, the normal form in which ethnic communities that believe in blood relationship and exclude exogamous marriage and social intercourse usually associate with one another. As mentioned before [ch. VI: vi: 6], such a caste situation is part of the phenomenon of pariah peoples and is found all over the world. These people form communities, acquire specific occupational traditions of handicrafts or of other arts, and cultivate a belief in their ethnic community. They live in a diaspora strictly segregated from all personal intercourse, except that of an unavoidable sort, and their situation is legally precarious. Yet, by virtue of their economic indispensability, they are tolerated, indeed frequently privileged, and they live interspersed in the political communities. The Jews are the most impressive historical example.

A status segregation grown into a caste differs in its structure from a mere ethnic segregation: the caste structure transforms the horizontal and unconnected coexistences of ethnically segregated groups into a vertical social system of super- and subordination. Correctly formulated: a comprehensive association integrates the ethnically divided communities into one political unit. They differ precisely in this way: ethnic coexistence, based on mutual repulsion and disdain, allows each ethnic community to consider its own honor as the highest one; the caste structure brings about a social subordination and an acknowledgement of 'more honor' in favor of the privileged caste and status groups. This is due to the fact that in the caste structure ethnic distinctions as such have become 'functional' distinctions within the political association (warriors, priests, artisans that are politically important for war and for building, and so on). But even pariah peoples who are most despised (for example, the Jews) are usually apt to continue cultivating the belief in their own specific 'honor', a belief that is equally peculiar to ethnic and to status groups. . . .

ECONOMIC CONDITIONS AND EFFECTS OF STATUS STRATIFICATION

. . . We have seen above that the market and its processes knows no personal distinctions: 'functional' interests dominate it. It knows nothing of honor. The status order means precisely the reverse: stratification in terms of honor and styles of life peculiar to status groups as such. The status order would be threatened at its very root if mere economic acquisition and naked economic power still bearing the stigma of its extra-status origin could bestow upon anyone who has won them the same or even greater honor as the vested interests claim for themselves. After all, given equality of status honor, property *per se* represents an addition even if it is not overtly acknowledged to be such. Therefore all groups having interest in the status order react with special sharpness precisely against the pretensions of purely economic acquisition. In most cases they react the more vigorously the more they feel themselves threatened. Calderon's respectful treatment of the peasant, for instance, as opposed to Shakespeare's simultaneous ostensible disdain of the *canaille* illustrates the different way in which a firmly structured status order reacts as compared with a status order that has become economically precarious. This is an example of a state of affairs that recurs everywhere. Precisely because of the rigorous reactions against the claims of property *per se*, the 'parvenu' is never accepted, personally and without reservation, by the privileged status groups, no matter how completely his style of life has been adjusted to theirs. They will only accept his descendants who have been educated in the conventions of their status group and who have never besmirched its honor by their own economic labor.

As to the general *effect* of the status order, only one consequence can be stated, but it is a very important one: the hindrance of the free development of the market. This occurs first for those goods that status groups directly withhold from free exchange by monopolization, which may be effected either legally or conventionally. For example, in many Hellenic cities during the 'status era' and also originally in Rome, the inherited estate (as shown by the old formula for placing spendthrifts under a guardian) was monopolized, as were the estates of knights, peasants, priests, and especially the clientele of the craft and merchant guilds. The market is restricted, and the power of naked property *per se*, which gives its stamp to class formation, is pushed into the background. The results of this process can be most varied. Of course, they do not necessarily weaken the contrasts in the economic situation. Frequently they strengthen these contrasts, and in any case, where stratification by status permeates a community as strongly as was the case in all political communities of Antiquity and of the Middle Ages, one can never speak of a genuinely free market competition as we understand it today. There are wider effects than this direct exclusion of special goods from the market. From the conflict between the status order and the purely economic order mentioned above, it follows that in most instances the notion of honor peculiar to status absolutely abhors that which is essential to the market: hard bargaining. Honor abhors hard bargaining among peers and occasionally it taboos it for the members of a status group in general. Therefore, everywhere some status groups, and usually the most influential, consider almost any kind of overt participation in economic acquisition as absolutely stigmatizing.

With some over-simplification, one might thus say that classes are stratified according to their relations to the production and acquisition of goods; whereas status groups are stratified according to the principles of their *consumption* of goods as represented by special styles of life. . . .

As to the general economic conditions making for the predominance of stratification by status, only the following can be said. When the bases of the acquisition and distribution of goods are relatively stable, stratification by status is favored. Every technological repercussion and economic transformation threatens stratification by status and pushes the class situation into the foreground. Epochs and countries in which the naked class situation is of predominant significance are regularly the periods of technical and economic transformations. And every slowing down of the change in economic stratification leads, in due course, to the growth of status structures and makes for a resuscitation of the important role of social honor.

PARTIES

Whereas the genuine place of classes is within the economic order, the place of status groups is within the social order, that is, within the sphere of the distribution of honor. From within these spheres, classes and status groups influence one another and the legal order and are in turn influenced by it. *'Parties'* reside in the sphere of power. Their action is oriented toward the acquisition of social power, that is to say, toward influencing social action no matter what its content may be. In principle, parties may exist in a social club as well as in a state. As over against the actions of classes and status groups, for which this is not necessarily the case, party-oriented social action always involves association. For it is always directed toward a goal which is striven for in a planned manner. This goal may be a cause (the party may aim at realizing a program for ideal or material purposes), or the goal may be personal (sinecures, power, and from these, honor for the leader and the followers of the party). Usually the party aims at all these simultaneously. Parties are, therefore, only possible within groups that have an associational character, that is, some rational order and a staff of persons available who are ready to enforce it. For parties aim precisely at influencing this staff, and if possible, to recruit from it party members.

In any individual case, parties may represent interests determined through class situation or status situation, and they may recruit their following respectively from one or the other. But they need be neither purely class nor purely status parties; in fact, they are more likely to be mixed types, and sometimes they are neither. They may represent ephemeral or enduring structures. Their means of attaining power may be quite varied, ranging from naked violence of any sort to canvassing for votes with coarse or subtle means: money, social influence, the force of speech, suggestion, clumsy hoax, and so on to the rougher or more artful tactics of obstruction in parliamentary bodies.

The sociological structure of parties differs in a basic way according to the kind of social action which they struggle to influence; that means, they differ according to whether or not the community is stratified by status or by classes. Above all else, they vary according to the structure of domination. For their leaders normally deal with its conquest. In our general terminology, parties are not only products of modern forms of domination. We shall also designate as parties the ancient and medieval ones, despite the fact that they differ basically from modern parties. Since a party always struggles for political control (*Herrschaft*), its organization too is frequently strict and 'authoritarian'. Because of these variations between the forms of domination, it is impossible to say anything about the structure of parties without discussing them first. Therefore, we shall now turn to this central phenomenon of all social organization.

Before we do this, we should add one more general observation about classes, status groups and parties. The fact that they presuppose a larger association, especially the framework of a polity, does not mean that they are confined to it. On the contrary, at all times it has been the order of the day that such association (even when it aims at the use of military force in common) reaches beyond the state boundaries. This can be seen in the [interlocal] solidarity of interests of oligarchs and democrats in Hellas, of Guelphs and Ghibellines in the Middle Ages, and within the Calvinist party during the age of religious struggles; and all the way up to the solidarity of landlords (International Congresses of Agriculture), princes (Holy Alliance, Karlsbad Decrees [of 1819]), socialist workers, conservatives (the longing of Prussian conservatives for Russian intervention in 1850). But their aim is not necessarily the establishment of a new territorial dominion. In the main they aim to influence the existing polity.

[*Economy and Society*, ed. Guenther Roth and Claus Wittich (2 vols.; University of California Press, Berkeley, 1978), ii. 926–40.]

3   on Estates and Classes

Estates and Classes Distinguished. Estates and *classes* are based essentially on the facts of economic life. But their significance reaches over into political affairs and into the intellectual and moral sphere. Estates are related to one another like the organs or limbs of a body; classes are engaged in a contractual relationship. Classes look upon, and deal with, one another basically as opponents, who depend on one another nevertheless as a result of their mutual interests. The relation between classes turns immediately into enmity, when one class is dissatisfied with the actions of the other, when one accuses the other that the contract is inadequate or that its conditions have not been observed. Hence, estates change over into classes, when they engage in hostile actions or engage one another in war. These struggles are class-struggles, even if they are called struggles between estates.

The terms 'estate' and 'class' are synonyms which are often used interchangeably. But scientifically we want to distinguish these terms in the sense that estates are conceived as *communal* and classes as *societal* collectives. Another distinction between them consists in the greater rigidity of estates as against the often extreme fluidity of classes. Classes are more frequently determined by environmental conditions, which as a rule remain the same for generations, but which become more changeable in the course of social development and which cause individuals and families to rise or fall to a higher or lower class. It follows, on the other hand, that an estate becomes more identical with a class, the more it disintegrates, i.e., the more the mobility of its members increases. But such a development, like all social developments is conditioned also by changes in political and in the moral and intellectual life, although these in turn are significantly influenced by economic changes.

Ruling estates. Ruling estates are the prototype of an estate with regard to their economic, political, intellectual as well as moral characteristics. We refer in the first place to those *ruling estates* (Herrenstände), whose activities are generally of a war-like or priestly character, and who lead and command as a result of these two functions. Estates are divided into a secular and a clerical nobility, although the term 'nobility' is reserved for the former. The great mass of the 'third' or peasant estate is distinguished from the ruling estates according to its principal occupation. The peasant-estate is distinguished in turn from the estate of craftsmen and of merchants, which together form the bourgeoisie (Bürgerstand) of the towns.

Consciousness of status is a characteristic feature of the ruling estates which is manifest in many different social forms. Pride is an especially noteworthy aspect of this consciousness, i.e. a heightened awareness of prominence, of adornment and beauty, which are based on one's estate, though in a petty way such pride may appear as vanity. Aristocratic pride is especially significant when it turns into an arrogance of status that has an effect on the lower strata of the governed.

The pride of the clerical estate is of a different kind, though it becomes more akin to aristocratic pride as its position and influence approximate or even surpass the great of this world and to the extent that the members of the two estates are in close personal contact. Clerical pride is derived from the presumption of, or the claim to, divine favor and grace. The priest feels that he is the representative, the delegate, and the confidant of supernatural powers and that he is sanctified by them. Therefore he wants to see his whole estate recognized as holy, even though his pride may be disguised by a denial of pride. By this humility the priest subordinates himself to those powers whose essence and will he alone can know and interpret, and if not completely then at any rate much better than laymen could. As a rule, this ability of the priest is readily trusted. In some relatively rare cases the priestly estate is not hereditary, but depends on election and appointment. In such cases its consciousness of status may be intensified, because members of the estate are not recruited through procreation and inheritance. Hence the replacement of the members seems to be based on supernatural sanction, in so far as it is attributed to the will of the Gods, or of one God.

Ever since the beginning of culture, this holiness of men has been the most favorable legitimation of authority, based on the reverence and humility of the people. And something of this holiness remains as an attribute of the secular ruling estates and their consummation, the princely estates and kingship. Closely related as it is to the original dignity of age, this element of holiness lends dignity to these estates. Moreover, the separation of the two ruling estates has always developed out of a common origin, from which they derived a natural affinity and a common magnificence, though this did not preclude the most bitter hatred and the most acute enmity between them. The self-assurance which goes with a consciousness of status has also moral effects, especially when it coincides with distinctive gifts. It can facilitate and encourage the development of these gifts, because it arouses and strengthens self-confidence and a sense of responsibility. This is true of all 'higher' social strata as well as of estates in the narrow sense; it is true, for example, of the remnants of the aristocracy, and of the higher clergy, in so far as they claim their high position or prove their worth through education and achievements. Analogous statements are true of any ruling class, in which the characteristics of the ruling estates are preserved.

Status honor. Estates in the sense discussed above have acquired a connotation of dignity as a result of the preeminent position of the ruling estates, both secular and clerical. And this connotation has been transferred easily to other preeminent strata or to their select circles, especially when these held privileged rank or possessed political power under the constitutional provisions of an estate-society. Ruling estates claim a special honor, they want to be honored by others. (A clerical estate wants to be honored especially by all those whom it represents and who worship its Gods.) But they also want to have and enjoy this honor as an inalienable possession that is highly prized, a *character indelebilis*. Consequently, ruling estates demand of their members that they should live in accordance with a code of honor which they must not violate, if they want to be members in good standing. A ruling estate, to a greater extent than other collectives, must insist on a certain level of performance and on a certain measure of dignified restraint. Such an estate must control or eliminate impropriety and lack of dignity, although it is not organized so as to decide and formally act upon the exclusion of people who belong to it. The public opinion of an estate has other means of ostracism; these are the more effective the more that opinion is unified.

But the conduct which is 'proper' to the estate (Standesgemäss) is not the only mark of honor. Another such mark is the way of life which is 'proper' in this sense and which finds special expression in the life of the family, especially as regards marriage. The nobility is *endogamous*. In the strict sense of the word, only the 'high' nobility is endogamous, and among its families hereditary succession depends upon equality of birth. But even the lower ranks of the nobility show the same tendency, although it is not really regarded as lacking in chivalrous conduct, if the family tree is 'enriched' by a bourgeois, or even by a Jewish marriage.

['Estates and Classes', repr. from *Class, Status, and Power: A Reader in Social Stratification*, ed. Reinhard Bendix and Seymour Martin Lipset (Free Press, Glencoe, 1953), 50–2.]

ROSEMARY CROMPTON

4 | The Development of the Classical Inheritance

Social class and inequality have been amongst the central topic areas within sociology. It is not surprising, therefore, that the investigation of these topics over the last half-century should have been significantly shaped by debates taking place within sociology itself. Thus debates in social theory, as well as the specific theoretical contributions of Marx and Weber, have also had an important impact on class analysis. Our primary objective in this chapter, besides giving an account of Marx's and Weber's classic contributions, will also be to explore the impact of these varying theoretical inputs on the developing project of class and stratification analysis.

The ideas of both Marx (1818–83) and Weber (1864–1920) continue to shape debates in class theory in the late twentieth century. However, their contributions have been extensively reinterpreted and reformulated by successive generations. Of these two 'founding fathers', Marx was primarily a political activist, rather than an academic social theorist. From the 1960s however, there was a revival of academic interest in Marx's work which ran in parallel with the theoretical debates in sociology which were then current—in particular, the developing critique of normative functionalism or the 'consensus' perspective.[1] As noted in chapter 1, the dominant paradigm in Anglo-American

[1] D. Lockwood, 'Social Integration and System Integration', in G. K. Zollschan and W. Hirsch (eds.), *Explorations in Social Change* (Houghton Mifflin, Boston, 1964).

sociology in the 1950s and early 1960s was essentially positivist—that is, it held to the view that sociology was the study of observable and objective *facts* about the social world (rather than being concerned with, for example, theological or metaphysical speculation). It had a primary emphasis on the study of social structures or systems, rather than individuals. As the conflict theorists claimed, it was also concerned mainly with the functional coherence and normative integration of these systems, rather than on any conflicts or underlying tensions.[1] These kinds of sociological assumptions had also shaped the 'industrial society' thesis—that is, the idea that all Industrial Societies have a tendency to converge in a similar, non conflictual, direction.[2]

However, critics of positivism argued that social facts cannot be objectively located but are theory-dependent—that is, they are not simply 'out there' but are socially *constructed*. Thus even apparently objective facts such as census data are gathered with regard to theoretical assumptions which may not always be explicit.[3] The emphasis on social structures or systems was criticized[4] for its 'oversocialized' conception of human nature. The recasting of social theory was associated with an increasing emphasis on the significance of human *action*; it was emphasized that human beings are neither (to paraphrase Garfinkel) structural nor cultural 'dopes' but act reflexively with the social world. The emphasis on stability and integration characteristic of normative functionalism was increasingly rejected in favour of perspectives that emphasized conflict rather than consensus, domination rather than integration.[5]

As a consequence of these theoretical debates, sociology has fragmented into a number of separate paradigms, and it would be difficult, if not impossible, to describe a 'dominant paradigm' in contemporary sociology. These divisions have also been reflected in its sub-fields. Despite a common origin in Marx's and Weber's work, therefore, class theory in sociology has developed in a number of different directions. However, these differences have not always been recognized explicitly by the many contributors to debates on 'class'.

Marxist theory has developed in a number of different directions. By the 1970s two broad strands within Marxism relating to the base/superstructure debate had emerged: 'humanist' and 'scientific'. As Urry[6] has noted, these perspectives incorporated 'the reproduction of certain of the problems which have already been encountered within orthodox sociology'. This was the structure/action

[1] N. J. Smelser (ed.), *Handbook of Sociology* (Sage, Beverly Hills, Calif., 1988), 10.
[2] C. Kerr, J. T. Dunlop, F. Harbison, and C. A. Myers, *Industrialism and Industrial Man* (Penguin, Harmondsworth, 1973 (1st edn. 1963)).
[3] B. Hindess, *The Use of Official Statistics in Sociology* (Macmillan, London, 1973).
[4] D. Wrong, 'The Oversocialized Conception of Man in Modern Sociology', repr. in L. A. Coser and B. Rosenberg (eds.), *Sociological Theory* (Collier-Macmillan, London, 1966).
[5] J. Rex, *Key Problems of Sociological Theory* (Routledge, London, 1961).
[6] J. Urry, *The Anatomy of Capitalist Societies* (Macmillan, London, 1981), 8.

debate; the contrast between, on the one hand, sociological perspectives which emphasize above all the significance of human action in explanations of social institutions and behaviour, and, on the other, the functionalist or structurally deterministic accounts of society which such 'action' approaches criticized. Thus, humanist Marxism—as in, for example, the work of Gramsci—tends to treat the base / superstructure distinction as a metaphor which can all too easily be interpreted in a deterministic fashion. Gramsci emphasizes the value of Marx's analysis as a means of developing a critique of the dehumanizing aspects of modern capitalism, a critique which will ultimately enable the actor to transcend his or her 'alienation'. As with the action approach within sociology, therefore, a central role is given to the human actor.

'Scientific' Marxism was the self-assigned label of French structural Marxists such as Althusser and Poulantzas.[1] Althusser argued that ideology and politics were not determined by the economy in a mechanistic fashion, as some simplistic interpretations of Marx had assumed. Rather, they should be seen as conditions of its existence and are therefore 'relatively autonomous'—although, echoing Engels, Althusser held that the economic was determinant in 'the last instance'. The work of Althusser and Poulantzas was also characterized by a distinctive epistomology, or view of how knowledge about the world is acquired. Knowledge about the social world, they argued, does not proceed by observation but through theoretical practice or 'science'—of which Marxism was an example. Thus we do not 'know' classes by observing them but rather through the theoretical identification and exploration of the class structure, and individuals are the 'bearers' or 'agents' of these structures of social relations. This approach, therefore, emphasizes above all the primacy of class *structures*. The manner in which individuals are distributed within these structures is, from their perspective, of comparatively minor importance; the important task for the 'scientist' is to identify the structure itself, and thus the 'real interests' of the individuals located within it. It is not difficult to see the parallels here with functionalism and structural over-determinism in sociology.[2] Different classes are being identified according to their 'functional' relationship to the capitalist mode of production as a whole, which is described in Marx's account of the exploitation of workers within the labour process and the way in which different groups in society are related to this process. [. . .]

Throughout the 1980s, the debate on class continued amongst Marxist theorists. Structural Marxism no longer has the influence it once had—at least in part, it may be suggested, because of the electoral failure of the left.[3] The

[1] L. Althusser, *For Marx* (Penguin, Harmondsworth, 1969); N. Poulantzas, *Classes in Contemporary Capitalism* (New Left Books, London, 1975).

[2] R. W. Connell, 'A Critique of the Althusserian Approach to Class', in A. Giddens and D. Held (eds.), *Classes, Power and Conflict: Classical and Contemporary Debates* (Macmillan, London, 1982).

[3] See T. Benton, *The Rise and Fall of Structural Marxism* (Macmillan, London, 1984), preface.

revival of Marxist scholarship in the 1960s was accompanied by an optimism of the left which persisted throughout much of the 1970s; the 1980s, however, witnessed the electoral rise of the 'New Right'—Thatcherism in Britain, Reaganomics in the United States. Political theorists including Przeworski, Laclau and Mouffe, and Wood have examined the possibilities of the development of socialism in these changing circumstances.[1] Much of this discussion has involved a fundamental revision of some basic Marxist political ideas. In particular, the central place which the proletariat or working class occupied within Marx's original writings has increasingly been called into question. Wood has summarized these revisions (which she describes, somewhat scathingly, as the 'New True Socialism') as follows: first, the absence of revolutionary politics amongst the working class reflects the fact that there is no necessary correspondence between economics and politics (that is, the link between base and superstructure is regarded as tenuous, even non-existent). Second, there is no necessary or privileged relation between the working class and socialism, and so a socialist movement can be constituted independently of class (thus dissolving the link between 'class' and 'consciousness'). Third, socialism is in any case concerned with universal human goals which transcend the narrowness of material class interests and may therefore address a broader public, irrespective of class. Thus the struggle for socialism can be conceived as a plurality of democratic struggles, bringing together a variety of resistances to many forms of inequality and oppression (for example, those associated with gender and race).[2]

These arguments amongst Marxist theoreticians have not been directly concerned with class and stratification research in sociology, but they have nevertheless had a considerable impact. The American sociologist Erik Wright has systematically developed both his 'class map' as well as his strategy of analysis in response to inputs from these sources.[3] More generally, however, it may be suggested that contemporary debates within theoretical Marxism have contributed to more general arguments to the effect that 'class' is no longer a relevant analytical concept as far as late twentieth-century societies are concerned. [. . .]

Class and Sociology after the Second World War

Sociology had been well established in the United States before the Second World War, and 'At the beginning of the 1950's . . . one could find large numbers of studies dealing with almost every aspect of behaviour in the United

---

[1] A. Przeworski, *Capitalism and Social Democracy* (Cambridge University Press, Cambridge, 1985); E. Laclau and C. Mouffe, *Hegemony and Socialist Strategy* (Verso, London, 1985); E. M. Wood, *The Retreat from Class* (Verso, London, 1986).

[2] *The Retreat from Class*, 3–4.

[3] E. O. Wright (ed.), *The Debate on Classes* (Verso, London, 1989).

States. No other society had ever been subjected to such detailed examination'.[1] A strong tradition of empirical investigation, therefore, was well established. This included research into social stratification, which, as in studies such as Warner's (1963) anthropologically inspired *Yankee City* series, first published in the 1940s, had a focus on occupational inequality and social mobility, often in small communities. As has frequently been noted, in such studies 'class' was in practice operationalized as a particular dimension of the Weberian concept of *status* in that it was mainly concerned with social prestige rankings within the community. The pre-eminent sociological theorist in the United States was Talcott Parsons; as we have seen, the structural functionalism which characterized his approach had a tendency to emphasize order rather than conflict, and thus to direct attention away from the conflict and tensions in society which are the focus of *class* (rather than status) analyses.

Sociology in Britain was relatively underdeveloped in the 1950s, and had been much influenced by the Fabian tradition of social improvement and reform. Thus a preoccupation with structured social inequality had always been present. An example of this tradition of British 'political arithmetic' would be Glass's *Social Mobility in Britain* (1954), which had used an occupational (class) scale in its statistical analyses of social mobility. In Continental Europe, sociology was more deeply rooted in established traditions of philosophy and social theory. The intellectual diaspora which was a consequence of the rise of fascism brought many European scholars to the United States and Britain, and with it an increasing emphasis on the significance of 'theory' in sociology.

The first major reader in the field of class and stratification to be published in English after the Second World War—*Class, Status, and Power* (1953; 2nd edn 1967), edited by Reinhard Bendix and S. M. Lipset—reflected this mingling of influences. The title was itself a deliberate play on a section of Weber's *Economy and Society*, 'Class, Status, and Party', which had been of considerable significance in shaping sociological thinking about 'social class'. The importance of the distinction between economic 'classes' and 'status rankings' (the latter describes the conceptualization of class in Warner's research) was increasingly emphasized. However, the use of the 'class' concept by the different contributors to the volume reflected the variety of definitions of the term which has been noted in chapter 1. Thus there were a number of papers on class theory, in which class was discussed as an abstract force, whereas other contributions used the same word—class—to describe the occupational aggregates used in, for example, empirical analyses of residential segregation. Bendix and Lipset's article—'Karl Marx's theory of social classes'[2]—provided a guide to 'Marx on Class' for a whole generation of sociology students in Britain and America.

[1] R. Bendix and S. M. Lipset, *Class, Status, and Power* (Routledge, London, 1967), 6.
[2] Ibid.

THE DEVELOPMENT OF THEORETICAL ACCOUNTS OF THE 'CLASS
STRUCTURE'

The way was laid open, therefore, for the analytical and empirical separation
of class structure from consciousness, between the 'objective' and 'subjective'
dimensions of class. Within this emerging sociological perspective, a central
problem is that of the identification of the class structure itself—that is, a
structure of positions which may or may not give rise to consciousness. The
structure of employment became the major focus of such attempts. Dahrendorf's work was extremely influential in this regard. In *Class and Class Conflict
in an Industrial Society* he drew upon the work of both Marx and Weber in
deriving the class structure from 'positions in associations (i.e. occupations)
co-ordinated by authority and defin[ing] them by the "characteristic" of participation in or exclusion from the exercise of authority'. In a similar vein to
Bendix and Lipset, he argued that: 'The general theory of class consists of two
analytically separable elements: the theory of class formation and the theory of
class action, or class conflict'.[1] This analytical separation of 'structure' and
'action', as we have seen, assumed considerable significance in sociology and
has had an important effect on the development of 'class analysis'.

Like Dahrendorf, Lockwood in *The Blackcoated Worker* drew upon the theoretical analyses of both Marx and Weber in his now-classic 1958 account of a
'socio-economic group that had long been a discomfort to Marxist theory: the
growing mass of lower non-manual or white-collar employees'.[2] (In fact,
Lockwood's research focused entirely on clerical occupations.) He described
'class position' as including three factors: 'market situation', that is 'the economic position narrowly conceived, consisting of source and size of income,
degree of job-security, and opportunity for upward occupational mobility';
secondly, 'work situation', or 'the set of social relationships in which the
individual is involved at work by virtue of his position in the division of
labour'; and finally, 'status situation', or the position of the individual in the
hierarchy of prestige in the society at large. Experiences originating in these
three spheres were seen as the principal determinants of class consciousness.[3]
It must be emphasized that Lockwood was not merely concerned descriptively
to locate clerks in the class structure. A central issue in his work is the question
of class consciousness and action, and he explored the differentiation of 'class
situation' within the clerical category which gave rise to variations in the level
and type of trade union activity amongst clerical workers—trade unionism is
here being viewed as an expression of class consciousness. Nevertheless, in
maintaining, like Dahrendorf, an analytical separation between structure (for-

---

[1] R. Dahrendorf, *Class and Class Conflict in an Industrial Society* (Routledge, London, 1959), 151;
153.
[2] D. Lockwood, *The Blackcoated Worker* (Allen & Unwin, London, 1958; 2nd edn. 1989), 218.
[3] 1989 edn., 15–16.

mation) and action, Lockwood's work left open the possibility that 'class analysis' might come to have a primary focus on one or the other. Although, therefore, his original work was concerned as much with the question of class consciousness and action as it was with class structure, it might be suggested that one of its enduring legacies has been that it provided, within a neo-Weberian framework, the means to locate empirically particular groups of occupations within the 'class structure'. In particular, Lockwood's concepts of 'work' and 'market' situation have been the key elements in Goldthorpe's development of a theoretical class scheme, based on the occupational structure, which has been widely employed in empirical research.[1]

Another sociologist who has devoted considerable effort to the theoretical identification of a 'class structure' within the structure of employment relationship is the American Marxist E. O. Wright. Wright's initial development of his Marxist 'class map', which was to become the basis of his own theoretical class scheme, was carried out in a conscious dialogue with structural Marxism.[2] Thus although Wright's theoretical perspectives are clearly very different from those of Lockwood, Dahrendorf, Goldthorpe and other 'left Weberians', his work is, like theirs, an attempt to identify sets of 'class positions' within the structure of employment. Wright's earlier work was much infuenced by Braverman, whose *Labor and Monopoly Capital*[3] was modelled on Marx's analysis of the labour process in *Capital*, vol. 1. Braverman argued that with the development of mass production, work had become increasingly routinized and, as a consequence, there had been a continuing 'proletarianization' of the labour force—despite the apparent increase in 'white-collar' or 'middle-class' employment. Braverman's account of the 'deskilling' of craft work and the rationalization of the labour process had a considerable impact on industrial sociology. In respect of class analysis, however, his work had the effect of driving a further wedge between structure and action: 'No attempt will be made to deal with the modern working class on the level of its consciousness, organization, or activities. This is a book about the working class as a class *in itself*, not as a class *for itself'*.[4] His account, therefore, focused entirely on developments within the labour process and did not discuss the possibility of class resistance or action. Thus although it is highly unlikely that Braverman would have had any sympathy with structural Marxism, his work had a similar impact. The 'analytical separation between class formation and

---

[1] J. H. Goldthorpe (with C. Llewellyn and C. Payne), *Social Mobility and Class Structure in Modern Britain* (Clarendon Press, Oxford, 1980; 2nd edn. 1987).

[2] E. O. Wright, 'Class Boundaries in Advanced Capitalist Societies', *New Left Review*, 98 (1976).

[3] H. Braverman, *Labor and Monopoly Capital* (Monthly Review Press, New York, 1974).

[4] Ibid. 26–7; emphasis in the original. It has to be said that, whatever Braverman's other strengths, his understanding of class analysis in sociology was rudimentary. His description of 'class analysis' in sociology was confined to a discussion of self-rated class which he took to

class action' (Dahrendorf) was increasingly coming to represent distinct areas of theoretical and empirical activity.[1]

Since the Second World War, therefore, we can trace the emergence of a distinctive sociological strand of 'class analysis'. Marxist and Weberian theories of social class are employed, as in the work of authors such as Lockwood, Dahrendorf and Braverman, to generate theoretical accounts of how particular jobs and occupations might be located within a structure of class positions. Increasingly, these accounts are used to elaborate and refine a predominant empirical approach within social stratification as a whole, in which employment aggregates are described as 'classes'. That is, 'classes' are identified theoretically within the structure of employment. Following from Bendix and Lipset's appropriation of Marx's distinction between a class 'in itself' and 'for itself', class structure and class action are regarded as analytically separable. Thus these theoretically identified employment aggregates may be regarded as 'classes'—although the question of class action is contingent, rather than inevitable. This strategy, therefore, brings together within a single framework theoretical analyses of social class with empirical analyses of inequality. It is an approach with tremendous explanatory and analytical promise but, as we shall see, it also embodies a number of serious, and probably irresolvable, difficulties.

[. . .] The development of theoretical class schemes, focused on the structure of employment, depends on the analytical separation of the study of class structure from that of class action, of 'subjective' and 'objective' dimensions, but the validity of this separation has always been contested—and not only by those committed to an ethnographic approach. For example, Stark has been highly critical of Braverman's separation of the investigation of a class 'in itself' from a class 'for itself'. He argues against the type of class analysis which 'proceeds by identifying the members who 'make up' the class; this aggregate is then given the properties of a purposive actor'.[2] As a consequence of this separation, he argues, Braverman's history was empirically inadequate in that it did not examine either worker resistance or the purposive strategies of the emergent managerial class. Rather than simply identifying classes as aggregates of 'places', Stark argues, in a manner reminiscent of Thompson, for a 'relational' approach:

a class is not 'composed of' individuals; it is not a collection or aggregation of individuals. *Classes*, like the social relations from which they arise, exist in an antagonistic and dependent relation to each other. Classes are constituted by these mutually

represent the investigation of class consciousness, and his discussion of Lockwood's work treats it as a historical, rather than a sociological, account of clerical work.

[1] R. Crompton and J. Gubbay, *Economy and Class Structure* (Macmillan, London, 1977).

[2] David Stark, 'Class Struggle and the Labour Process', *Theory and Society*, 9/1 (1980), 96–7.

antagonistic relations. In this sense . . . the object of study is not the elements themselves but the relations between them.[1]

Thus the transformation of method, he argues, must also be accompanied by a shift in the level of abstraction of class analysis, away from an obsessive over-concern with the 'mode of production' to the study of the *interaction* of organizations and groups.

Stark's arguments, therefore, may be seen as an example of the ongoing parallel between debates in Marxist theory and those in mainstream sociology during the 1960s and 1970s. Giddens, whose work was influential in developing the critique of positivism, first developed his ideas on 'structuration', which has become the core of his social theory, in his book *The Class Structure of the Advanced Societies*. He introduced the concept of 'structuration' as a means of focusing upon '*the modes in which "economic" relationships become translated into "non-economic" social structures*'—that is, *social* classes.[2] [. . .]

[. . .] Giddens's account of the 'class structure', therefore, reflected the developing critique of positivism and structural over-determination within sociology itself, in that class relationships were presented as being *actively* structured, rather than simply being taken as given.

[. . .] The possibilities of the development of class consciousness and action consequent upon class formation has also been a continuing focus of empirical research in British sociology. Much of this work was stimulated by Lockwood's influential article, 'Sources of Variation in Working Class Images of Society'. For the most part, Lockwood argued, individuals 'visualise the . . . structure of their society from the vantage points of their own particular *milieux*, and their perceptions of the larger society will vary according to their experiences . . . in the smaller societies in which they live out their daily lives'.[3] He thus developed a typology of working-class images of society ('traditional proletarian', 'traditional deferential', and 'privatised'), which corresponded to variations in the characteristic 'work' and 'community' situations experienced within the working class. Thus particular structural locations are seen as corresponding to particular societal images.

Lockwood's work stimulated a number of empirical studies which explored the link between particular occupational groups, structural locations, and social imagery—for example, Newby's study of agricultural workers, Brown and Brannen's study of shipbuilders, as well as wide-ranging review and debate

---

[1] Ibid. 97.

[2] A. Giddens, *The Class Structure of the Advanced Societies* (Hutchinson, London, 1973; 2nd edn. 1981), 105. It is of interest that Giddens uses P. Willis, *Learning to Labour: How Working class Kids get Working Class Jobs* (Saxon House, London, 1977), a 'cultural' investigation of the 'class structure', as an example of the empirical application of 'structuration'; A. Giddens, *The Constitution of Society* (Polity Press, London, 1984), 289 ff.

[3] D. Lockwood, 'Sources of Variation in Working Class Images of Society', *Sociological Review*, 14/3 (1966), 244–67, at 249.

(Bulmer). This work makes no empirical separation between the investigation of structure and action, and was often consciously related to the 'action' perspective which developed within sociology from the 1960s (Willener). Thus within sociology there has been a continuing exploration of the origins and significance of class action. This kind of research, however, has more usually taken the form of the case study, rather than relying primarily on the large-scale sample survey (Marshall).[1]

The concept of social class has occupied a central position in both urban sociology and radical geography. These sub-disciplines have been highly responsive to current developments in social thought, and have been much influenced, in succession, by structuralist Marxism (Castells), political economy, the rediscovery of the labour process and the 'deskilling' debate (Massey), philosophical realism (Sayer), and, most recently, debates about 'postmodernism' (Harvey).[2] There has also been a continuing focus on the interpretation of contemporary social developments; in particular the debates relating to the restructuring of Western economies following the recession of the late 1970s and early 1980s have loomed large in empirical and theoretical discussions in Britain. This flexibility and openness of approach has been a source of both strength and weakness. [. . .]

Urban sociology has also been much influenced by the 'realist' theoretical approach. Philosophical realism became influential as a possible solution to the theoretical problems raised by the critique of positivism.[3] 'Realism' directs attention not just at events, but at the underlying processes or mechanisms which produce them. These relatively enduring social entities are held to have causal properties which give rise to events—but the mere existence of a causal property does not mean that an event *will* occur. The realization of particular causal properties often depends on the blocking, or realization, of others, and empirical investigations guided by 'realist' principles have reflected this complexity.[4] 'Realist' accounts have tended to focus on class *formation*, which has many parallels with Gidden's account of 'structuration'. In the 'realist' ap-

[1] H. Newby, *The Deferential Worker* (Allen Lane, London, 1977); R. Brown and P. Brannen, 'Social Relations and Social Perspectives amongst Shipbuilding Workers, I and II', *Sociology*, 4/1 (1970), 71–84; 197–211; M. Bulmer, *Working Class Images of Society* (Routledge & Kegan Paul, London, 1975); A. Willener, *The Action-Image of Society* (Tavistock, London, 1970); G. Marshall, 'The Politics of the New Middle Class: History and Predictions', paper presented at the annual conference of the British Sociological Association, 1988.

[2] M. Castells, *The Urban Question* (Edward Arnold, London, 1977); D. Massey, *Spatial Divisions of Labour* (Macmillan, London, 1984); A. Sayer, *Method in Social Science: A Realist Approach* (Hutchinson, London, 1984); D. Harvey, *The Condition of Postmodernity* (Blackwell, Oxford, 1990).

[3] R. Keat and J. Urry, *Social Theory as Science* (Routledge, London, 1975; 2nd edn. 1981).

[4] P. Bagguley, J. Mark-Lawson, D. Shapiro, J. Urry, S. Walby, and A. Warde, *Restructuring Place, Class and Gender: Social and Spatial Change in a British Locality* (Sage, London, 1989).

proach, therefore, the separation of the investigation of class structure from that of class action would be rejected.

Thus for example Keat and Urry claim that:

> The term 'class' is used by Marx in a realist manner. It refers to social entities which are not directly observable, yet which are historically present, and the members of which are potentially aware of their common interests and consciousness. The existence of classes is not to be identified with the existence of inequalities of income, wealth, status or educational opportunity. For Marx, and generally for realists, class structures are taken to cause such social inequalities. The meaning of the term, 'class', is not given by these inequalities. Rather it is the structure of class relationships which determines the patterns of inequality.[1]

It may be noted, however, that Keat and Urry's description of Marx as a 'realist' incorporates an 'objectivist' characterization of the class structure, despite their stress on class *relationships*. Nevertheless, Keat and Urry are particularly critical of what they describe as the 'positivisation' of class in American stratification studies that is the identification of 'classes' as aggregates of individuals without reference to 'causal properties' but 'in terms of various kinds of demographic, social, and psychological criteria'.[2] Thus in his subsequent work Urry has taken a socio-historical approach in his empirical investigations of the class structure. In particular, he has devoted considerable attention to exploring the emergence of the 'service class', and its 'causal powers' in contemporary capitalism.[3]

Theoretical 'realism' within urban sociology, therefore, sees classes as having 'causal powers' which are 'realized' in the struggle with other classes. Thus empirical analysis informed by this approach is socio-historical. Savage *et al.*'s recent work on the middle classes in Britain provides a clear statement of this approach to 'class analysis'.[4] As indicated above, the major focus of the 'realist' approach is upon class *formation*, and this is reflected in their work. They argue that the 'middle classes' have access, to varying degrees, to three assets—or potential 'causal powers'. These are, first, property; second, organizational assets (that is, access to positions in organizational hierarchies, and the power that goes with them); and third, cultural assets, that is, the 'styles of life', or 'habitus', which serve to buttress and perpetuate structures of power and advantage (there are obvious parallels between cultural assets and the Weberian concept of status). Savage *et al.* draw upon a wide range of empirical

[1] *Social Theory as Science*, 94–5. Note that Pawson has argued convincingly that although their critique may be valid, Keat and Urry's methodological prescriptions are essentially structuralist; R. Pawson, *A Measure for Measures* (Routledge, London, 1989).

[2] *Social Theory as Science*, 95.

[3] N. Abercrombie and J. Urry, *Capital, Labour, and the Middle Classes* (Allen & Unwin, London, 1983); S. Lash and J. Urry, *The End of Organized Capitalism* (Polity Press, Cambridge, 1987).

[4] M. Savage, J. Barlow, A. Dickens, and T. Fielding, *Property, Bureaucracy and Culture: Middle Class Formation in Contemporary Britain* (Routledge, London, 1992).

material to suggest how relatively stable social collectivities have emerged on the basis of these 'causal powers'.

The 'realist' approach, therefore, may be characterized as having its major empirical focus upon processes of class formation, rather than upon descriptions of the class structure. The emphasis upon the contingency of the realization of particular 'causal powers' means that, in practice, empirical accounts of the processes of class structuring carried out within this framework are multidimensional. [. . .]

Marx and Weber, despite their very real theoretical differences, both conceptualized social classes as groups structured out of *economic* relationships, and both saw classes as significant social 'actors' in the context of capitalist industrialism. For Marx, class struggle would have a central role in the ultimate transformation of capitalism. Weber did not hold to this view, but there can be little doubt that he saw class conflict as a major phenomenon in capitalist society. In the late twentieth century, a criticism that is increasingly made of both authors (particularly Marx), and indeed, of 'class analysis' in general is that such arguments place too much emphasis on the significance of economically determined classes at the expense of other, competing sources of social identity such as nationality, gender, locality, or ethnic group. In short, it is argued, nineteenth-century sociology cannot adequately grasp the complexities of late twentieth-century society.

[. . .] In sociology (and history), however, the question of class consciousness has been incorporated into a more general debate concerning the nature of social reality, which has crucially shaped the perspectives of a number of different authors who would all claim to be doing 'class analysis'—although the diversity of their work belies the common label.

In the course of this chapter, there have emerged a series of dichotomies relating to both sociology and class analysis, some of which may be summarized as follows:

Sociology	
structure	action
Class analysis	
class in itself	class for itself (Marx)
objective	subjective (Braverman)
class formation	class action (Dahrendorf)
aggregational	relational (Stark)

The persistence of such dichotomies in the social sciences has often been criticized, as when, for example, Bourdieu writes that:

One can and must transcend the opposition between the vision which we can indifferently label realist, objectivist or structuralist on the one hand, and the constructivist, subjectivist, spontaneist vision on the other. Any theory of the social universe must include the representation that agents have of the social world and, more precisely, the contribution they make to the construction of the vision of that world and consequently, to the very construction of that world.[1]

It might be argued, however, that although Bourdieu has described the essence of sociological 'good practice', the overarching theory that would successfully achieve this integration has not yet been developed—or rather, there is certainly no consensus that it has been.

[*Class and Stratification: An Introduction to Current Debates* (Polity Press, Cambridge, 1993), 21–3, 26–7, 27–8, 33–6, 39–40, 41–2, 42–5, 45–6.]

HOWARD NEWBY ET AL.
....
5 **An Inheritance Reaffirmed: Weber**

The second half of our report addresses the thesis that class conflict has somehow been restructured. In particular we concentrate on the themes of sectionalism, egoism, privatism, and fatalism. These have been well summarized by, among others, Lukes and Hobsbawm. The argument here, it will be remembered, is that technological change, the increased participation of women in paid labour, and 'politicization of the market' via state intervention in economic processes, together with the shift from manufacturing to service industries, have made the distinction between manual and nonmanual labour largely irrelevant. Indeed, with the rise of mass production and consumption, labour or work itself has become less central to the identity and consciousness of workers. More and more the working class is concerned with issues of consumption—of housing and of state benefits for example. According to Lukes, Hobsbawm and others, recent events show Britain to be a society divided against itself in new ways: those with a stake in private property and those without; the self-sufficient on wages versus welfare claimants; the populations of declining regions against those resident in economically buoyant areas; those in relatively secure occupational or company career-ladders against the unemployed and subemployed who are on the economic margins of society. These new sectional interests are reflected, so the argument goes, in the growth of instrumental, pecuniary, egoistic (that is capitalist) values and attitudes, and in a corresponding decline in older forms of solidarity based on community, unionism, or class itself. British workers, having come to terms with the acquisitive society, now seek their private satisfactions at home and

---

[1] P. Bourdieu, 'What Makes a Social Class?', *Berkeley Journal of Sociology*, 22 (1987), 1–18, at 10. To avoid confusion, it should be pointed out that Bourdieu is here using the term 'realist' to describe those who, having determined empirically the properties and boundaries of the class structure, argue that these are 'real' classes.

in leisure. Disillusioned with their class organization they pursue conflicting sectional demands in the workplace.

Our investigation of these arguments (the issues of socio-political class formation) is less thorough than the study of demographic class formation conducted in the first part of the book because our data are rather less full. The relevant findings are correspondingly more tentative. We have argued that sectionalism, privatism, and instrumentalism among the British working class are not characteristics somehow peculiar to recent years of economic recession. The working class has long been stratified internally yet this has not prevented it from developing class organizations in order to pursue solidaristic as well as sectional objectives. Nor has its longstanding privatism necessarily been associated with status rather than class concerns. The so-called labour aristocracy, for example, supported collective action on behalf of the working class and sectional or individualized status politics in more or less equal measure. Of course there are well-documented difficulties of interpretation here, especially where pecuniary orientations to distributional struggles are concerned, but an historical perspective suggests that sectionalism, privatism, and instrumentalism have always been close to the surface of working-class life.

Conversely, data from our own survey confirm that class solidarities retain an importance that undermines recent accounts of the alleged demise of class consciousness and class politics, and associated rise of aggressive consumerism. Social class is to the fore among conceptions of collective identity. It is still the case that important differences in shared beliefs and values are structured more obviously by class than by other sources of social cleavage. It is true that the commitment to class organizations seems to be instrumental rather than expressive in tenor. However, this can be explained as an evaluative rather than cognitive phenomenon, the result of a realistic appraisal—based on past experience—of the likely outcome of the economic and social policies pursued by all political parties. This 'informed fatalism' is reflected in an overt cynicism about *party* politics. *Class* politics is far from exhausted. Social class still structures voting intentions in complex though quite definite ways and does so no less today than in the recent past. Labour and Conservative supporters continue to vote, on the whole, for principled reasons of party policy. Many of the disillusioned say that they will vote for the political centre or else not vote at all. But this is not the demise of class politics. It is, rather, class politics with a volatile and perhaps none too permanent protest option. The protest is not against class politics as such—so, as Heath has shown, there has been no secular and persistent decline in relative class voting. Changes in the pattern of voting reflect political factors rather than a long-term loosening of class processes.

Of course class awareness and class-based voting are not what most sociologists intend by the term 'class consciousness'. Among our interviewees, class was a salient source of social identity, but few were inclined to the systematic pursuit of clear class objectives. This would require a degree of logical, technical, and normative consistency in world-views for which we can find no evidence in our data. Our replication of Erik Wright's study of 'class consciousness' must be set in this context, as well as that of our historically grounded observations. We would argue that there has been no secular decline in the tendency for collective identities and collective action to develop on a class basis. But class consciousness is not, and never has been, mass consciousness. Rather, class consciousness becomes evident in the propensity to take collective action in pursuit of class objectives, rather than purely personal or sectional gains. Such actions are shaped by the institutional and organizational frameworks within which they occur. They will be successful only to the extent that free-rider problems are solved. Our evidence suggests that there is a rather widespread support for a greater measure of social justice within capitalist socio-economic arrangements. This is consistent with the predominant view of class inequalities as differences in income and life-style. There is no obvious polarization in the values and attitudes of the different classes. Class ideologies are not that neatly packaged. Rather, the longstanding absence of class consciousness in Britain lies in the failure of class organizations to convert sectional and conventional struggles into solidaristic and legal ones. The decentralized structure of free collective bargaining in this country militates against such a process. The failure of successive Labour governments to pursue a more generalized social justice by controlling union sectionalism makes many sceptical of the party's ability or even its willingness to do so.

But these are speculations which take us far beyond our data and are the subject of detailed study elsewhere. Our own objectives have been much more limited. Examining 'class consciousness' in modern Britain we can find no evidence of the demise of class identities. As Weberians we find this result somewhat gratifying. It confirms the general principle that the frame of reference within which action takes place—the 'definition of the situation'—carries significant implications for social conduct. Certainly, as far as Britain is concerned, perceptions of class identity are at least as important to any plausible explanations of the patterning of votes as are the more objective aspects of social class. The class structure does not determine social outcomes. People are not simply bearers of class relationships. Moreover, in so far as class locations are associated with voting behaviour (as clearly they are), class effects are more obvious if class is derived from a conception of market situation and work situation rather than relationship to the means of production. 'Semi-autonomous employee', 'expert non-manager', and the like are less coherent and meaningful class categories than are John Goldthorpe's more straightforwardly named alternatives, when judged according to the criterion of analytical utility.

II

Our one remaining task in this volume is to attempt, however briefly, to relate these rather disparate findings—about the class schemata of Erik Wright and John Goldthorpe, on the one hand, and the structuring of social consciousness on the other—to more general statements about class processes in advanced western societies. Our rather specialized research monograph has concentrated, for reasons that are by now well documented, on a strictly limited number of issues and perspectives. But there are more things in class analysis than have been thought of by our theoretical mentors—no matter how convincing their respective contributions may seem to be. How then, if at all, can our conclusions about social mobility, class identities, attitudes to distributional justice and the like, be fitted into the broader canvas of debates in class analysis as a whole?

These debates have been very broad-ranging. In recent years, for example, close attention has been given to a large number of perceived and alleged changes in the class structures of western societies. These include the decline of traditional proletarian occupations and communities; the expansion of working-class 'affluence'; the growth of service sector and white-collar employment; the professionalization of certain nonmanual occupations and routinization or deskilling of others; and the increasing participation of women in paid employment. Commonly, however, these processes have been interpreted within one or other of two overarching theoretical frameworks. These make rather different predictions about long-term transformations in the class stratification of advanced western societies.

One perspective is typified by the work of liberal theorists such as Daniel Bell. The image that is presented here is one of societies in which the labour process is decreasingly proletarianized, requiring a higher proportion of workers with technical expertise, in occupations demanding less routinization of tasks and more responsibility. Tendencies intrinsic to production itself—in particular the sectoral shifts in economic activity due to technological change—are seen to accord workers greater control over their conditions of work and more freedom within it. This 'upgrading' of employment leads to a shrinkage of the working class—the proportion of the employed population involved in routine manual activities for which no specialized knowledge is required—and the emergence of a 'new middle class' of salaried and highly qualified nonmanual employees. Necessarily, therefore, the transformation in the structure of employment—the move from manufacturing to services and unskilled to skilled occupations—creates high levels of class mobility. Since the demand for highly trained administrators, managers, and professionals cannot be met by self-recruitment, the structure itself generates substantial net upward mobility, as those from working-class origins move into the new middle-class positions. Additionally, however, the widespread use of more 'meritocratic' criteria in selection procedures enhances the rates of mobility as the new 'post-industrial' society becomes more open and egalitarian. Class structures give way, at least in some liberal accounts, to gradational and fluid socioeconomic hierarchies.[1]

The other framework is distinctively Marxist in provenance and most recently has been evident in debates about the work of Harry Braverman. This perceives changes in the labour process as being almost the complete opposite of those outlined by the theorists of post-industrialism. Work is regarded as becoming generally more proletarianized, real technical expertise is thus confined to a smaller proportion of the labour force, routinization of activities is more pervasive and responsibilities less meaningful. Far from the material basis of alienation being undermined it is here argued that deskilling is prevalent and alienation correspondingly intensified. The expansion of middle-class positions is therefore more apparent than real, since many of the new nonmanual jobs are 'degraded' or 'deskilled' to such an extent that they are indistinguishable from those performed by manual workers, for whom those in the 'proletarianized' or 'contradictory' middle layers form a natural class ally. The reality of all wage labour under capitalism is that it is necessarily exploitative and is organized only in the interests of capital. Putative rates of upward mobility out of manual into nonmanual employment therefore serve only to mystify the class struggle and obscure the continuing dynamics of class stratification.[2]

Different conclusions about the nature of 'working-class consciousness' follow from these contrasting accounts. Liberals argue that the openness of modern industrial societies undermines class identities and so lessens the potential for collective action in general and class conflict in particular. As consciousness of class steadily declines, so workers become more individualistic, more consumer-oriented, and correspondingly less inclined to pursue any form of class politics. In meritocratic post-industrial societies they strive for pleasure and status in a strictly personal fashion. The transition from 'class' to 'mass' society dissolves all sub-cultural particularisms in favour of the hitherto middle-class norms of individualism, consumerism, and privatism. Marxists, on the other hand, maintain that the newly proletarianized workers of late capitalism will be pushed to collective resistance against the managerial strategy of deskilling tasks and policing the labour process ever more closely. In their view, work (and in particular the process of production) is still central to the creation of class-based images of society, and so to the development of

---

[1] Daniel Bell, The Coming of Post-Industrial Society (Penguin, Harmondsworth, 1976); P. B. Blau and O. D. Duncan, The American Occupational Structure (Wiley, New York, 1967); Clark Kerr et al., Industrialism and Industrial Man (Harvard University Press, Cambridge, Mass.; 1960).

[2] Harry Braverman, Labour and Monopoly Capital (Monthly Review Press, London, 1974); G. Carchedi, On the Economic Identification of Classes (Routledge & Kegan Paul, London 1977); Ernest Mandel, Late Capitalism (Verso, London, 1978).

oppositional social consciousness. In due course the inherent tendency of workers towards workplace and communal solidarism will re-emerge from the alienation induced by social relationships that rest exclusively on the cash nexus. Class-based action, in the political and industrial spheres, will eventually challenge the structures of property and power which underpin late capitalism.[1]

To some extent the contrast between these frameworks simply reflects the changed economic circumstances of the long post-war boom as compared with those of the recessionary 1970s and 1980s. As the age of affluence has given way to economic stagnation so the liberal perspective has become less fashionable among class theorists. In part, however, the contradictory interpretations arise as a consequence of determined efforts by the two groups of social theorists to shackle the activities of certain social groups (most commonly the working class) to their own socio-political goals. For this reason the two perspectives actually converge in their logic—despite wide-ranging and explicit substantive disagreements. Both have taken the western working classes as the essential means to achieving liberal or (conversely) socialist political and social goals; both are prone to implicit historicism since they share a common tendency to view present events as part of a predetermined long-term historical trend; and, in consequence, both are inclined to wishful rather than critical thinking in the interpretation of empirical materials.

As will already be obvious our own findings about class structure and class consciousness vindicate neither perspective. For those with no particular political axe to grind the picture seems somewhat more complicated than is allowed for by straightforward arguments about embourgeoisement or proletarianization.

It is true that, at first sight, much of the evidence presented in the above chapters seems to substantiate the liberal position. In recent years there has been a marked expansion of the salariat and corresponding decline in the working class. Perhaps as many as one-third of those presently in service-class positions have arrived there from working-class origins. Around 10 per cent of those from working-class backgrounds whose own initial class at entry to employment was itself working class will nevertheless arrive at service-class destinations during the course of their occupational careers. Meanwhile, the working class has itself shrunk by about one-third during the years covered by our mobility data, perhaps somewhat less if one treats routine 'sales and service' employees as proletarians. Upward mobility on this scale is clearly at odds with Marxist theories about the rigidity of class structures in advanced capitalism. Nor can these theories be salvaged by recourse to arguments about the proletarianization of the middle layers of the structure. There is nothing in

---

[1] F. Zweig, *The Worker in an Affluent Society* (Heineman, London, 1961); Paul E. Willis, *Learning to Labour* (Saxon House, Westmead, Hants, 1979).

our data to suggest that routine nonmanual jobs, or those who perform them, are somehow degraded or deskilled. The jobs themselves characteristically allow more autonomy to their incumbents than do manual occupations. Very few of those involved report any deskilling of the associated tasks. In any case, even where the working conditions for routine nonmanual jobs *are* largely indistinguishable from those found in manual employment, it is clear that socio-political proletarianization does not necessarily follow. Most of those recruited to routine sales and service or administrative jobs have been women, and as we have seen, they tend to take the socio-political lead from their male partners—only about one-third of whom are themselves in the working class. Finally, we might note that the individuals performing the various routine 'middle layer' jobs are themselves not subject to a process of proletarianization, since there is no evidence that relative mobility rates for this stratum have changed over the years—even when these are calculated separately for men and women. It would seem, then, that during the post-war periods of economic growth and recession alike, the numbers involved in specialized and routine nonmanual activities have continued to grow at the expense of those involved in traditional (manual) working-class occupations.

However, despite this seemingly extensive corroborating evidence there are serious flaws in the liberal account of advanced western societies, at least where the case of modern Britain is concerned. The notion of relative mobility provides the key to these. Our data show clearly that, calculating the likely transitions from class of origin to class destinations as a series of odds ratios, the chances of someone from a service-class background securing service-class rather than working-class employment for himself or herself are somewhere between seven and thirteen times greater than those for someone arriving at service-class employment rather than working-class employment from working-class origins. Moreover, since there is no evidence that the degree of 'social fluidity' or equality of opportunity has altered over successive mobility cohorts, then it is reasonable to conclude that the expansion of the salariat that is evident in the comparison between the class distribution of parents and children is almost entirely due to structural factors. That is, the 'room at the top' created by the transformation in the occupational division of labour has not been accompanied by greater equality in the chances of getting there, since the most privileged groups have shown themselves to be more rather than less successful at using their relative advantages to prevent downward mobility among their offspring. As a result, the association between an individual's class of origin and his or her eventual destination has proved remarkably stable, despite economic expansion, egalitarian social policies, and educational reform. Moreover, whether one looks at mobility trajectories or conditions of employment, women tend to be generally disadvantaged when compared to men. They are no less divided by class differences, but tend to have inferior market situations and work situations to those of class-comparable men, and to receive proportionately fewer rewards for their educational achievements. Finally, nowhere in liberal theories is it envisaged that the expansion of professional and skilled occupations will be accompanied by large-scale unemployment, yet this is precisely what has happened in recessionary Britain. Our concern with class theories and employment as such has meant that, in this volume at least, we have had relatively little to say about joblessness. We intend to rectify this in subsequent publications. For the moment, it is sufficient merely to note that extensive evidence from research elsewhere points overwhelmingly to the conclusion that unemployment and subemployment are predominantly working-class fates, and that many both inside and outside this class have only a precarious employment in 'secondary' labour markets based on non-standard types of work.[1] We have reserved the study of this phenomenon—of part-time work, subemployment, and 'dualism' or 'segmentation' of labour markets—for a separate volume. Already, however, there is more than sufficient evidence from other economic and sociological studies to cause serious doubts, in our minds at least, about the optimistic scenario for longterm changes in the structure of stratification that is presented in liberal theories of industrialism.

Not surprisingly, therefore, these theories are equally suspect in their predictions about the progressive disappearance of classes and increasing stability of western industrial societies. There is nothing in our data to suggest that collective identities and collective action of a class-based kind are in the process of long-term decline. It is true that individualism, consumerism, and privatism are readily apparent. But there is no evidence to support the claim that these tendencies indicate a decomposition of classes resulting from social mobility or the extension of meritocratic criteria to processes of occupational selection. Our own belief is that the explanation for working-class instrumentalism in Britain is to be found in the strategies and policies of working-class movements rather than putative changes in the structure of inequality itself. Naturally, we cannot directly substantiate this belief here, since a study of organizational dynamics, class strategies, and political processes would take us far beyond the confines of our particular data set. What we can do, however, is rule out the alternative possibility that any obvious changes in 'class consciousness' can be attributed to a long-term 'loosening of the class structure'.[2]

The debate about the so-called decline of class politics provides a good illustration of this. Class dealignment—a weakening in the association between class and vote—has popularly been advanced as an explanation for the

---

[1] J. H. Goldthorpe and C. Payne, 'Trends in Intergenerational Mobility in England and Wales, 1979–1983', *Sociology*, 20 (1986), 1–24; B. Showler and A. Sinfield (eds.), *The Workless State* (Martin Robertson, Oxford, 1981); Bryan Roberts *et al.*, (eds.), *New Approaches to Economic Life* (Manchester University Press, 1984).

[2] For a more detailed account which reaches the same conclusions see the forthcoming revised edition of Goldthorpe's *Social Mobility and Class Studies in Modern Britain* (esp. ch. 12).

recently poor performances of Labour at the polls and corresponding rise of the Liberal/Social Democratic Alliance. The Labour Party was said to be in decline precisely because it was a class party: it did not appeal to the growing numbers of white-collar workers and failed to detect a 'sea-change' in the attitudes of manual employees away from traditional class loyalties and concerns. In fact, however, longitudinal data support the countervailing claim advanced by Heath and his colleagues that relative class voting has remained more or less constant throughout the period of so-called dealignment. The fact that such variations as can be found to exist in the association between vote and class take the form of 'trendless fluctuations' suggests that Labour's electoral failures have a political rather than a sociological source. It has performed badly as a party across its entire electoral base, and not simply among the working class, because (among other things) many of its policies (such as those on defence) have been unpopular, it lacks coherence as a movement, and it has failed to convince voters as a whole that a Labour government could offer credible alternatives to Thatcherite 'realism' in the economic sphere. True, the decline in the relative size of the working-class electorate has damaged the Labour vote, since the largest proportion of its support comes from this quarter. But neither of these factors suggest that there has been a decline in the political cohesiveness or class identity of the working class. Class interests are seemingly still central to the political process. There has been no transition to a post-industrial society in which the structure of class inequalities, together with class-based political action, have given way to the purely status politics of the open society. There is, seemingly, no 'logic of industrialism' to which our data lend credibility.

On the other hand there is nothing in our findings to support the claims of Marxist authors that the working class share in an intrinsic commitment to communal rather than individual concerns. Historical evidence suggests that class and status politics have always coexisted. Only a determinedly historicist reading of instrumentalism among the working class can impute an 'objective' collectivism—socialist 'resistance'—to the beliefs and values of our respondents. Wright's assertion that the overall trajectory of historical development is 'progressive' is no more plausible than Kerr's supposition that there is a 'logic of industrialism'.[1]

Thus, to take up the specific concerns of class analysts, routine nonmanual employees cannot be regarded as a new proletariat in the making. The systematic degradation of labour is Marxist myth. Rather, as our evidence confirms, the proletarianization of intermediate layers in the class structure is historically contingent. Routine clerical and sales and service workers are not an undifferentiated mass soon to be shackled to the historical destiny of the

---

[1] Erik Olin Wright, *Classes* (Verso, London, 1985); Clark Kerr, *The Future of Industrial Societies* (Harvard University Press, Cambridge, Mass., 1983).

proletariat. On the other hand, they can no more plausibly be described as part of a 'new middle class', willing to endorse unambiguously the reward structure embraced by existing socio-political arrangements. In fact these workers have widely varying worklife trajectories. If class differences and interests are there-fore to be mobilized for political purposes, as Marxists claim, then this will result from political will rather than a spontaneous process of class polariza-tion. In the British case, the Labour Party must find some means of transcend-ing its class constituency, without losing the support of manual workers. Our data suggest that a broad-based appeal to social justice would attract support, not only among those routine nonmanual employees whose market and work situation is similar to that of manual workers, but also among many in more privileged class positions. Previous Labour governments have in fact suc-ceeded in achieving Wright's political objective. That is, they have created class alliances around social democratic issues having popular support across manual and nonmanual groupings alike, particularly those issues associated with the extension of the various rights of citizenship—education, social wel-fare, and the like. Our own belief is that the party's best hope for the future lies in precisely the same direction—but this is to let our personal political beliefs spill over into our sociological analysis. We can claim, from sociological reasoning alone, that whatever happens will not be the result of some under-lying logic or dialectic in the development of industrial-capitalist societies. Our analysis of demographic and socio-political class formation offers no support to historicists either on the left or the right.

[Gordon Marshall, Howard Newby, David Rose, and Carolyn Vogler, *Social Class in Modern Britain* (Hutchinson, London, 1988), 266–74.]

ELLEN MEIKSINS WOOD

6   An Inheritance Reaffirmed: Marx

Both the historical record and the structural antagonism between capital and labour tell a story very different from the one we are offered by the NTS.[1] One cannot, then, help wondering what exactly we are being told when the NTS deny the connection between the working class and socialism, or even be-tween economic conditions and political forces in general. Again, we are reminded that the NTS has come to fruition not at a time when the opposition between labour and capital has receded into the background, but rather when the antagonisms of class have been especially urgent and visible. It would be interesting to speculate about the historical and sociological reasons for this curious detachment from reality—for example, about whether it is the ideo-

---

[1] This term is explained in Rosemary Crompton, above.

logical representation of a specific social interest in its own right; at any rate, we can at least expose its faulty theoretical foundations.

The NTS is based on a profound misunderstanding of what it means to say, as Marxists traditionally have done, that capitalism has laid the foundation for socialism and that the working class is the revolutionary class. According to the straw-Marxism conjured up and then knocked down by the NTS, there will be an automatic, mechanical, and non-contradictory transition from capitalism to socialism. More specifically, this Marxism is a crude technological determinism according to which the development of productive forces—conceived as a natural, neutral process—will inevitably and mechanically produce a united and revolutionary working class. In other words, Marxism stands or falls according to whether a unified working class immediately committed to socialism is directly given by capitalist production relations and the development of productive forces. Since history has clearly denied any such mechanical determination, say the NTS, the whole Marxist project collapses. There is no sense here of Marx's own complex and subtle understanding of the ways in which capitalism creates not the mechanical inevitability of socialism, but the possibilities and contradictions which put it on the historical agenda as it never could have been before. Missing too is his conception of the working class not as a mechanical reflex of technological development, whose 'historic task' is nothing more than (automatically) to appropriate collectively the forces of production created by capitalism, but rather a class which contains the possibility of a classless society because its own interests cannot be fully served without the abolition of class and because its strategic location in the production of capital gives it a unique capability to destroy capitalism.

The problem, however, lies not simply in a faulty interpretation of Marx, but more fundamentally, in a thoroughly inadequate, indeed non-existent, conception of history as a determinate process—indeed as a process at all, as distinct from an arbitrary series of contingencies, at best held together by the logic of discourse. For underlying this interpretation of Marxism is the crudely dualistic view, which we have already noted as a characteristic of the NTS (and which is part of its structuralist legacy), that where there is no absolute determination there is absolute contingency. There is little room here for historical *relations, conditions,* or *possibilities;* there are only contingent juxtapositions or 'conjunctures'.

There is perhaps yet another element in the NTS rejection of the working class as revolutionary agent. Somehow the notion has gained currency, even on the left, that the very idea of a collective historical agent is a metaphysical abstraction, and one of the more pernicious Hegelian legacies surviving in Marxism, fraught with dangers of despotism and oppression. There is no crime so heinous that it cannot, according to this view, be justified by those who claim to act 'in the name of' the 'universal class', that mythical collective agent, the revolutionary proletariat.

But why should this be so? Consider the alternatives. Failing a collective agent, history must be made by individuals acting independently, or by Great Men and/or Great Women, or else there are no human agents in history at all—in which case *any* political movement is clearly a delusion and a waste of time. Even the most limited political intervention, even the most 'moderate' political programme which presupposes that people can deliberately intervene in the shaping of social arrangements, however modestly, inevitably assumes the possibility of a collective agent, even if only a political party. There is nothing metaphysical about this assumption, nor is it fanciful to assume that people can be joined by some principle of unity, some common purpose and commitment, in the pursuit of certain common goals.

It is not even unreasonable, or metaphysical, to assume that such common purposes and commitments are likely to be grounded in certain common social circumstances and experiences. In fact, the assumption that political movements need *not* be grounded in existing social identities and interests would at best be highly fanciful, and at worst profoundly dangerous. Is it conceivable that a political programme could be devised in complete abstraction from the immediate social conditions and interests of any living human being, without any presuppositions about the kinds of people that are likely to congregate around it? And is it possible to imagine a political movement constructed simply by announcing a programme and sitting back to wait while it exerts its own magnetic force? It is probably safe to say that political movements generally draw upon existing collective identities and appeal to existing collective interests—that is, interests in which people partake by virtue of belonging to identifiable collectivities. Political movements without a sound basis in existing social collectivities and not firmly guided by existing social interests have tended to go one of two ways: at best, for lack of their own social roots they have become instruments of the dominant interest—as social-democratic parties have more than once, whether willingly or not, become the agents of capital when they have uprooted themselves from their working-class foundations. At worst, political movements without firm social roots have degenerated into precisely the despotic arbitrariness which critics have wrongly attributed to the Marxist conception of the revolutionary proletariat. In fact, it can be argued that the most metaphysical—and potentially danger-ous—view of historical agency is that historical agents are constituted by nothing but Discourse or Idea. If the threat of despotism is to be found anywhere, it is surely here, in the notion of Idea incarnate in the bearers of discourse, who will create social collectivities—such as the 'people'—where none existed before, out of a shapeless mass with no social identity of its own.

What, then, is specific to the Marxist conception of the collective agent, the revolutionary working class? The first premise, of course, is that production is essential to human existence and the organization of social life. (It cannot be emphasized enough that the NTS rejection of Marxism begins here, with an effective denial of this elementary fact and everything that follows from it.) On the assumption that political movements must be grounded in social relations and interests, the critical question for Marxism is, what social relations and interests are commensurate with, and provide the surest grounding for, a political project that has as its object the transformation of production relations and the abolition of class? Marxism's answer is that there is such a thing as a working class, people who by virtue of their situation in the relations of production and exploitation share certain fundamental interests, and that these class interests coincide with the essential objective of socialism, the abolition of class, and more specifically, the classless administration of production by the direct producers themselves.

This is not to say that the condition of the working class directly determines that its members will have socialism as their immediate class objective. It does, however, mean that they can uniquely advance the cause of socialism (though not completely achieve it) even *without* conceiving socialism as their class objective, by pursuing their material class interests, because these interests are by nature essentially opposed to capitalist class exploitation and to a class-dominated organization of production. Since the material interests of the working class cannot be satisfied within the existing framework of social relations, and since a pursuit of these interests will inevitably encounter the opposing interests of capital, the process of struggle will tend to expose its own limitations, spill over into the political arena, and carry the battle closer to the centres of capitalist power. Furthermore, since the working class itself *creates* capital, and since the organization of production and appropriation place the collective labourer at the heart of the whole capitalist structure, the working class has a unique capacity to destroy capital. The conditions of production, and of working-class struggle, are also such as to encourage the organization of workers into a collective force potentially suited to carry out this project. This does not mean that the working class is immediately available as a political organization ready-made to prosecute the struggle for socialism. It simply means that the organizational and political efforts of socialists will most fruitfully be devoted to unifying the working class and serving its interests, while the boundaries of class struggle are pushed forward. To say—as the NTS repeatedly do—that *classes* are never political agents, while undoubtedly true in its limited way, is therefore quite beside the point.

There is one unique characteristic of socialism which adds an even greater force to the Marxist argument that the revolution must come by the self-emancipation of the working class: although the struggle between exploiting and exploited classes has been a major force in every transformation of production relations, no other social revolution has ever placed the exploited class of the old social order in command of the new one. No transformation of production relations has had as its principal object the interests of the exploited class, however much those interests may have moved the revolution forward. Even more specifically, socialism alone presupposes both a continuity between the direct producers of the old order and the new, and a social organization of production administered by those direct producers themselves. The Marxist project is based on the premise that the collective labourer of advanced industrial capitalism will be the direct producer of the socialist order, and that socialist democracy will be constituted by the self-organization of freely associated producers. This places the collective labourer in capitalism at the centre of the socialist project as no exploited class has ever been in any other social revolution. Thus, unless the class interests of the working class themselves direct them into political struggle and to the transformation of the mode of production, the socialist project must remain an empty and utopian aspiration. This does not mean that socialism is inevitable, only that it will come about in this way or not at all.

[*The Retreat from Class: A New True Socialism* (Verso, London, 1986), 186–90.]

PART B

An Inheritance in Question

Zygmunt Bauman dwells on the failings of what he terms a postmodern sociology. These include the employment of a modernist category of truth as objective and absolute, but the central failing is held to be its inability to become a sociology of postmodernity, and so to analyse the social changes that make up contemporary reality, the 'postmodern' condition which society is now in. None the less, the insights of a postmodern sociology are put to work to produce a sociology of postmodernity. Though not employing these terms, Alain Touraine arrives at a similar understanding of the contemporary world, one in which class has lost its significance, in favour of the concept of movement. Both writers reveal the utility of new concepts and tools ('sociality', 'self-institution', 'movement', and so on) as ways of understanding the present.

However, in employing these tools, and an understanding of the historical movement out of the 'modernist' era which informs their employment, both writers reveal modernity to be a normative project that was the product of its own historical times. By doing so they alert us to the fact that the conceptual apparatus of 'modernist' social thought did not merely reflect the reality of its day but actively created it. Both writers recognize how the model of the nation state, and the concern with order and change, that marked classical social thought, both did and did not accurately depict their object of study, the object—among other things—of 'society' and the classes that gave this society form. This reader is more historical in interest than both these contributions, and the historical inadequacies of classical social thought need emphasis beyond that given them by Bauman and Touraine. None the less, in both writers there is the recognition that even in its heyday the nation state was in reality a very imperfect model for the concept of society as a systemic totality. In describing the operations of this nation state, and the 'society' that purported to be not only its abstract model but its concrete embodiment, little account was taken of how unlike a system the nation state was, how 'porous' it was (Bauman's term), and how much it was characterized by developments exogenous and not endogenous to its geographic boundaries. Traditional social thought and sociology did not, therefore, even do justice to this major reality of their own day.

When the concepts of a postmodernist sociology/sociology of postmodernism are seen to reveal the historical context of former sociologies, then it becomes possible to suggest that these new sociologies may reveal the reality of the past as well as the present. Of course, the new conceptual tool-kits indicated here, like those of 'modernity', are themselves a historical product of their own day, with all the limitations for understanding the past an awareness of this entails. None the less, though Bauman and Touraine confine themselves to the analysis of the present, they may be unduly unambitious in this, or unduly present-minded. A general perspective on the *processual* nature of social reality suggests itself as of as much use in interpreting the past as the present, especially when it so successfully reveals the tendency of traditional accounts to privilege structure over process in interpreting the very past these accounts purported to describe. The nation state in its heyday, for example, needs to be interpreted as much in terms of process as of structure.

The emphasis on action, agency, randomness, and self-creation in this pro-cessual perspective on social reality is of course corrosive of traditional notions of the dichotomy of structure and culture, objective and subjective, and so on. This critique is developed in the readings that form Section (*b*), 'Arguments'. Baudrillard's work may be regarded as the polar opposite of notions of the 'objectivity' of social structure. Baudrillard regards the social as a regime of power and truth in much the same way as Foucault. It has profound practical consequences though it is also an 'ideology'. Its aspect as both is evident in Baudrillard's potted 'history' of the social, with its three possible routes. For historians this is an unusual form of history no doubt, doubly so as we are not told which of the routes history has taken. But of the present strength of a 'simulated', 'hyperreal', social there is no doubt in this account. The social is real because of its very unreality. It is also no longer a feasible basis for political alignments.

The search for new alignments is evident in Haraway's work. From her avowed and impassioned postmodernist position previous social categories like race and class have been irretrievably 'de-essentialized', robbed of their power to found a politics on the basis of a stable identity. In the same way the identity of women has been 'de-natured'. Haraway here dwells on the failure of a Marxist 'essentialism', this time of 'labour', to produce a workable identity for women, and a workable basis for politics (though her accent elsewhere is on how to build on a postmodern conception of identity).

The rest of the contributors to this section could hardly be called postmod-ern, but their work points in a very similar direction. In both of the Bourdieu readings, Bourdieu's prioritizing of 'material determinants' is, however, appar-ent. 'Habitus' is a product of the structures constitutive of the conditions of existence within which it is acquired. Despite Bourdieu's reputation for uniting structure and action, his emphasis on the 'relative autonomy' of classificatory schemes recalls the very dualisms he attempts to expel. Giddens's account of 'structuration' presents a more neutral account. Here the dualism of action and structure becomes the 'duality of structure' in which 'social structures are both constituted *by* human agency, and yet at the same time are the *medium* of this constitution'. Sharrock and Watson's ethnomethodology argues that we *im-pose* the dualism of action and structure on ourselves. It is posited on a taken-for-granted separation of society seen-from-within and seen-from-with-out, whereas both structure and agency are present in the fundamental activity of comprehending social life itself. They may not be separated, for one is a modification of the other. Ethnomethodology is therefore interested in this 'primitive', 'originary' activity of comprehending social life, for it is in this hermeneutic activity of 'being-in-the-world' in the first place that all subsequent understandings of social life are grounded. This position is not interested in the *correct* form of theorizing, but in how the work of theorizing is itself constituted.

These authors point to the resulting difficulties of integrating ethnomethodology and other sociologies. The latter take for granted what this hermeneutics posits as the object of scrutiny, the business of 'going on' in life. However, they leave open the questions of the validity of other traditions, and whether starting from their position we would be better able to answer the questions posed in these traditions. These open questions invite an affirmative answer, as does the possibility of starting from other positions and answering better the questions posed in ethnomethodology. In working out the points of connection between different positions, the assumptions of the phenomenological philosophy underlying ethnomethodology need to be brought to the surface, as well as historicized. Ethnomethodology tends to be decidedly 'foundationalist' in its assumptions.

Finally, Castoriadis presents a very different tradition, a post-Marxism that unlike Bourdieu actually breaks with Marxism, albeit quixotically in the name of revolution (the idea of alienation is still present, though in a radically new key, that of ignorance that society is self-instituting). The revolutionary credentials of this have not worn well, but what is challenging is the uncompromising emphasis on the self-creation of society and the social. The symbolic realm is in this account what makes the real possible. The 'central social imaginary significations' of a society cannot be thought of in terms of their 'referents', for these significations are what renders referents, and the relation to them, possible. The symbolic, and the 'social imaginary', have a life and logic of their own, which cannot be reduced to their function. In writing the history and sociology of 'society' and 'class' this logic needs to be accounted for. In accounting for it we need to ask questions like that asked by Castoriadis, 'How can we grasp God?' In answering them the irreducibility of society's 'imaginary significations' and 'fundamental fantasies' becomes apparent.

(a) Positions

ZYGMUNT BAUMAN

7 **Sociology and Postmodernity**

Postmodern Sociology

At the threshold of postmodernity, sociology arrived in the form aptly called by Anthony Giddens the orthodox consensus. This form was constituted by the widely shared strategy of rational analysis of society, understood as a nation state; such a society, it was agreed, was subject to the processes of continuing rationalization, not necessarily free from contradictions and upsets (or, indeed, temporary retreats), yet sufficiently dominant to offer a safe frame against which information about social reality could be plotted. Constantly lurking behind the scene in the orthodox vision of social reality was the powerful image of the social system—this synonym of an ordered, structured space of interaction, in which probable actions had been, so to speak, pre-selected by the mechanisms of domination or value-sharing. It was a 'principally coordinated' space (in Talcott Parsons's rendition of Weber's imagery); one inside which the cultural, the political and the economic levels of supra-individual organization were all resonant with each other and functionally complementary. In Parson's memorable phrase, sociology was best understood as an ongoing effort to solve the 'Hobbesian problem': the mystery of non-randomness, the regularity of behaviour of essentially free and voluntary subjects. The orthodox consensus focused accordingly on mechanisms which trimmed or eliminated the randomness and multidirectionality of human action and thus imposed co-ordination upon otherwise centrifugal forces; order upon chaos.

The first victim of advancing postmodernity was the invisibly present, tacitly assumed spectre of the system, the source and the guarantee of the meaningfulness of the sociological project and, in particular, of the orthodox consensus. The immediate outcome was a widespread feeling of unease and erosion of confidence. Well before the exact nature of postmodern change was articulated, the signs had appeared of growing disaffection with the way the business of sociology had been conducted in the era of orthodox consensus. Symbols of that era (Parsons's structural functionalism above all) came increasingly under attack, often for reasons only tenuously connected with the character of sensed change. Truly at stake was the overall de-legitimation of the orthodox consensus, rather than the ostensible topic of the assault; the replacement of specific theoretical assumptions or strategic principles. As T. H. Marshall wrote on a different occasion, sociologists knew what they were running from; they did not know yet where to.

At the time the rebellion started, there was little awareness of the link between the new spirit of theoretical and strategical restlessness and the changing social reality. The call to revise the practice of sociology was expressed in universalistic terms. It was not supposed that the orthodox consensus had outlived its usefulness and hence was ripe for reform; instead, the consensus was proclaimed wrong from the start; a sad case of error, of self-deception, or ideological surrender. Paradoxically (though not unexpectedly) the effort to discredit the modern view of the social world needed the thoroughly modern understanding of truth for self-validation. Without necessarily saying this in so many words, the rebels aimed at the substitution of the new consensus for the old (they often spoke of the search for a 'new paradigm'). In reality, their efforts led to the constitution of what one would best call a postmodern sociology (as distinct from the sociology of postmodernity).

Postmodern sociology received its original boost from Garfinkel's techniques conceived to expose the endemic fragility and brittleness of social reality, its 'merely' conversational and conventional groundings, its negotiability, perpetual use and irreparable underdetermination. Soon it adopted Alfred Schutz as its spiritual ancestor, with his contemplation of the marvel of social action and its self-propelling capacity, with his debunking of 'because-of' explanations as hidden 'in-order-to' motives, with his dissolution of systemic order into a plethora of multiple realities and universes of meaning. Shortly afterwards it turned to Wittgenstein and Gadamer for philosophical inspiration and the certificate of academic respectability. From Wittgenstein, the idea of language games was borrowed and skilfully adapted to justify the elimination of all 'tougher', extra-conversational constituents of social reality. From Gadamer came the vision of the life-world as a communally produced and traditionally validated assembly of meanings, and the courage to abandon the search for universal, supra-local, 'objective' (i.e. referring to none of the communally confined experiences) truth.

It was a postmodern world which lent animus and momentum to postmodern sociology; the latter reflects the former much in the same way the collage of the postmodern art 'realistically represents' (in the 'conceptual sense of realism')[1] randomly assembled experience of postmodern life. And yet postmodern sociology is distinguished by avoiding confrontation with postmodernity as a certain form of social reality, as a new departure set apart by new attributes. Postmodern sociology denies its kinship with a specific stage in the

---

[1] Cf. Rosalind E. Kraus, *The Originality of Avant-Garde and Other Modernist Myths* (MIT Press, 1985), 52–4. The concept has been suggested by G. M. Luquet.

history of social life. In a curious way, this sociology which took impetus from dissatisfaction with visions born of the universalistic aspiration of the western, capitalist form of life, conceives of itself in universalistic, extemporal and exspatial, terms. It prefers to see its attainment as rectification of blunder, discovery of truth, finding of right direction, rather than as a self-adaptation to the transformed object of study. The attributes of social reality, made salient by the fading hopes of missionary culture and brought into relief by the postmodern world-view, postmodern sociology promoted to the status of perpetual (though heretofore overlooked) essences of social life in general.

One may say that postmodern sociology does not have the concept of postmodernity. One suspects that it would find it difficult to generate and legitimate such a concept without radically transforming itself. It is precisely because it is so well adapted to the postmodern cultural setting—that postmodern sociology (its tendency to argue the non-universality of truth in universalistic terms notwithstanding) cannot conceive of itself as an event in history. Indeed, it is singularly unfit to conceptualize the twin phenomena of the logic of historical succession and of the social embeddedness of ideas.

Postmodern sociology has responded to the postmodern condition through mimesis; it informs of that condition obliquely, in a coded way: through the isomorphism of its own structure, through commutation (Hjelmslev) between its structure and the structure of that extra-sociological reality of which it is a part. One can say that postmodern sociology is a signifier, with the postmodern condition as its signified. One can obtain a valid insight into the postmodern condition through the analysis of the practices of postmodern sociology. For the discursive knowledge of postmodernity as a type of social reality with a place in history and social space, one needs however to turn to other sociological responses. [. . .]

Sociology at the Age of Postmodernity

Constructing a new model of contemporary society, necessitated by profound changes in its organization and functioning, is but one task with which sociology has been confronted by the advent of postmodernity. Another, no less complex task, is that of rethinking major sociological categories shaped, as it were, under conditions now fast receding into the past.

From its birth, sociology was an adjunct of modernity. It took the accomplishment of modernity—the construction of the free individual through cutting him loose from visible, tangible 'pinpointable' bonds—for granted, and hence defined its task as the study and the service of unfreedom—all those processes of *socialization, cultural hegemony, control, power, culture, civilization,* which could account for the mystery of 'de-randomizing' the voluntary actions of free agents. It translated the 'rationalization spurt', the disciplinary practices, the uniforming ambitions of modernity from a normative project into the analytical framework for making sense of reality, and thus made the 'structure' those pre-individual forces which bring order into the otherwise chaotic and potentially damaging drives of the free agents—the pivot of its discourse. It drew its cognitive horizons with the leg of the compass placed firmly in the very spot from which the levelling, uniforming, proselytizing tendencies of modern times emanated—and thus identified 'society', the largest analytical totality meant to incorporate and accommodate all analysis—with the nation state.

Not only did sociology develop as a theory and a service discipline of modernity. Its underlying world-view, its conceptual apparatus, its strategy, were all geared to the latter's practices and declared ambitions. It seems unlikely, therefore, that with those practices and ambitions undergoing profound change, the business of sociology can go on 'as usual'. There seems to be little in the orthodox lore of sociology which can a priori claim exemption from re-thinking.

The first to have come under scrutiny is the very imagery of the social world as *a cohesive totality with a degree of stiffness and resilience against change, with a neatly arranged hierarchy of power and value prior to the interaction between individual and group agents*. Such an imagery was most conspicuously epitomized in the concept of structure, characterized first and foremost by the attributes of relative inflexibility and autonomy in relation to the level of interaction. No wonder it is the concept of structure which has been treated with most suspicion by the theorists seeking the 'new paradigm' for sociology—one better geared to the time of systemic indifference to cultural plurality and, indeed, to the waywardness of constitutive agencies. Previous emphasis on structurally determined constraints to interaction gives way to a new concern with the process in which ostensibly 'solid' realities are construed and reconstrued in the course of interaction; simultaneously, the ascribed potency of agency is considerably expanded, the limits of its freedom and of its reality-generating potential pushed much further than the orthodox imagery would ever allow. The overall outcome of such revisions is a vision of a fluid, changeable social setting, kept in motion by the interaction of the plurality of autonomous and unco-ordinated agents.

And so Alain Touraine promoted for more than a decade the substitution of the idea of social movement for that of the social class as the basic unit of societal analysis. The latter concept is most intimately related to the imagery of structure and structural constraints and determination. The first, in Touraine's rendering, implies a vision of pliable, under-determined, unfinished reality amenable to ideational and practical remoulding by motivated social actors. In a recent expression of this vision, Touraine rejects the idea of 'class in itself'; workers' action, he insists,

is not a reaction to an economic and social situation; it is itself a blueprint which determines the state of social relations. . . . It follows from this that the working class cannot be defined 'objectively', and therefore that the concept governing the analysis is no longer one of class position, but of social movement.[1]

The most crucial attribute ascribed to a social movement is its *self-constituting* capacity: social movement is not an emanation, epiphenomenon, reflection of anything else; it is fully its own creation; it generates its own subject; it constitutes itself into a social agent.

Anthony Giddens directs his attention to the revisions which the teaching of the 'founding fathers' of sociology, and the concepts and visions they bequeathed, require in order to be of use in the analysis of contemporary society (though it is not entirely clear in Giddens's writings whether that 'contemporaneity' which makes revisions necessary, is one of *social theory*, or of the *social world* it theorizes). In the successive rewritings of his new theoretical synthesis, Giddens redefines structure as a process which incorporates motivated agents and their interaction as its, simultaneously, building material and operating force. Indeed, Giddens substitutes the concept of structuration for that of structure, rightly assuming that in this new, 'action-oriented' and 'action-expressive' form, the pivotal concept of social analysis is better geared to the task of theorizing an un-predetermined, flexible social reality which pre-empts none of its options, which is open to the influence of a plurality of only loosely co-ordinated power centres, and which emerges from an interaction between only partly translatable, communally grounded meanings.

A most important point has been promoted for some time by S. M. Eisenstadt in his seminal comparative study of civilizations. Eisenstadt insists that the very idea of the *social system* is in need of a radical reconsideration. He suggests that no human population is confined within a single system, 'but rather in a multiplicity of only partly coalescing organizations, collectivities and systems'.

Unlike the view found in many sociological and anthropological studies—namely that social systems are natural or given, and that they change through internal processes of differentiation—we stress that these systems are constructed through continuous process and that this construction is always both there and very fragile. . . . These systems never develop as entirely self-enclosed ones. . . . Different structures evince differences in organization, continuity and change and, together with their patterns may change to different degrees or in different constellations within the 'same' society.[2]

Thus the current sociological theory (at least in its most advanced versions) takes cognizance of the increasingly apparent plurality and heterogeneity of the sociocultural world, and on the whole abandons the orthodox imagery of a co-ordinated, hierarchized, deviance-fighting social system in favour of a

[1] Alain Touraine, Michel Wieviorka, François Dubet, *The Workers' Movement*, trans. Ian Patterson (Cambridge University Press, 1987), 20, 21.

[2] S. N. Eisenstadt, *A Sociological Approach to Comparative Civilisation: The Development and Directions of a Research Program* (The Hebrew University, Jerusalem, 1986), 29–30.

much more fluid, processual social setting with no clear-cut distinction between order and abnormality, consensus and conflict. There is, however, another large group of theoretical issues posited by the advent of postmodernity, which have not attracted as yet sufficient attention. These are issues related to the adequacy of the concept of 'society' as the horizon and the most inclusive category of social analysis.

For reasons which can be both understood and justified, the concept of 'society' has been historically cut to the measure of the nation state; however defined, this concept invariably carried ideas intimately associated with a situation which only a nation state (in its reality or in its promise) could bring about and sustain: a degree of normative—legal and moral—unity, an all-embracing system of classification which entailed and located every unit, a relatively unambiguous distribution of power and influence, and a setting for action sufficiently uniform for *similar actions* to be expected to bring *similar consequences* for the whole and thus to be interpreted in a similar way. Moreover, the nation state prototype for the concept of society endowed the latter with a visible *developmental tendency*; a self-sustained and self-propelled tendency, with all its relevant explanatory factors to be found *inside* the society in question—so that all *outside* factors could be theoretically reduced to the role of environment and accounted for, if at all, by the *caeteris paribus* formula.

Sociologists were always aware that the theoretical concept of society as a compact, sealed totality merely approximates the reality of any nation state, however large and justified in its ecumenical ambitions. In reality, the nation states, those prototypes of theoretical 'societies', were porous, and porous in a double sense; much of what went on inside could not be fully explained without a reference to factors uncontrolled by the inside authorities—and factors which had to be interpreted in terms of motives and agencies, not just in terms of the passive resistance of an environment treated solely as an *object* of action; and much of what was going on inside the nation states revealed its true significance only when traced through its consequences outside the boundaries of its home society—consequences which could look very different when seen in such a wider perspective. One could indeed find in sociological literature frequent warnings and rejoinders to this effect; yet few, if any, conclusions were drawn from them in sociological practice. It seems that most sociologists of the era of modern orthodoxy believed that—all being said—the nation state is close enough to its own postulate of sovereignty to validate the use of its theoretical expression—the 'society' concept—as an adequate framework for sociological analysis.

In the postmodern world, this belief carries less conviction than ever before. With the sovereignty of nation states vividly displaying its limitations in the 'input' as much as in the 'output' sense, the traditional model of society loses its credence as a reliable frame of reference, while the consequences of its persistent use in sociological analysis gain in gravity. Given the centrality of the notion of society in sociological analysis (indeed, its tacit presence in *all* sociological analysis, if only as the condition for the given space being an appropriate object of sociological treatment), this new situation confronts sociological theory with tasks whose total dimension it is too early to ascertain.

Conditions of Theoretical Emancipation

What the theory of postmodernity must discard in the first place is the assumption of an *'organismic'*, equilibrated social totality it purports to model in Parsons-like style: the vision of a 'principally co-ordinated' and enclosed totality (*a*) with a degree of cohesiveness, (*b*) equilibrated or marked by an overwhelming tendency to equilibration, (*c*) unified by an internally coherent value syndrome and a core authority able to promote and enforce it and (*d*) defining its elements in terms of the function they perform in that process of equilibration or the reproduction of the equilibrated state. The sought theory must assume instead that the social condition it intends to model is essentially and perpetually *unequilibrated*: composed of elements with a degree of autonomy large enough to justify the view of totality as a kaleidoscopic—momentary and contingent—outcome of interaction. The orderly, structured nature of totality cannot be taken for granted; nor can its pseudo-representational construction be seen as the purpose of theoretical activity. The randomness of the global outcome of uncoordinated activities cannot be treated as a departure from the pattern which the totality strives to maintain; any pattern that may temporarily emerge out of the random movements of autonomous agents is as haphazard and unmotivated as the one that could emerge in its place or the one bound to replace it, if also for a time only. All order that can be found is a local, emergent and transitory phenomenon; its nature can be best grasped by a metaphor of a whirlpool appearing in the flow of a river, retaining its shape only for a relatively brief period and only at the expense of incessant metabolism and constant renewal of content.

The theory of postmodernity must be free of the metaphor of progress that informed all competing theories of modern society. With the totality dissipated into a series of randomly emerging, shifting and evanescent islands of order, its temporal record cannot be linearly represented. Perpetual local transformations do not add up so as to prompt (much less to assure) in effect an increased homogeneity, rationality or organic systemness of the whole. The postmodern condition is a site of constant mobility and change, but no clear direction of development. The image of Brownian movement offers an apt metaphor for this aspect of postmodernity: each momentary state is neither a necessary effect of the preceding state nor the sufficient cause of the next one. The postmodern condition is both *undetermined* and *undetermining*. It 'unbinds' time; weakens the constraining impact of the past and effectively prevents colonization of the future.

Similarly, the theory of postmodernity would do well if it disposed of concepts like *system* in its orthodox, organismic sense (or, for that matter, *society*), suggestive of a sovereign totality logically prior to its parts, a totality bestowing meaning on its parts, a totality whose welfare or perpetuation all smaller (and, by definition, subordinate) units serve; in short, a totality assumed to define, and be practically capable of defining, the meanings of individual actions and agencies that compose it. A sociology geared to the conditions of postmodernity ought to replace the category of *society* with that of *sociality*; a category that tries to convey the processual modality of social reality, the dialectical play of randomness and pattern (or, from the agent's point of view, of freedom and dependence); and a category that refuses to take the structured character of the process for granted—which treats instead all found structures as emergent accomplishments.

With their field of vision organized around the focal point of system-like, resourceful and meaning-bestowing totality, sociological theories of modernity (which conceived of themselves as sociological theories *tout court*) concentrated on the vehicles of homogenization and conflict-resolution in a relentless search for a solution to the 'Hobbesian problem'. This cognitive perspective (shared with the one realistic referent of the concept of 'society'—the national state, the only totality in history able seriously to entertain the ambition of contrived, artificially sustained and managed monotony and homogeneity) a priori disqualified any 'uncertified' agency; unpatterned and unregulated spontaneity of the autonomous agent was pre-defined as a destabilizing and, indeed, anti-social factor marked for taming and extinction in the continuous struggle for societal survival. By the same token, prime importance was assigned to the mechanisms and weapons of order-promotion and pattern-maintenance: the state and the legitimation of its authority, power, socialization, culture, ideology, etc.—all selected for the role they played in the promotion of pattern, monotony, predictability and thus also manageability of conduct.

A sociological theory of postmodernity is bound to reverse the structure of the cognitive field. The focus must be now on agency; more correctly, on the *habitat* in which agency operates and which it produces in the course of operation. As it offers the agency the sum total of resources for all possible action as well as the field inside which the action-orienting and action-oriented relevancies may be plotted, the habitat is the territory inside which both freedom and dependency of the agency are constituted (and, indeed, perceived as such). Unlike the system-like totalities of modern social theory, habitat neither determines the conduct of the agents nor defines its meaning; it is no more (but no less either) than the setting in which both action and meaning-assignment are *possible*. Its own identity is as under-determined and motile, as emergent and transitory, as those of the actions and their meanings that form it.

There is one crucial area, though, in which the habitat performs a determining (systematizing, patterning) role: it sets the agenda for the 'business of life' through supplying the inventory of ends and the pool of means. The way in which the ends and means are supplied also determines the meaning of the 'business of life': the nature of the tasks all agencies confront and have to take up in one form or another. In so far as the ends are offered as potentially alluring rather than obligatory, and rely for their choice on their own seductiveness rather than the supporting power of coercion, the 'business of life' splits into a series of choices. The series is not pre-structured, or is pre-structured only feebly and above all inconclusively. For this reason the choices through which the life of the agent is construed and sustained is best seen (as it tends to be seen by the agents themselves) as adding up to the process of *self-constitution*. To underline the graduated and ultimately inconclusive nature of the process, self-constitution is best viewed as *self-assembly*.

I propose that sociality, habitat, self-constitution and self-assembly should occupy in the sociological theory of postmodernity the central place that the orthodoxy of modern social theory had reserved for the categories of society, normative group (like class or community), socialization and control.

Main Tenets of the Theory of Postmodernity

1. Under the postmodern condition, habitat is a *complex system*. According to contemporary mathematics, complex systems differ from mechanical systems (those assumed by the orthodox, modern theory of society) in two crucial respects. First, they are unpredictable; second, they are not controlled by statistically significant factors (the circumstance demonstrated by the mathematical proof of the famous 'butterfly effect'). The consequences of these two distinctive features of complex systems are truly revolutionary in relation to the received wisdom of sociology. The 'systemness' of the postmodern habitat no longer lends itself to the organismic metaphor, which means that agencies active within the habitat cannot be assessed in terms of functionality or dysfunctionality. The successive states of the habitat appear to be unmotivated and free from constraints of deterministic logic. And the most formidable research strategy modern sociology had developed—statistical analysis—is of no use in exploring the dynamics of social phenomena and evaluating the probabilities of their future development. Significance and numbers have parted ways. Statistically insignificant phenomena may prove to be decisive, and their decisive role cannot be grasped in advance.

2. The postmodern habitat is a complex (non-mechanical) system for two closely related reasons. First, there is no 'goal setting' agency with overall managing and co-ordinating capacities or ambitions—one whose presence would provide a vantage point from which the aggregate of effective agents appears as a 'totality' with a determined structure of relevances; a totality

which one can think as of an *organization*. Second, the habitat is populated by a great number of agencies, most of them single-purpose, some of them small, some big, but none large enough to subsume or otherwise determine the behaviour of the others. Focusing on a single purpose considerably enhances the effectiveness of each agency in the field of its own operation, but prevents each area of the habitat from being controlled from a single source, as the field of operation of any agency never exhausts the whole area the action is affecting. Operating in different fields yet zeroing in on shared areas, agencies are *partly* dependent on each other, but the lines of dependence cannot be fixed and thus their actions (and consequences) remain staunchly under-determined, that is autonomous.

3. Autonomy means that agents are only partly, if at all, constrained in their pursuit of whatever they have institutionalized as their purpose. To a large extent, they are free to pursue the purpose to the best of their mastery over resources and managerial capacity. They are free (and tend) to view the rest of the habitat shared with other agents as a collection of opportunities and 'problems' to be resolved or removed. Opportunity is what increases output in the pursuit of purpose, problems are what threatens the decrease or a halt of production. In ideal circumstances (maximization of opportunities and minimization of problems) each agent would tend to go in the pursuit of their purpose as far as resources would allow; the availability of resources is the only reason for action they need and thus the sufficient guarantee of the action's reasonability. The possible impact on other agents' opportunities is not automatically re-forged into the limitation of the agent's own output. The many products of purpose-pursuing activities of numerous partly interdependent but relatively autonomous agents must yet find, *ex post facto*, their relevance, utility and demand-securing attractiveness. The products are bound to be created in volumes exceeding the pre-existing demand motivated by already articulated problems. They are still to seek their place and meaning as well as the problems that they may claim to be able to resolve.

[*Intimations of Postmodernity* (Routledge, London, 1992), 39–42, 53–7, 189–93.]

8 Sociology and the Study of Society

The acceleration and expansion of change has modified our image of social life. The latter is dominated by the level of action through which human societies create and transform themselves. The analysis of modern societies, which is the specific field of sociology, was at first identified with the study of political and juridical institutions, because the most important things in these societies were the movement of commodities and capital, the security of roads, the respect of contracts and the standardization of weights and measures; this gave rise to a juridical interpretation of social life as a totality of regulated exchanges. By contrast, industrial society gave priority to production over exchange and work over transport. While the central categories of social analysis in the first phase were those of the market and the city, money and law, the guardians and the law-breakers, industrial society shifted the emphasis to the machine and the factory, social relations of production, wages and profits, strikes and managerial power, the latter often supported by public authority. Before the industrial revolution, the analysis of change was separated from that of order, because the causes of change were mainly external: the availability of new raw materials or the discovery of new markets, conquests or the replacement of one dynasty by another. But sociology—as the offspring of industrial society—naturally inclined to define society in terms of change. This is the underlying significance of the distinction between community (*Gemeinschaft*) and society (*Gesellschaft*), first formulated by Tönnies and later developed by Durkheim in terms of forms of integration and division of labour. For Weber, Durkheim and Parsons, modern society is above all characterized by a movement towards modernity, i.e. the process of rationalization and secularization. This image of a society in permanent movement is linked to the philosophy of the Enlightenment, but it was not sufficient for the purposes of sociological analysis. From the sociological point of view, modernization was as destructive as it was creative: it uprooted individuals from their original environment, destroyed local solidarities, proletarized the workers and created dangerous and unhealthy cities. Moreover, it proved impossible to conceptualize the whole of social life as change, because industrialization only affected the means of production and did not directly modify needs, ideas and languages. Sociology could take a reformist or a neo-conservative turn, but in either case, it was always trying to re-establish order within change and integration against a background of fragmentation. Hence the peculiar ambiguity of this discipline: it was oriented towards progress and modernity, but also engaged in the search for a principle of order which would be for modern societies what religion, political institutions and education had been for traditional ones. The ambiguity is built into the very idea of society, a basic but by no means simple concept of classical sociology; an unstable mixture of social modernity and political order, it reflects the historical reality of the nation-state. In fact, the analysis of change or development is always concerned with concrete totalities, nations dominated by states whose task is to maintain or construct the unity of the nation in the context of ongoing transformations. Classical sociology thus tends to identify the study of social change with that of political and institutional order, and this spontaneous identification is today reproduced by sociologists of the emerging nations, particularly in Latin America and the Arab world. The convergence of social and political categories in the central concept of *institution* is thus characteristic of classical sociology and corresponds to a limited scope of social change. This helps to pinpoint one of the most far-reaching changes in experience and thought during the last century: when people lived within a national (or even infra-national) space, the nation was synonymous with society, but the obvious dissociation of these two realities in our era of economic and cultural inter-nationalization (accompanied by a reactive search for more immediate ident-ities and communities) undermines the received image of society.

There is another image, still in the process of formation, which reflects more adequately our increased ability to transform our own existence. During the last fifty years, we have discovered that we can not only organize the exchange of material goods and produce them more efficiently on the basis of the division and mechanization of labour; we can also produce symbolic goods, languages and informations and modify our relationship to ourselves, most obviously through the progress of biology and medicine. Social life is no longer perceived as a restricted space for liberty in a universe of necessity but as an indefinite and perhaps infinite space, so that we must abandon not only the conception of the human world as a microcosm within a macrocosm, but also the idea that social life takes place within essential limits which in practice coincide with those of the nation-state and its juridical institutions or educa-tional programmes. [. . .]

As we shall see, this also changes our understanding of social actors and social conflicts. In this context—the most global perspective on social change—the contrast with classical and pre-classical sociology is particularly pronounced. The social philosophers—e.g. Locke and Montesquieu—were interested in the preconditions of social order; sociology, born of the industrial revolution, was concerned with ways and means of reimposing order on the 'great transformation' (K. Polanyi). Today we can no longer rely on principles of order or images of the just society; we can only think in terms of action, change and social relations, and theorize in terms of strategies, politics, or—as I prefer—the conflictual self-production of society.

It is true that the sixties and seventies saw the emergence of another image of social life, diametrically opposed to the one sketched above. Some French philosophers adopted the ideas of Marcuse, who had stressed the increasing capacity of modern societies to control and contain themselves. In different ways, Althusser, Foucault and Bourdieu developed and diffused the image of society as an implacable machine which serves to maintain inequality, power and privilege. This idea of sociology as a critique of order has been popular among the intellectuals and the social groups most directly influenced by them (particularly teachers and social workers); it will always have an important role to play in social thought, because every 'open' complex of social and political relations tends to transform itself into a 'closed' system of integration and exclusion, reproduction of privileges, and justification of the established order. In a similar way, a sociology of crises must be added to the sociology of action and order. The classics were already interested in anomie and the effects of proletarization, and the current emphasis on action and change makes us more sensitive to the obstacles which still prevent the formation of new social actors, especially in the case of social, ethnic and cultural minorities. [. . .]

By contrast, a sociology of action and change casts doubt on all interpretations which describe social life in terms of a system of an organism capable of self-regulation and striving for equilibrium. Not only do the roles of institution and socialization lose much of their importance; more fundamentally, the very idea of *society* should be eliminated. In an earlier phase, sociology was the study of society; it should now be defined as the study of social relations and—increasingly—social change. The idea of society, which was—as noted above—inseparable from the triumph of the nation-state, was an image of order. As if change could only be understood with reference to an order, as if the various aspects of social life were the organs of a body regulated by a central mechanism; as if outside the social order there was only chaos, private interest and violence.

The limited separation of state and civil society, which goes back to the 18th century, is now being accentuated to such an extent that it destroys the very idea of society. The most extreme version of the division separates a complex and changing field of social relations from a state which is above all charged with international responsibilities. This leads to the decomposition of the political field itself. [. . .]

The fundamental fact of the growing separation of society and the state can also be interpreted as the progressive constitution of civil society. Where the concept of the latter appeared in the 18th century, it was associated with the idea of social classes and their conflicts, centring on the control and use of the results of economic production. Today it is even more true that society is the totality of stakes of social conflicts. Because industrial societies have increased their ability to intervene in their own structures—in other words: their capacity of self-production—the field of conflicts has been broadened and at the same time separated more clearly from political struggles in the strict sense, i.e. those that have to do with the conquest of state power. The real centre of social life is the general and permanent debate about the utilization of new technologies, new instruments for the transformation of personal and collective life. If we look back at the long century of industrialization, our first impression is that the workers' movement played a central role for which there is no successor. But a closer examination shows that the contemporary debate has become much more multi-faceted, ramified and comprehensive than the social question then was. From nuclear industry to genetic engineering, from the media to the universities—in all those domains we see the development of discussion and of currents of opinion which all relate to the same central question: under what conditions can our technological potential be used to enhance the liberty and security of every individual, instead of subordinating individuals and groups to a technocratic power? This question is not only important in itself; it also shows us the limits of the image of social life as pure change. We should not think of ourselves as simply consumers or, at best, strategists, defending our interests within complex organizations and controlled markets. Change is not simply the sum total of modifications of the environment; it is also a sign of cultural creativity and of a power which has expanded beyond the spheres of economy and politics into the production and diffusion of informations and—in a more general sense—symbolic goods, i.e. culture. In this sense, contemporary sociology can take the guidelines of classical sociology to their most extreme consequences. Even more than before, it is concerned with the study of modernity, the self-transforming capacity of society; and it sees the struggle for social control over this capacity as the structuring principle of social life.

Social Relations and Social Movements

We are now witnessing the decomposition of previously central analytical categories. When we talked about social classes, we were at least implicitly alluding to the idea of the *estate* (in the sense of a 'third estate'), i.e. to the combination of economic conditions of life and hereditary privileges (or exclusion from privileges). Even today, the word 'bourgeois' suggests the rentier rather than the industrialist. But such inequalities, reinforced by symbols and institutional mechanisms are less and less relevant to our societies. The notion of class therefore tends to disappear and it is most frequently replaced by the abovementioned image of society which separates a central mass from a privileged minority at the top and the more numerous marginals at the bottom. The sociologists who try to defend the image of a highly stratified and hierarchical society have to rely on an ideological construction to make themselves heard; they compare real societies with an ideal society that would be characterized by perfect mobility. But this model bears no semblance to reality: who would want to live in a society where children would be separated from their parents at birth, in order to prevent the consolidation of inequality during the first years of their life? This kind of abstract egalitarianism is sometimes invoked to show how far the democratic societies have departed from their principles. But concrete experience has another story to tell: social barriers are constantly lowered, even if it is true that some luxury goods become common among the rich before they are diffused more slowly among the rest of the population. A shared mass culture has become the predominant pattern in the countries where the majority of households owns television sets, radios, refrigerators, washing machines and cars; where schooling has been extended by several years; where the signs of social hierarchies (especially with regard to clothing) are disappearing; and where economic growth has led to a geographical and social mobility which is often underestimated. These obvious facts do not add up to the picture of an egalitarian society, not even in the sense of equal opportunities, but they show the inadequacy of concepts which have more to do with a society of reproduction than with a society of growth, change and mass consumption.

But if we go beyond these initial observations, we must raise the question of the nature of social actors and hence also conflicts and negotiations in societies that are characterized by change rather than by order. And here we arrive at one of the most important shifts in social thought. For a long time, it was taken for granted that an objective situation determines collective and individual behaviour and that the conditions of peasants, tradesmen and workers, defined in economic and political terms, would give rise to peasant, popular or worker's movements. In the Hegelian–Marxist tradition, theorists talked about the transition from a 'class-in-itself' to a 'class-for-itself', thus assuming that a class can be defined without reference to a class consciousness, and that specific actors, such as political parties or groups of intellectuals, have the ability to 'give' consciousness to the social strata which do not develop it in a natural fashion. This idea has been substantiated by historical research; it was very often a crisis of the state accentuated by the rebellion of privileged groups, such as the French aristocracy at the end of the 18th century, that created an opening for the expression of popular discontent, and the resultant movement was radicalized as the social and political order disintegrated. But in contemporary industrial societies, situations do not determine actions, it is, rather, action that brings to light relations of domination and subordination which lack a visible juridical or political expression. The concept of class must therefore be replaced, as a central category of sociological analysis, by the concept of the *social movement*. The main reason for this is that the actions of those who hold power now tend to effect the whole of social life, because they produce models which determine the patterns of a mass society. Consequently, at the receiving and potentially resisting end, we no longer find clearly delimited groups, such as the wage-labourers in a factory but rather a *public*—the public which watches television or receives medical treatment. The action which it can undertake is not objectively pre-determined; on the contrary, an actor is only constituted by the detachment from the situation of the consumer who oscillates between the attitudes of dependent conformism and global rejection. [. . .]

To sum up: in a society dominated less by the transmission of privileges than by the power to model collective experience, the existence of social actors no longer precedes their action—it is produced by it. The idea of a 'class-in-itself', defined without reference to its consciousness of itself, is therefore unacceptable. Slaves and serfs lived in social conditions defined by the law, and the constraints to which they were subjected made collective action difficult and prevented the development of a conflictual class consciousness. The workers' movement was, by contrast, resisting a power that was more economic than political and defined in general rather than personal terms; it therefore emphasized possible action more than imposed domination. The new social movements have moved further in this direction. They are more concerned with active intervention, rather than simply with breaking the links of dependence; and above all, the social actor who resists domination now appeals more and more directly to the values of creation and change, which in the past seemed to be monopolized by the ruling groups, whereas the dominated ones were more inclined to envisage a return to the past and to condemn historical evolution as a fall from a golden to an iron age.

Classical sociology hesitated between the study of social integration and the construction of a meaning of history. Society was seen as existing in history and as moved by it from tradition to modernity; its main task was to defend its cohesion while completing the mutation. Today the idea of evolution has disappeared and been replaced by the more neutral concept of change. On the other hand, actors are now recognized as more than simply the components of society or the limbs of a social body; they are real actors who transform the increased ability of society to act upon itself into actions, conflicts and negotiations which give rise to forms of social and cultural organization.

['Is Sociology still the Study of Society?', *Thesis Eleven*, 23 (1989), 174–6, 177, 178, 181–2, 182–5, 185–6.]

(b) Arguments

9   The End of the Social

The social is not a clear and unequivocal process. Do modern societies correspond to a process of socialisation or to one of progressive desocialisation?
Everything depends on one's understanding of the term and none of these
is fixed; all are reversible. Thus the institutions which have sign-posted the 'advance of the social' (urbanisation, concentration, production, work, medicine,
education, social security, insurance, etc.) including capital, which was undoubtedly the most effective socialisation medium of all, could be said to
produce and destroy the social in one and the same movement.

If the social is formed out of abstract instances which are laid down one after
the other on the ruins of the symbolic and ceremonial edifice of former
societies, then these institutions produce more and more of them. But at the
same time they consecrate that ravenous, all-consuming abstraction which
perhaps devours precisely the 'essential marrow' of the social. From that point
of view, it could be said that the social regresses to the same degree as its
institutions develop.

The process accelerates and reaches its maximal extent with mass media and
information. Media, *all* media, information, *all* information, act in two directions: outwardly they produce more of the social, inwardly they neutralise
social relations and the social itself.

But then, if the social is both destroyed by what produces it (the media,
information) and reabsorbed by what it produces (the masses), it follows that
its definition is empty, and that this term which serves as universal alibi for
every discourse, no longer analyses anything, no longer designates anything.
Not only is it superfluous and useless—wherever it appears it conceals something else: defiance, death, seduction, ritual, repetition—it conceals that it is
only abstraction and residue, or even simply an *effect* of the social, a simulation
and an illusion.

Even the term 'social relation' is enigmatic. What is a 'social relation', what
is the 'production of social relations'? Here everything is spurious. Is the social
instantaneously, and as if by definition, a 'relation', which already presupposes
a serious abstraction and a rational algebra of the social—or else is it something
different from what the term 'relation' neatly rationalises? Does the 'social
relation' perhaps exist *for something different*, namely for what it destroys? Does
it perhaps ratify, perhaps inaugurate the end of the social?

The 'social sciences' came to consecrate this obviousness and agelessness of the social. But we must change our tune. There were *societies without the social*, just as there were societies without history. Networks of symbolic ties were precisely neither 'relational' nor 'social'. At the other extreme, our 'society' is perhaps in the process of putting an end to the social, of burying the social beneath a simulation of the social. There are many ways for it to die—as many as there are definitions. Perhaps the social will have had only an ephemeral existence, in the narrow gap between the symbolic formations and our 'society' where it is dying. Before, there is not yet any social; after, there is no longer any. Only 'sociology' can seem to testify to its agelessness, and the supreme gibberish of the 'social sciences' will still echo it long after its disappearance.

For two centuries now, the uninterrupted energy of the social has come from deterritorialisation and from concentration in ever more unified agencies. A centralised perspective space which orientates everything inserted into it by simple convergence along the 'line of flight' towards infinity (in effect, the social, like space and time, opens up a perspective towards infinity). The social can only be defined from this panoptic point of view.

But let us not forget that this perspective space (in painting and architecture as in politics or the economy) is only one simulation model among others, and that it is characterised only by the fact that it gives rise to effects of truth, of objectivity, unknown and unheard of in the other models. Perhaps, even this is only a *delusion*? In which case everything that has been contrived and staged in this 'comedy of errors' of the social has never had any deep significance. Ultimately, things have never functioned socially, but symbolically, magically, irrationally, etc. Which implies the formula: capital is a *defiance* of society. That is to say that this perspective, this panoptic machine, this machine of truth, of rationality, of productivity which is capital, is without objective finality, without reason: it is above all a violence, and this violence is perpetrated by the social on the social, but basically it is not a social machine, it doesn't care a damn about capital or likewise about the social in their equally interdependent and antagonistic definition. This is to say, once more, that there is no contract, no contract is ever exchanged between distinct agencies according to the law—that is all sound and fury—there are only ever stakes, defiances, that is to say something which does not proceed via a 'social relation'.

Here several hypotheses are possible:

1. *The social has basically never existed*. There never has been any 'social relation'. Nothing has ever functioned socially. On this inescapable basis of challenge, seduction and death, there has never been anything but *simulation* of the social and the social relation. In which case, there is no point dreaming about a 'real' sociality, a hidden sociality, an ideal socialist: this just hypostatises a simulacrum. If the social is a simulation, the only likely turn of events

is that of a brutal *de-simulation*—the social ceasing to take itself as a space of reference and to play the game, and putting an end at last to power, to the effect of power and to the mirror of the social which perpetuates it. A de-simulation which itself captures the style of a challenge (the reverse of capital's challenge of the social and society): a challenge to the belief that capital and power exist according to their own logic—*they have none*, they vanish as apparatuses as soon as the simulation of social space is undone.[1] This is really what we are seeing today: the disintegration of the whole idea of the social, the consumption and involution of the social, the breakdown of the social simulacrum, a genuine defiance of the constructive and productive approach to the social which dominates us. All quite suddenly, as if the social had never existed. A breakdown which has all the features of a catastrophe, not an evolution or revolution. No longer a 'crisis' of the social, but the reabsorption of its system. Without having anything to do with those marginal defections (of the mad, women, druggies, delinquents), which, on the contrary, supply new energy to the failing social. This reabsorption process can no longer be resocialised. Like a ghost at dawn, its principle of reality and of social rationality simply fades away.

2. *The social has really existed, it exists even more and more*, it invests everything, it alone exists. Far from being volatilised, it is the social which triumphs; the reality of the social is imposed everywhere. But, contrary to the antiquated idea which makes the social into an objective progress of mankind, everything which escapes it being only residue, it is possible to envisage that *the social itself is only residue*, and that, if it has triumphed in the real, it is precisely as such. Litter piling up from the symbolic order as it blows around, it is the social as remainder which has assumed real force and which is soon to be universal. Here is a more subtle form of death.

In this event, we are really even deeper in the social, even deeper in pure excrement, in the fantastic congestion of dead labor, of dead and institution-alised relations within terrorist bureaucracies, of dead languages and grammars (the very term 'relation' already has something dead about it, something about death to it).

Then of course it can no longer be said that the social is dying, *since it is already the accumulation of death*. In effect we are in a civilisation of the super-social, and simultaneously in a civilisation of non-degradable, indestructible residue, piling up as the social spreads.

Waste and recycling: such would be the social in the image of a production whose cycle has long escaped the 'social' finalties to become a completely described spiral nebula, rotating and expanding with every 'revolution' it

---

[1] But defying the social can take the reverse form of a renewed outbreak of the social simulacrum, of social demand, of demand *for* the social. An exacerbated, compulsive hypercon-formity, a much more pressing demand for the social as norm and as discourse.

makes. Thus one sees the social expanding throughout history as a 'rational' control of residues, and a rational *production* of residues.

1544 saw the opening of the first great poor-house in Paris: vagrants, lunatics, the sick, everyone not integrated by the group and discarded as remainders were taken in charge under the emerging sign of the social. This was extended to the dimensions of National Assistance in the nineteenth century, then Social Security in the twentieth century. Proportional to the reinforcement of social reason, it is the whole community which soon becomes residual and hence, by one more spiral, the social which piles up. When the remainders reach the dimensions of the whole of society, one has a perfect socialisation. Everybody is completely excluded and taken in charge, completely disintegrated and socialised.

Symbolic integration is replaced by a functional integration, functional institutions take charge of the residue from symbolic disintegration—a social agency appears where there was none, nor even any name for it. 'Social relations' fester, proliferate, grow proportionately richer with this disintegration. And the social sciences cap it off. Whence the piquancy of an expression like: 'the responsibility of society vis-a-vis its underprivileged members', when we know the 'social' is precisely the agency which arises from this dereliction.

Whence the interest of *Le Monde*'s 'Society' column where paradoxically only immigrants, delinquents, women, etc. appear: precisely those who have not been socialised; the social 'case' being analogous to the pathological case. Pockets to be absorbed, segments which the social isolates the more it spreads. Designated as *refuse* on the horizon of the social, they thus fall under its jurisdiction and are fated to find their place in a widening sociality. It is on these *remainders* that the social machine starts up again and finds support for a new extension. But what happens when everybody is socialized? Then the machine stops, the dynamic is reversed, and it is *the whole social system which becomes residue*. As the social progressively gets rid of all of its residue, it becomes residual itself. By placing residual categories under the rubric 'Society', the social *designates itself as remainder*.

3. *The social has well and truly existed, but does not exist any more.* It has existed as coherent space, as reality principle: the social relation, the production of social relations, the social as dynamic abstraction, scene of conflicts and historical contradictions, the social as structure and as stake, as strategy and as ideal—all this has had an end in view, all this has meant something. The social has not always been a delusion, as in the first hypothesis, nor remainder, as in the second. But precisely, it has only had an end in view, a meaning as power, as work, as capital, from the perspective space of a rational distribution, from the finalised space of an ideal convergence, which is also that of production—in short, in the narrow gap of second-order simulacra, and, absorbed into third-order simulacra, it is dying.

End of the perspective space of the social. The rational sociality of the contract, dialectical sociality (that of the State and of civil society, of public and private, of the social and the individual) gives way to the sociality of contact, of the circuit and transistorised network of millions of molecules and particles maintained in a random gravitational field, magnetised by the constant circulation and the thousands of tactical combinations which electrify them. But is it still a question of the *socius*? Where is sociality in Los Angeles? And where will it be later on, in a future generation (for Los Angeles is still that of TV, movies, the telephone and the automobile), that of a total dissemination, of a ventilation of individuals as terminals of information, in an even more measurable—not convergent, but connected—space: a space of connection? The social only exists in a perspective space, it dies in the space of simulation, which is also a space of deterrence.

The space of simulation confuses the real with the model. There is no longer any critical and speculative distance between the real and the rational. There is no longer really even any projection of models in the real (which is still equivalent to the substitution of the map for the territory in Borges), but an in-the-field, here-and-now transfiguration of the real into model. A fantastic short-circuit: the real is hyperrealised. Neither realised, nor idealised: but hyperrealised. The hyperreal is the abolition of the real not by violent destruction, but by its assumption, elevation to the strength of the model. Anticipation, deterrence, preventive transfiguration, etc.: the model acts as a sphere of absorption of the real.

It also puts an end to the social in the same way. The social, if it existed with second-order simulacra, no longer even has the opportunity to be produced with third-order ones: from the beginning it is trapped in its own 'blown up' and desperate staging, in its own obscenity. Signs of this hyperrealisation of the social, signs of its reduplication and its anticipated fulfilment are everywhere. The transparency of the social relation is flaunted, signified, consumed everywhere. The history of the social will never have had time to lead to revolution: it will have been outstripped by signs of the social and of revolution. The social will never have had time to lead to socialism, it will have been short-circuited by the hypersocial, by the hyperreality of the social (but perhaps socialism is no more than this?). Thus the proletariat will not have even had time to deny itself as such: the concept of class will have dissolved well before, into some parodic, extended double, like 'the mass of workers' or simply into a retrospective simulation of the proletariat. Thus, even before political economy leads to its dialectical overthrow, to the resolution of all needs and to the optimal organisation of things, before it would have been able to see whether there was any basis to all that, it will have been captivated by hyperreality of the economy (the stepping up of production, the precession of the production of demand before that of goods, the indefinite scenario of crisis).

Nothing has come to the end of its history, or will henceforth any more, for nothing escapes this precession of simulacra. And the social itself has died before having given up its secret.[1]

Nevertheless let us tenderly recall the unbelievable naivety of social and socialist thinking, for thus having been able to reify as universal and to elevate as ideal of transparency such a totally ambiguous and contradictory—worse, such a residual or imaginary—worse, such an already abolished in its very simulation—'reality': the social.

[*In the Shadow of the Silent Majorities, or, The End of the Social and Other Essays*, trans. Paul Foss, John Johnston, and Paul Patton (Semiotexte, New York, 1983), 65–9, 70–5, 82–4, 85–6.]

DONNA HARAWAY

10   Fractured Identities

It has become difficult to name one's feminism by a single adjective—or even to insist in every circumstance upon the noun. Consciousness of exclusion through naming is acute. Identities seem contradictory, partial, and strategic. With the hard-won recognition of their social and historical constitution, gender, race, and class cannot provide the basis for belief in 'essential' unity. There is nothing about being 'female' that naturally binds women. There is not even such a state as 'being' female, itself a highly complex category constructed in contested sexual scientific discourses and other social practices. Gender, race, or class consciousness is an achievement forced on us by the terrible historical experience of the contradictory social realities of patriarchy, colonialism, and capitalism. And who counts as 'us' in my own rhetoric? Which identities are available to ground such a potent political myth called 'us', and what could motivate enlistment in this collectivity? Painful fragmentation among feminists (not to mention among women) along every possible fault line has made the concept of *woman* elusive, an excuse for the matrix of women's dominations of each other. For me—and for many who share a similar historical location in white, professional middle-class, female, radical, North American, mid-adult bodies—the sources of a crisis in political identity are legion. The recent history for much of the US left and US feminism has been a response to this kind of crisis by endless splitting and searches for a new essential unity. But there has also been a growing recognition of another response through coalition—affinity, not identity.[2] [. . .]

---

[1] Fourth hypothesis: *The implosion of the social into the masses*. This hypothesis is akin to hypothesis 3 (simulation/deterrence/implosion) in another form. It is developed in the main text.

[2] Powerful developments of coalition politics emerge from 'Third World' speakers, speaking from nowhere, the displaced centre of the universe, earth: 'We live on the third planet from the

The theoretical and practical struggle against unity-through-domination or unity-through-incorporation ironically not only undermines the justifications for patriarchy, colonialism, humanism, positivism, essentialism, scientism, and other unlamented-isms, but *all* claims for an organic or natural standpoint. I think that radical and socialist/Marxist-feminisms have also undermined their/our own epistemological strategies and that this is a crucially valuable step in imagining possible unities. It remains to be seen whether all 'epistemologies' as Western political people have known them fail us in the task to build effective affinities.

It is important to note that the effort to construct revolutionary standpoints, epistemologies as achievements of people committed to changing the world, has been part of the process showing the limits of identification. The acid tools of postmodernist theory and the constructive tools of ontological discourse about revolutionary subjects might be seen as ironic allies in dissolving Western selves in the interests of survival. We are excruciatingly conscious of what it means to have a historically constituted body. But with the loss of innocence in our origin, there is no expulsion from the Garden either. Our politics lose the indulgence of guilt with the *naïveté* of innocence. But what would another political myth for socialist-feminism look like? What kind of politics could embrace partial, contradictory, permanently unclosed constructions of personal and collective selves and still be faithful, effective—and, ironically, socialist-feminist?

I do not know of any other time in history when there was greater need for political unity to confront effectively the dominations of 'race', 'gender', 'sexuality', and 'class'. I also do not know of any other time when the kind of unity we might help build could have been possible. None of 'us' have any longer the symbolic or material capability of dictating the shape of reality to any of 'them'. Or at least 'we' cannot claim innocence from practising such dominations. White women, including socialist feminists, discovered (that is, were forced kicking and screaming to notice) the non-innocence of the category 'woman'. That consciousness changes the geography of all previous categories; it denatures them as heat denatures a fragile protein. Cyborg feminists have to argue that 'we' do not want any more natural matrix of unity and that no construction is whole. Innocence, and the corollary insistence on victimhood as the only ground for insight, has done enough damage. But the constructed revolutionary subject must give late-twentieth-century people pause as well. In the fraying of identities and in the reflexive strategies for

sun'—*Sun Poem* by Jamaican writer, Edward Kamau Braithwaite, review by Nathaniel Mackey, *Sulfur*, 2 (1984), 200–5. Contributors to Barbara Smith (ed.), *Home Girls: A Black Feminist Anthology* (Women of Color Press, New York, 1983), ironically subvert naturalized identities precisely while constructing a place from which to speak called home: see esp. Bernice Johnson Reagon, 'Coalition Politics: Turning the Century', on pp. 356–68, Trinh T. Minh-ha, 'She, the Inappropriat/ed Other', *Discourse* 8 (1986–7).

constructing them, the possibility opens up for weaving something other than a shroud for the day after the apocalypse that so prophetically ends salvation history.

Both Marxist/socialist-feminisms and radical feminisms have simultaneously naturalized and denatured the category 'woman' and consciousness of the social lives of 'women'. Perhaps a schematic caricature can highlight both kinds of moves. Marxian socialism is rooted in an analysis of wage labour which reveals class structure. The consequence of the wage relationship is systematic alienation, as the worker is dissociated from his (sic) product. Abstraction and illusion rule in knowledge, domination rules in practice. Labour is the pre-eminently privileged category enabling the Marxist to overcome illusion and find that point of view which is necessary for changing the world. Labour is the humanizing activity that makes man; labour is an ontological category permitting the knowledge of a subject, and so the knowledge of subjugation and alienation.

In faithful filiation, socialist-feminism advanced by allying itself with the basic analytic strategies of Marxism. The main achievement of both Marxist feminists and socialist feminists was to expand the category of labour to accommodate what (some) women did, even when the wage relation was subordinated to a more comprehensive view of labour under capitalist patriarchy. In particular, women's labour in the household and women's activity as mothers generally (that is, reproduction in the socialist-feminist sense), entered theory on the authority of analogy to the Marxian concept of labour. The unity of women here rests on an epistemology based on the ontological structure of 'labour'. Marxist/socialist-feminism does not 'naturalize' unity; it is a possible achievement based on a possible standpoint rooted in social relations. The essentializing move is in the ontological structure of labour or of its analogue, women's activity.[1] The inheritance of Marxian humanism,

---

[1] The central role of object relations versions of psychoanalysis and related strong universalizing moves in discussing reproduction, caring work, and mothering in many approaches to epistemology underline their authors' resistance to what I am calling postmodernism. For me, both the universalizing moves and these versions of psychoanalysis make analysis of 'women's place in the integrated circuit' difficult and lead to systematic difficulties in accounting for or even seeing major aspects of the construction of gender and gendered social life. The feminist standpoint argument had been developed by: Jane Flax, 'Political Philosophy and the Patriarchal Unconscious: A Psychoanalytic Perspective on Epistemology and Metaphysics', in Sandra Harding and Merill Hintikka (eds.), *Discovering Reality: Feminist Perspectives on Epistemology, Metaphysics, Methodology and Philosophy of Science* (Reidel, Dordrecht, 1983), 245–82; Sandra Harding, *The Science Question in Feminism* (Cornell University Press, Ithaca, NY, 1986); Harding and Hintikka (eds.), *Discovering Reality*; Nancy Hartsock, 'The Feminist Standpoint: Developing the Ground for a Specifically Feminist Historical Materialism', in Harding and Hintikka, and *Money, Sex and Power* (Longman, New York, 1983); Mary O'Brien, *The Politics of Reproduction* (Routledge, New York, 1981); Hilary Rose, 'Hand, Brain and Heart: A Feminist Epistemology for the Natural Sciences', *Signs*, 9/1 (1983); Dorothy Smith, 'Women's Perspective as a Radical Critique of Sociology', *Sociological Inquiry*, 44 (1974) and 'A Sociology of Women', in J. Sherman

with its pre-eminently Western self, is the difficulty for me. The contribution from these formulations has been the emphasis on the daily responsibility of real women to build unities, rather than to naturalize them. [. . .]

Beyond either the difficulties or the contributions in the argument of any one author, neither Marxist nor radical feminist points of view have tended to embrace the status of a partial explanation; both were regularly constituted as totalities. Western explanation has demanded as much; how else could the 'Western' author incorporate its others? Each tried to annex other forms of domination by expanding its basic categories through analogy, simple listing, or addition. Embarrassed silence about race among white radical and socialist feminists was one major, devastating political consequence. History and poly-vocality disappear into political taxonomies that try to establish genealogies. There was no structural room for race (or for much else) in theory claiming to reveal the construction of the category woman and social group women as a unified or totalizable whole. The structure of my caricature looks like this:

socialist feminism—structure of class//wage labour//alienation
labour, by analogy reproduction, by extension sex, by addition race
radical feminism—structure of gender//sexual appropriation//objectification
sex, by analogy labour, by extension reproduction, by addition race

In another context, the French theorist, Julia Kristeva, claimed women ap-peared as a historical group after the Second World War, along with groups like youth. Her dates are doubtful; but we are now accustomed to remembe-ring that as objects of knowledge and as historical actors, 'race' did not always exist, 'class' has a historical genesis, and 'homosexuals' are quite junior. It is no accident that the symbolic system of the family of man—and so the essence of woman—breaks up at the same moment that networks of connection among people on the planet are unprecedentedly multiple, pregnant, and complex. 'Advanced capitalism' is inadequate to convey the structure of this historical moment. In the 'Western' sense, the end of man is at stake. It is no accident that woman disintegrates into women in our time. Perhaps socialist feminists were not substantially guilty of producing essentialist theory that suppressed women's particularity and contradictory interests. I think we have been, at least through unreflective participation in the logics, languages, and practices of white humanism and through searching for a single ground of domination to secure our revolutionary voice. Now we have less excuse. But in the consciousness of our failures, we risk lapsing into boundless difference and giving up on the confusing task of making partial, real connection. Some

and E. T. Beck (eds.), *The Prism of Sex* (University of Wisconsin Press, Madison, 1979). For rethinking theories of feminist materialism and feminist standpoints in response to criticism, see Harding, *The Science Question*, 163–96; Hilary Rose, 'Women's Work: Women's Knowl-edge', in J. Mitchell and A. Oakley (eds.), *What is Feminism? A Re-examination* (Pantheon, New York, 1986).

differences are playful; some are poles of world historical systems of domination. 'Epistemology' is about knowing the difference.

[*Simians, Cyborgs and Women: The Reinvention of Nature* (Free Association Books, London, 1991), 155, 157–8, 160–1.]

PIERRE BOURDIEU

11   The Reality of Representation and the Representation of Reality

The classifying subjects who classify the properties and practices of others, or their own, are also classifiable objects which classify themselves (in the eyes of others) by appropriating practices and properties that are already classified (as vulgar or distinguished, high or low, heavy or light etc.—in other words, in the last analysis, as popular or bourgeois) according to their probable distribution between groups that are themselves classified. The most classifying and best classified of these properties are, of course, those which are overtly designated to function as signs of distinction or marks of infamy, stigmata, especially the names and titles expressing class membership whose intersection defines social identity at any given time—the name of a nation, a region, an ethnic group, a family name, the name of an occupation, an educational qualification, honorific titles and so on. Those who classify themselves or others, by appropriating or classifying practices or properties that are classified and classifying, cannot be unaware that, through distinctive objects or practices in which their 'powers' are expressed and which, being appropriated by and appropriate to classes, classify those who appropriate them, they classify themselves in the eyes of other classifying (but also classifiable) subjects, endowed with classificatory schemes analogous to those which enable them more or less adequately to anticipate their own classification.

Social subjects comprehend the social world which comprehends them. This means that they cannot be characterized simply in terms of material properties, starting with the body, which can be counted and measured like any other object in the physical world. In fact, each of these properties, be it the height or volume of the body or the extent of landed property, when perceived and appreciated in relation to other properties of the same class by agents equipped with socially constituted schemes of perception and appreciation, functions as a symbolic property. It is therefore necessary to move beyond the opposition between a 'social physics'—which uses statistics in objectivist fashion to establish distributions (in both the statistical and economic senses), quantified expressions of the differential appropriation of a finite quantity of social energy by a large number of competing individuals, identified through 'objective indicators'—and a 'social semiology' which seeks to decipher meanings and bring to light the cognitive operations whereby agents produce and decipher them. We have to refuse the dichotomy between, on the one hand, the aim of arriving at an objective 'reality', 'independent of individual consciousnesses and wills', by breaking with common representations of the social world (Durkheim's 'pre-notions'), and of uncovering 'laws'—that is, significant (in the sense of non-random) relationships between distributions—and, on the other hand, the aim of grasping, not 'reality', but agents' representations of it, which are the whole 'reality' of a social world conceived 'as will and representation'.

In short, social science does not have to choose between that form of social physics, represented by Durkheim—who agrees with social semiology in acknowledging that one can only know 'reality' by applying logical instruments of classification[1]—and the idealist semiology which, undertaking to construct 'an account of accounts', as Harold Garfinkel puts it, can do no more than record the recordings of a social world which is ultimately no more than the product of mental, i.e., linguistic, structures. What we have to do is to bring into the science of scarcity, and of competition for scarce goods, the practical knowledge which the agents obtain for themselves by producing—on the basis of their experience of the distributions, itself dependent on their position in the distributions—divisions and classifications which are no less objective than those of the balance-sheets of social physics. In other words, we have to move beyond the opposition between objectivist theories which identify the social classes (but also the sex or age classes) with discrete groups, simple countable populations separated by boundaries objectively drawn in reality, and subjectivist (or marginalist) theories which reduce the 'social order' to a sort of collective classification obtained by aggregating the individual classifications or, more precisely, the individual strategies, classified and classifying, through which agents class themselves and others.

One only has to bear in mind that goods are converted into distinctive signs, which may be signs of distinction but also of vulgarity, as soon as they are perceived relationally, to see that the representation which individuals and groups inevitably project through their practices and properties is an integral part of social reality. A class is defined as much by its *being-perceived* as by its *being*, by its consumption—which need not be conspicuous in order to be symbolic—as much as by its position in the relations of production (even if it is true that the latter governs the former). The Berkeleian—i.e., petit-bourgeois—vision which reduces social being to perceived being, to seeming, and which, forgetting that there is no need to give theatrical performances (*représentations*) in order to be the object of mental representations, reduces the social world to the sum of the (mental) representations which the various

[1] One scarcely needs to point out the affinity between social physics and the positivist inclination to see classifications either as arbitrary, 'operational' divisions (such as age groups or income brackets) or as 'objective' cleavages (discontinuities in distributions or bends in curves) which only need to be recorded.

groups have of the theatrical performances put on by the other groups, has the virtue of insisting on the relative autonomy of the logic of symbolic representations with respect to the material determinants of socio-economic condition. The individual or collective classification struggles aimed at transforming the categories of perception and appreciation of the social world and, through this, the social world itself, are indeed a forgotten dimension of the class struggle. But one only has to realize that the classificatory schemes which underlie agents' practical relationship to their condition and the representation they have of it are themselves the product of that condition, in order to see the limits of this autonomy. Position in the classification struggle depends on position in the class structure; and social subjects—including intellectuals, who are not those best placed to grasp that which defines the limits of their thought of the social world, that is, the illusion of the absence of limits—are perhaps never less likely to transcend 'the limits of their minds' than in the representation they have and give of their position, which defines those limits.

[*Distinction: A Source Critique of the Judgement of Taste*, trans. Richard Nice (Routledge, London, 1984), 482–4.]

JOHN B. THOMPSON

12 Bourdieu on 'Habitus'

Such a disposition, or system of dispositions, is what Bourdieu calls 'habitus', the main features of which are summed up (rather densely) in the following passage:

the structures constitutive of a particular type of environment . . . produce the habitus, systems of durable *dispositions*, structured structures predisposed to function as structuring structures, that is, as the principle of generation and structuration of practices and representations which can be objectively 'regulated' and 'regular' without in any way being the product of obedience to rules, objectively adapted to their goal without presupposing the conscious orientation towards ends and the express mastery of the operations necessary to attain them and, being all that, collectively orchestrated without being the product of the organizing action of a conductor.[1]

Let us unpack a few of these features. The habitus is a system of durable, transposable dispositions which mediates between structures and practices. It is a product of the structures constitutive of the conditions of existence within which it is acquired—for example, the conditions of existence of a particular class in a class-divided society. The dispositions are acquired through a gradual process of inculcation, the specific modes and characteristics of which depend

---

[1] Pierre Bourdieu, *Esquisse d'une théorie de la pratique*, 175 (*Outline of a Theory of Practice*, trans. Richard Nice (Cambridge University Press, 1977), 73).

upon the institutional arrangements of the society concerned. The dispositions are inculcated in a *durable* way: the body is literally moulded into certain forms, so that the habitus is reflected in the whole way that one carries oneself in the world, the way that one walks, speaks, acts, eats. The dispositions are 'transposable' in the sense that they are capable of generating practices in fields other than that in which they were originally acquired. As durably installed systems of dispositions, the habitus tends to generate practices and perceptions which concur with the conditions of existence of which they are the product, and which those practices and perceptions thereby reproduce. This does not mean, Bourdieu stresses, that actors are to be regarded as mere dupes of the social structures which determine their every action. On the contrary, actors have numerous strategies at their disposal and they often act in reflective and deliberative ways; but their action and reflection always takes place within a structured space of possibilities that defines a certain *style of life*.[1]

The *linguistic* habitus is a specific instance of the system of dispositions which govern practice. Acquired in the course of learning to speak in particular markets (most importantly, in a family occupying a determinate position in the social space), the linguistic habitus governs both our subsequent linguistic practices and our anticipation of the value that our linguistic products will receive on other markets, such as the school or the labour market. 'The system of successive reinforcements or refutations thus constitutes in each of us', observes Bourdieu, 'a sense of the social value of linguistic usages and of the relation between different usages and different markets which organizes all subsequent perceptions of linguistic products, tending to give them a high degree of stability.'[2] The sense of the value of one's own linguistic products is a fundamental dimension of the sense of one's position in the social space; it governs not only the expressions one produces, but also the very relation one adopts to different markets. For members of the dominant class, whose linguistic habitus incorporates the dominant norm, there is a concordance between the necessities of most markets and the dispositions of the habitus; whence the confident if circumspect ease with which they speak, the *relaxation within tension* which underlies all the distinctive traits of the dominant mode of expression. The hyper-correction of the *petits-bourgeois*, on the other hand, is the consequence of a class divided against itself, seeking to produce, at the cost of a constant anxiety and tension, linguistic expressions which bear the mark of a habitus other than their own. For members of the lower class, whose conditions of existence are least conductive to the acquisition of the dominant norm, there are many markets in which their linguistic products are assigned,

---

[1] For a discussion of the relation between habitus and life-styles, see Pierre Bourdieu, *La Distinction* (Les Éditions de Minuit, Paris, 1979), 189–97.

[2] Pierre Bourdieu, *Ce que parler veut dire: L'Économie des échanges linguistiques* (Fayard, Paris, 1981), 83–4.

by others as well as by themselves, a limited value. Hence the tendency of lower-class children to eliminate themselves from the educational system, or to resign themselves to devalorized courses of training.[1] Hence also the unease, the hesitation leading to silence, which, as previously noted, over-comes many members of the lower class on occasions defined as official.

As a durably installed system of dispositions, the linguistic habitus is in-scribed in the body, forming 'one dimension of the corporeal hexis where the whole relation to the social world, and the socially inculcated relation to the world, is expressed'.[2] The inculcation of habitus is the incorporation of habitus: through countless forms of linguistic-corporeal discipline ('sit up straight', 'don't talk with your mouth full', etc.), social structures are transformed into patterns of behaviour which are withdrawn from consciousness and which define our way of being in the world.

[*Studies in the Theory of Ideology* (Cambridge University Press, 1984), 53–5.]

JOHN B. THOMPSON
....

13 Giddens on 'Structuration'

Let me begin by outlining the central themes of Giddens's account. This account is formulated with a view towards building upon the strengths, while avoiding the weaknesses, of certain theoretical orientations in the social sciences. Functionalism has rightly emphasized the institutional features of the social world and has focused attention on the ways in which the unintended consequences of action serve to maintain existing social relations. Structur-alism and 'post-structuralist' approaches have developed novel conceptions of structure, of structuring processes and of the subject, conceptions which have been applied with particular efficacy to the analysis of texts and cultural objects. But what functionalism and structuralism lack, in spite of much discus-sion of the 'action frame of reference' and the 'theory of the subject', is an adequate account of action and agency. The latter have been principal con-cerns of 'analytical philosophy' during the last two decades, as well as of the 'interpretative sociologies' influenced by Husserl, Wittgenstein and others. In various ways these philosophers and sociologists have portrayed individuals as competent agents who know a great deal about the social world, who act purposively and reflectively and who can, if asked, provide reasons for what they have done. But where functionalism and structuralism are strong,

---

[1] Mechanisms of self-elimination from the educational system are examined by Bourdieu and Passeron in *La Reproduction*, 185–202 (*Reproduction: In Education, Society and Culture*, trans. Richard Nice (Sage, London, 1977), 152–64).

[2] Bourdieu, *Ce que parler veut dire*, 90.

analytical philosophy and interpretative sociology are weak, for they largely neglect problems of institutional and structural analysis.

Giddens seeks to move beyond these various orientations by rethinking the notions of, and the relations between, action and structure. Rather than seeing action and structure as the counteracting elements of a dualism, they should be regarded as the complementary terms of a duality, the 'duality of structure'. 'By the *duality of structure*', writes Giddens, 'I mean that social structures are both constituted *by* human agency, and yet at the same time are the very *medium* of this constitution.'[1] Every act of production is at the same time an act of reproduction: the structures that render an action possible are, in the performance of that action, reproduced. Even action which disrupts the social order, breaking conventions or challenging established hierarchies, is mediated by structural features which are reconstituted by the action, albeit in a modified form. This intimate connection between production and reproduction is what Giddens calls the 'recursive character' of social life. His theory of structuration is a sustained attempt to tease out the threads that are woven into this apparently unproblematic fact.

Action, according to Giddens, should be conceived as a continuous flow of interventions in the world which are initiated by autonomous agents. Action must be distinguished from 'acts', which are discrete segments of action that are cut out of the continuous flow by explicit processes of categorization and description. Not all action is 'purposeful', in the sense of being guided by clear purposes which the agent has in mind; but much action is 'purposive', in the sense that it is *monitored* by actors who continuously survey what they are doing, how others react to what they are doing, and the circumstances in which they are doing it. An important aspect of this reflexive monitoring of action is the ability of agents to explain, both to themselves and to others, why they act as they do by giving reasons for their action. Individuals are, Giddens repeatedly emphasizes, *knowledgeable agents* who are capable of accounting for their action: they are neither 'cultural dopes' nor mere 'supports' of social relations, but are skilful actors who know a great deal about the world in which they act. If the 'rationalization of action' refers to the reasons which agents offer to explain their action, the 'motivation of action' refers to the motives or wants which prompt it. Unconscious motivation is a crucial feature of human conduct and Giddens takes on board, primarily through a critical appraisal of the so-called 'ego-psychology' of Erikson and Sullivan, a cluster of psychoanalytic concepts. However, in place of the psychoanalytic triad of ego, super-ego and id, Giddens adheres to distinctions between the unconscious, practical consciousness and discursive consciousness. While the latter two are separated from the unconscious by the barrier of repression, the boundary between

---

[1] Anthony Giddens, *New Rules of Sociological Method: A Positive Critique of Interpretative Sociologies* (Hutchinson, London, 1976).

practical consciousness and discursive consciousness is a vague and fluctuating one. Much of what actors know about the world is part of their 'practical consciousness', in the sense that it is known without being articulated as such; but that such knowledge *could* be rendered explicit and incorporated into 'discursive consciousness' is a vital consideration which has important consequences for the status of social scientific research.

These various aspects of action and agency are part of what Giddens calls the 'stratification model of action'. The model could be represented as in Fig. 6.[1]

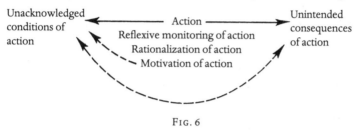

Fig. 6

This model brings out the limitations of any attempt to analyse action by focusing on the individual agent. For the accounts which agents are able to give of their actions are 'bounded', both by unintended consequences of action and by unacknowledged conditions of action (including unconscious sources of motivation). The significance of the unintended consequences of action is stressed by Merton, who introduces the concept of 'latent function' in order to show that practices may serve to maintain institutions and organizations, regardless of whether this outcome is intended by the agents concerned. Giddens firmly rejects any suggestion that such a demonstration would *explain* the existence of the practice: 'there is *nothing*', he asserts, 'which can count as "functionalist explanation" '.[2] But he wishes to preserve the insight that action may have unintended consequences which become the unacknowledged conditions of further action. There are two principal ways, on Giddens's account, in which this feedback process can occur. Unintended consequences can become unacknowledged conditions by being incorporated in 'homeostatic causal loops', such as the so-called 'poverty cycle' of material deprivation → poor schooling → low-level employment → material deprivation. Unintended consequences can also become unacknowledged conditions in so far as the unintended consequence of action is the reproduction of the *structure* which renders further action possible. To clarify the latter process we must take up Giddens's discussion of the concept of structure.

---

[1] Adapted from *Central Problems in Social Theory: Action, Structure and Contradiction in Social Analysis* (Macmillan, London, 1979), 56.

[2] Anthony Giddens, *A Contemporary Critique of Historical Materialism*, vol. i: *Power, Property and the State* (Macmillan, London, 1981), 17.

In the sociological literature 'structure' is often conceived in a quasi-mechanical, quasi-visual way, like the girders of a building, the skeleton of a body or the 'patterning' of social relationships. Giddens does not dismiss this connotation altogether; as we shall see, he preserves elements of it in his notion of 'social system'. To the concept of structure, however, he ascribes a different sense. Here I shall focus on the sense ascribed in *New Rules of Sociological Method*, reserving for later a consideration of certain modifications which are presented in subsequent works. In *New Rules of Sociological Method* Giddens approaches the concept of structure through a comparison of language and speech—'not because society is like a language', he hastens to add, 'but on the contrary because language as a practical activity is so central to social life that in *some* basic respects it can be treated as exemplifying social processes in general'.[1] Thus, whereas speech is spatially and temporally situated, presupposing a subject as well as another to whom it is addressed, language is 'virtual and outside of time' and is 'subject-less', in the sense that it is neither the product of any one subject nor is it oriented towards any other. Giddens employs this comparison to draw a similar distinction between *interaction* and *structure* in social analysis. Whereas interaction is constituted in and through the activities of agents, structure has a 'virtual existence': it consists of 'rules and resources' which are implemented in interaction, which thereby structure interaction and which are, in that very process, reproduced. As Giddens explains, 'by the term "structure" I do not refer, as is conventional in functionalism, to the descriptive analysis of the relations of interaction which "compose" organizations or collectivities, but to systems of generative rules and resources'.[2]

[*Studies in the Theory of Ideology* (Cambridge University Press, 1984), 150–3.]

ANTHONY GIDDENS

14 The Concept of Structure

Interpreting agency within the context of its duration helps link the notion of action to those concepts—that is, structure, institutions and so on—which have been so important to objectivist social scientists. To see how these connections might be made, we have however to consider afresh the concept of structure. Among English-speaking social scientists, the concept of structure has ordinarily been a received notion. In contrast, for example, to the concept of function, the idea of structure has received remarkably little discussion. Why should this be so? The reason is probably that most English-speaking social scientists have a clear idea of how the concept of structure should be

---

[1] Giddens, *New Rules of Sociological Method*, 127.   [2] Ibid.

understood. When they talk of structure, or of 'the structural properties of institutions', they have in mind a sort of visual analogy. They see the structural properties of institutions as like the girders of a building, or the anatomy of a body. Structure consists of the patterns or relationships observable in a diversity of social contexts. Now this notion of structure needs to be examined just as closely as the idea of action.

In the traditions of structuralism and post-structuralism, the concept of structure is used in a fashion quite divergent from that characteristic of Anglo-Saxon social science and philosophy. The easiest way to indicate this is by reference to Saussure's classic discussion of the structural qualities of language. Structural features of language do not exist as patterns situated in time and space, like patterns of social relationships; they consist of relations of absences and presences embedded in the instantiation of language, in speech or in texts.[1] Structure here presumes the idea of an absent totality. To understand a sentence which a speaker utters means knowing an enormous range of rules and strategies of a syntactical and semantical kind, which are not contained with the speech act, but are nevertheless necessary to either understand it or to produce it. It is such a notion of structure (as an absent totality) which I hold to be important as a concept for the social sciences as a whole and basic to the notion of duality of structure. The problem with conceptualizing structure as a set of relations of 'presences', is that structure then appears as a constraint which is 'external' to action.[2]

If we conceive of structure in this fashion, it is not surprising that action appears to be limited by structural constraints which have essentially nothing to do with it. For structures limit behaviour, although it may be that within those limits—so one would have to presume—the agent is capable of acting freely. According to the notion of the duality of structure, by contrast, structure is not as such external to human action, and is not identified solely with constraint. Structure is both the medium and the outcome of the human activities which it recursively organizes. Institutions, or large-scale societies, have structural properties in virtue of the continuity of the actions of their component members. But those members of society are only able to carry out their day-to-day activities in virtue of their capability of instantiating those structural properties.

[*Social Theory and Modern Sociology* (Polity Press, Oxford, 1986), 60–1.]

[1] Ferdinand de Saussure, *Course in General Linguistics* (Fontana, London, 1974).
[2] Emile Durkheim, *The Rules of Sociological Method* (Macmillan, London, 1982).

15 The Incarnation of Social Structure

Sociology thrives and stumbles on dualisms. Dualisms provide it with its problems, but at the same time they prove stubborn, resistant to quick disposal, focuses of polarized controversy, sources of persistent puzzlement. One can, of course, take one's stand within the space defined by such dualisms, one can opt for one side or the other, or one can attempt to overcome the duality. In doing this, though, one is asking what to do about the problem of this or that duality, rather than how one comes to be in possession of such a dualism to begin with. What is the relationship between 'structure' and 'agency'? The two seem inimical: 'structure' apparently means givenness, constraint, stability, whilst 'agency' seemingly implies creativity, autonomy, fluidity. How, then, do structure and agency relate in society: is it primarily one or the other? Does emphasis on structure marginalize or eliminate agency, does emphasis on agency dispose of structure? Which should we favour? Or should we seek an appropriate balance between them, saying that society is both structure and agency, that agency requires structure (or is only possible within structure) whilst structure is engendered by but emergent from agency? Asking about 'structure and agency' in this way, though, is to disregard the first way in which these two are related: they are presented as a dualism, given as terms in which to define our problematic. It is, though, possible to ask whether it is not the relationship of agency-to-structure within our theories which gives the problematic, but the character of our theories which sticks us with the dualism of agency-and-structure, and thus our attitude to theorizing which is problematic. Ethnomethodology approaches these matters in this way. It does not stand within the same conception of theorizing, does not affiliate itself to the received tradition of theorizing, but steps outside of that and thus outside of the collection of dualisms (including structure-and-agency) which comprise sociology's institutionalized dilemmas.

The opposition of agency to structure is not, itself, primary but derivative. It is also pretty directly derivative from yet another, more primeval, duality, between society-seen-from-within and society-seen-from-without. Structure-and-agency originates in a contrast of points of view, that between society as it appears to us within the sphere of our daily lives where we appear to be free agents, capable of deciding and choosing, and society as it appears from the larger, longer view, in which our actions appear as dictated not by our individual subjectivities, but by the objective requirements of historically assembled, large-scale organized structures. It is at just this point, though, that ethnomethodology rejects the dichotomization which will result if we treat society-seen-from-within and society-seen-from-without as distinct and finished alternatives. If we treat them thus, then we appear to have two independent alternatives, and a problem as to how to relate them: here are two views of (in some sense) the same thing, but in these two views the same thing appears very different. Which of these views are we to take, if either? Ethnomethodology (for reasons which we do not go into) looks into the origins of these views and finds that we do not have two *entirely distinct and contrasting views* but that one is a *modification* of the other. Society-as-seen-from-without is produced by idealization from society-as-seen-from-within. That society-as-seen-from-without is an idealization is no objection to it, for idealization has utility within the traditional framework of theorizing; however, this kind of idealization does not have utility for ethnomethodology, since it does not undertake those tasks in terms of which a conception of society-as-seen-from-without can find a place and a use. Ethnomethodology does not set out to provide a specific mode of comprehending society, a theoretical framework *within* which a substantive conception of society is to be construed, but determines (instead) to inquire into the *comprehensibility of society*, into the ways in which social life can be understood and described when seen from within by members, or when seen under the auspices of the idealizations of social science. It does not, in other words, concern itself with theorizing as an epistemological and cognitive matter, but with theorizing as a social and organized affair: it does not, that is, pursue arguments about the correct form of theorizing but seeks to identify and describe those activities which are constituent of the work of theorizing. Those working within the tradition of social science theorizing can—indeed must—disregard the extent to which their activities are rooted in and organized through an understanding of society-seen-from-within, since these matters are (from the point of view of theorizing) entirely irrelevant. However, ethnomethodology cannot so disregard them, for it is concerned with precisely the ways in which these *theoretically* irrelevant matters are *practically* essential and consequential.

We bring out these basic points because they show how far back the divergences between ethnomethodology and other sociologies go, and how considerable are the differences between them. It is wholly misleading to treat ethnomethodology as though it were a different view of the same things that other sociologies are interested in, when it is, in truth, interested in very different things than they are, so much so that there is a sharp discontinuity between them, with ethnomethodology directing its attention to the very things which (under the rules of their tradition of theorizing) other sociologies must *systematically* disregard. Ethnomethodology must with equal systematicity give sustained attention to them.

This should indicate why we are deeply sceptical of the suggestion that ethnomethodology's point of view could, with relative ease, be reconciled with that of other sociologies or accommodated within some overall scheme which incorporates it and those other sociologies. The relationship between ethnomethodology's point of view and that of any other sociology is not like that between two perspectives on the same thing, such that these can be conjoined to produce a more 'rounded' picture of the object of attention. The relationship between these points of view is, rather, much more like that between the elements in a *gestalt* switch such that there is—again—a discontinuity: one can look at things one way or the other, but they are discrete and alternate, not additive, ways of seeing things, such that what is seen from one point of view 'disappears' when seen from the other. Those things which are the very stuff of ethnomethodology's inquiries are the same ones as must, perforce, be counted out of attention if other exercises in sociological theorizing are to proceed coherently and the attempt to take notice of them (without otherwise and massively readjusting themselves) will simply *distract* them from their intended business. It would make absolutely no sense for ethnomethodology to urge other sociologies to improve themselves by taking on board its concerns, for it is clear that those are directed to matters which are not casually overlooked by those sociologies, but which are necessarily and persistently excluded from their consideration (though they are, of course, ones to which a close and detailed practical attention must be pervasively sustained). [. . .]

Thus, many topics which have been extensively discussed as substantive problems in sociological theory (like the structure-versus-agency dilemma) are, for ethnomethodology, ones which are better considered as products of methodological decisions which antedate the formation of the theories themselves and which require, therefore, re-examination at the most primitive pre-theoretical level, rather than within the given framework of dualisms, dichotomies, and dilemmas which, in view of the received traditions of sociological theorizing, we apparently face as immutable, granted suppositions of our sociological reasoning. Ethnomethodology offers the possibility that they are not the unavoidable dualisms which must frame our thinking about how to examine the organization of social life, but are dilemmas which we impose upon ourselves by the adoption of a particular (albeit widespread, and widely approved of) way of thinking. Thus, what many see as the thoroughly empiricist character of ethnomethodology might be better understood as an attempt to retrace the steps involved in some of sociology's most elementary methodological decisions.

To invite ethnomethodology to conceive itself through the opposition of 'structure' or 'agency' or to contribute to the mediation-and-resolution of this opposition is to ask it to situate itself in the terms of a dualism whose very constitution it finds problematic. Worse, to understand ethnomethodology as though it acquired its sense and role within a discussion conducted on the unquestioned basis of that decision (as if, for example, it were an instance of 'radical subjectivism') is to misread its entire character. Does it not, though, offer itself as just such a subjectivism, for does it not invite us to consider social phenomena as 'achieved' phenomena, as locally and interactionally accomplished outcomes of practical sociological reasoning, proposing to portray the ways in which such phenomena are made to happen? Is not this the same as saying that society is created by individuals, necessarily—and even fatally—overlooking the fact that individuals are created by society? Worse, is it not exactly the same as proposing that society is made up afresh, *de novo*, by individuals, as if they were free to make it happen however they wished? And does this not clearly—even fatally—underplay the fact that the members of society are not free to make it happen as they like, that there are tremendous constraints given by society itself on how they can produce social reality? They do not, indeed, produce society, they reproduce it.

There are numerous misconceptions compounded into such characterizations. One is, of course, that it supposes that ethnomethodology strives to produce the same kind of theoretical output as standard sociologies do, namely a synoptic characterization of society, or of 'social reality'. What is taken for an oversight with respect to the given and constraining effect of society-in-the-large is in fact a consequence of the refusal to begin from the dichotomization of society seen from without and within. A methodological decision, to study society purely as encountered from within the world of daily life, is treated as though it were an ontological or causal claim. The second significant mistake is that of taking ethnomethodology's aim as being that of the synoptic overview yielding a *causal portrayal* of individual action and/or the constitution of social structures. However, it is also to overlook the most rudimentary point of all, which is that ethnomethodology does not take as its puzzle the fact that people act in stable, regular ways (such that we have the problem of what keeps them behaving like that) but the quite different one of how it is that the stability and regularity of conduct is recognizable and discoverable, and recognizable and discoverable from within its own midst (which gives us the problem of how we go about the business of identifying people's actions and finding explanations for them). The third crucial mistake (and the last one we will discuss here) is to take the suggestion that social phenomena be viewed as 'achievements' as an argument about the causal production of social structure (as these are understood within the conventions of more standard sociological frameworks). We are, again, dealing with a methodological step, and one which encourages us to examine social phenomena as procedural affairs, replacing the questions 'why do people do X in the first place?' and 'what keeps people doing X?' with 'what do people have to do to be (routinely, unremarkably, but recognizably and readily so) doing X?' This formulation serves one purpose quite satisfactorily. It shows just how different the central question which ethnomethodology puts is from those to which sociological theory conventionally gives priority. We make no comment on whether this question of ethnomethodology's should take priority over or even entirely displace those others, or whether starting from ethnomethodology's question we would eventually be in a better position to answer the other ones. In another respect, our formulation may not be so satisfactory. It can be misinterpreted as focusing upon individual action, opening the way to a repetition of the claim: it ignores 'social structures'. There are ways in which one can formulate ethnomethodology in such a way that 'the individual' drops out entirely and one can say, quite firmly, that ethnomethodology is interested in actions, activities and courses of action, and not in individuals at all (thus, one can talk about 'the member' not as a 'person' at all, but as a 'mastery of natural language'),[1] but we avoid these since they make argument cumbersome and elaborate, and perhaps even harder to understand. The way to avoid this kind of misapprehension on this occasion is (perhaps) to say something about the way in which we ask 'what is involved in doing X?' which is not to be understood as 'what is involved in an individual doing action X?' since this gratuitously formulates the question in a way which isolates individual and action, when the question will, for ethnomethodology, be more characteristically (say) 'what actions are involved in carrying on the orderly business of a history lesson in junior school?' or 'what actions are involved in making up a crowd following a football match?' or, again, 'what actions are involved in executing the day-to-day tasks of a medium-sized business?' These are all queries about how actions make up orderly patterns, how actions comprise the day-to-day business.

Furthermore, we may suggest that the procedural emphasis together with the construal of the queries in this way combine to highlight the collective / collaborative character of the matters being investigated, allowing (indeed!) an emphasis on this to a degree that cannot be matched (and certainly cannot be exceeded) by sociologies which are (supposedly) vastly less individualistic than ethnomethodology. It is not, after all, that ethnomethodology conceived social phenomena individualistically, for it conceives them as essentially collaborative phenomena. Thus, for example, ethnomethodology should ask not 'how does a teacher maintain the order of a classroom?' but 'how do teacher, pupils and others not necessarily present there collectively engender a-classroom-routinely-and-recognizably-going-about-its-business?' This last question is not at all the same order of question as the first.

For many sociologists, the notion of showing that something is 'social' involves, essentially, establishing that it takes place within society, and that it bears the marks of the society within which it takes place. Ethnomethodology has a different notion: showing that something is social involves showing how it is done together. The conception of society from a collectivist or

[1] See H. Garfinkel and H. Sachs, 'On Formal Structures of Practical Actions', in John C. McKinsey and E. A. Tiryakian (eds.), *Theoretical Sociology: Perspectives and Developments* (Appleton-Century-Crofts, New York, 1970), esp. pp. 342–5.

individualist point of view involves an emphasis on the relation and connection of positions and persons respectively but for ethnomethodology it involves the connection of activities with, as far as we know, a unique concentration on the way in which actions are co-ordinated and concerted. Just to avoid any impression that there is some underlying—and erroneous—assumption about the amount of consensus in real life, let us say that the expressions 'collaborative' and 'co-ordinated' are not to be understood as meaning (for example) 'done in a spirit of collaboration' or 'done with the aim of helping each other out'. From this point of view, a radical disagreement would be a collaborative production, would be 'made to happen' by the various parties to it.

[. . .] the idea of an opposition of 'individual action' and 'social structure' is entirely incongruous with ethnomethodology's root conceptions. The whole point of it is to show that we cannot conceive of an individual action except as an-action-in-a-social-structure, any more than we can conceive of a single word as other than a-word-in-a-language. What the word is depends upon which language it is part of, and what someone's action is depends upon which social setting it is part of. The relationship between 'action' and 'social structure' is not to be conceived at this level as one between cause and consequence (whichever way the causal connection is supposed to run, from action to structure or vice versa or dialectically between them). It is, instead, to be conceived as that of pattern and particular, where the articulation of the two provides for their mutual visibility: the particular is recognizable for what it is as part of the pattern but the pattern itself is made out of and manifested in the particulars (as the elements of a mosaic and the mosaic-as-a-whole comprise one another). The pattern and particular are mutually constitutive and that is why ethnomethodology cannot make the analytic separation of action and social structure, nor face the problems which arise from it: an action 'isolated' from its social structure can only be discovered in and through the actions which make it up.

['Autonomy among Social Theories: The Incarnation of Social Structure', in N. G. Fielding (ed.), *Actions and Structure* (Sage, London, 1988), 58–60, 61–3, 64.]

JOHN B. THOMPSON

16 **Castoriadis on the Imaginary Institution of Society**

Institution of the Social-Historical

It is Castoriadis's view that the nature of society and history has been obscured by certain emphases which run throughout the whole tradition of Western thought. For this tradition, to which Marx belongs, has always situated reflection on the social-historical within an ontology of determinacy; it has always assumed that 'to be' has one sense: 'to be determined'. Traditional thought thus misses the essential feature of the social-historical world, namely that this world is not articulated once and for all but is in each case the creation of the society concerned. In instituting itself society *creates* in the fullest sense of the term; it posits a new *eidos* which could not be deduced from or produced by a prior state of affairs. Just as the social cannot be conceived within traditional schemata of the coexistence of elements, so too the historical cannot be subsumed to traditional schemata of succession. 'For what is given in and by history is not a determinate sequence of the determined, but the emergence of radical alterity, immanent creation, non-trivial novelty.'[1] To conceptualize time and history one must reject the traditional ontology of determinacy. Genuine time is not merely in-determination but the emergence of *new* and *other* determinations. Time is the auto-alteration of what is; time 'is', as Castoriadis says, only in so far as it is 'being towards' (*à-être*).

Each society institutes a specific type of temporality which defines its specific mode of auto-alteration. What we call 'capitalism', for instance, would have been impossible outside the specific mode of auto-alteration which, in a sense, *is* capitalism. More precisely, Castoriadis distinguishes between two layers in the capitalist institution of temporality. There is the layer of homogeneous uniform, measurable time, the time of accumulation, rationalization and the conquest of nature. This is the temporality *explicitly* instituted by capitalism, but it is not its *effective* temporality. The effective temporality of capitalism is the time of incessant rupture, of recurrent crises, of the perpetual tearing up of what is. It is this effective temporality which, as Marx perceived, distinguishes capitalism from most archaic and traditional societies. In the latter societies, the explicitly instituted temporality is much closer to the effective temporality, which appears more like regular pulsations than radical ruptures. There is, nonetheless, a striking feature which is common to all hitherto existing societies, irrespective of their particular differences. For in all hitherto existing societies, the effective temporality of alterity and auto-alteration seems to get covered over and excluded from view. Castoriadis's account of this remarkable process is worthy of extended quotation:

Thus everything happens as if the time of social doing, essentially irregular, accidental, altering, must always be imaginarily reabsorbed through a denial of time by means of the eternal return of the same, its representation as pure usury and corruption, its levelling out in the indifference of the merely quantitative difference, its annulment before Eternity. Everything happens as if the terrain where the creativity of society is manifested in the most trangible manner, the terrain where it makes, makes be and makes itself be in making be, must be covered over by an imaginary creation ordered in such a way that the society can conceal from itself what it is. Everything happens as if

---

[1] Cornelius Castoriadis, *L'Institution imaginaire de la société* (Seuil, Paris, 1975), 256.

the society must negate itself as society, hide its social being in negating the temporality which is first and above all its own temporality, the time of alteration-alterity which it makes be and which makes it be as society. Another way of saying the same thing: everything happens as if society could not recognize itself as making itself, as institution of itself, as self-institution.[1]

The misrecognition by society of its own social-historical being corresponds to a certain necessity of the social institution such as we know it, that is, such as it has been instituted hitherto. Obliging its subjects to integrate themselves into the time which is explicitly instituted, society also provides them with the means to compensate for this negation of effective temporality, endowing them with the comfort of the unchanging and the routine. Castoriadis insists, however, that this misrecognition is not an 'ontological necessity'; it must not be assumed a priori that society could not recognize itself as instituting, as the source of its own alterity and alteration. For *that* is the question of revolution: the setting up of a society which makes and remakes itself as an explicitly self-instituting collectivity.

Social Imaginary

To acknowledge the fundamental and irreducible creativity in the institution of the social-historical is to encounter what Castoriadis calls the 'social imaginary' (*l'imaginaire social*). The imaginary element of the social-historical world has, like the social-historical itself, been persistently misunderstood by traditional thought. For it has always been assumed that the imaginary is a mere reflection, a specular image of what is already there. Rejecting this assumption and the classical ontology upon which it rests, Castoriadis contends that the imaginary is what renders possible any relation of object and image; it is the creation *ex nihilo* of figures and forms, without which there could be no reflection *of* anything. On the level of the social-historical,[2] it is the imaginary which accounts for the orientation of social institutions, for the constitution of motives and needs, for the existence of symbolism, tradition and myth. Here, once again, it is worth quoting Castoriadis:

This element, which endows the functionality of each institutional system with its specific orientation, which overdetermines the choice and connections of symbolic networks, which creates for each historical period its singular way of living, seeing and making its own existence, its world and its relations to it, this originary structuring, this central signifier-signified, source of what is each time given as indisputable and indisputed sense, support of the articulations and distinctions of what matters and of what

---

[1] Ibid. 293.
[2] There is also a specifically psychic level of the imaginary, which Castoriadis calls the 'radical imagination'. For Castoriadis's discussion of this level, and for his views on the psyche and on psychoanalysis more generally, see *L'Institution imaginaire de la société*, ch. VI; and *Les Carrefours du labyrinthe* (Seuil, Paris, 1978), part one.

does not, origin of the augmented being (*surcroît d'être*) of the individual or collective objects of practical, affective and intellectual investment—this element is nothing other than the *imaginary* of the society or period concerned.[1]

No society could exist without organizing the production of material goods and the reproduction of its members; but neither of these forms of organization is dictated by natural laws or by purely technical considerations. What is important in the dimension of the social-historical is not that human beings always eat and have children, but that they do so in an infinite variety of ways. It is precisely this infinite variety, this indeterminate range of possibilities which builds upon but always exceeds the material conditions of human life, which is the domain of the social imaginary.

The social imaginary is expressed primarily through the constitution of a world of significations. By means of these significations—these symbols and myths in which a society represents its present and its past—a society is endowed with an identity and distinguished both from other societies and from an undifferentiated chaos. The creative and constitutive character of significations can be seen in the operation of language, which Castoriadis regards as a particular sphere of the symbolic. Here signification is the co-belonging of a term and that to which it 'refers', both in the Saussurian sense of *signifié* and in the broader sense of 'referent'. In both senses the cluster of references is necessarily open, for the referent itself is an indeterminate being. Hence 'a signification is indefinitely determin*able* (and this "indefinitely" is evidently essential), although that does not mean that it is determin*ed*'.[2] It follows that no rigorous and ultimately valid distinction can be made between the proper and the figurative sense of a word, since all language is essentially 'tropical'. It also follows that any attempt to treat language as a self-enclosed system of interrelating terms, in the manner of structuralism, is at best a partial approach. Such an attempt draws upon a logic which is implicit in all social activity, *la logique ensembliste-identitaire*, but it can never grasp the open and creative character of language. Social imaginary significations necessarily escape from the confines of a self-enclosed system, comprising a *magma* of meanings which cannot be organized into a logically structured whole. When one considers, moreover, the central imaginary significations of a society, one sees that they cannot be thought of in terms of their relations to referents, however open this relation may be; for these significations are what renders 'referents', and hence the relation to them, possible. What is the referent of the word 'God', asks Castoriadis, if not the individual representations of God which are created by means of the institution of the central imaginary signification which is God? The central imaginary significations of a society, far from being mere epiphenomena of 'real' forces and relations of production, are the

---

[1] *L'Institution imaginaire de la société*, 203.   [2] Ibid. 465.

laces which tie a society together and the forms which define what, for a given society, is 'real'.

[*Studies in the Theory of Ideology* (Cambridge University Press, 1984), 21–4.]

 17   The Social Imaginary

That which, since 1964, I have termed the social imaginary—a term which has since been used and misused in a number of different ways—and, more generally, that which I call the imaginary has nothing to do with the representations currently circulating under this heading. In particular, it has nothing to do with that which is presented as 'imaginary' by certain currents in psychoanalysis: namely, the 'specular' which is obviously only an image *of* and a reflected image, in other words a *reflection*, and in yet other words a byproduct of Platonic ontology (*eidolon*) even if those who speak of it are unaware of its origin. The imaginary does not come from the image in the mirror or from the gaze of the other. Instead, the 'mirror' itself and its possibility, and the other as mirror, are the works of the imaginary, which is creation *ex nihilo*. Those who speak of 'imaginary', understanding by this the 'specular', the reflection of the 'fictive', do no more than repeat, usually without realizing it, the affirmation which has for all time chained them to the underground of the famous cave: it is necessary that this world be an image *of* something. The imaginary of which I am speaking is not an image *of*. It is the unceasing and essentially *undetermined* (social-historical and psychical) creation of figures/forms/images, on the basis of which alone there can ever be a question *of* 'something'. What we call 'reality' and 'rationality' are its works. [. . .]

II. The Institution and the Symbolic

Everything that is presented to us in the social-historical world is inextricably tied to the symbolic. Not that it is limited to this. Real acts, whether individual or collective ones—work, consumption, war, love, child-bearing—the innumerable material products without which no society could live even an instant, are not (not always, not directly) symbols. All of these, however, would be impossible outside of a symbolic network.

We first encounter the symbolic, of course, in language. But we also encounter it, to a different degree and in a different way, in institutions. Institutions cannot be reduced to the symbolic but they can exist only in the symbolic: they are impossible outside of a second-order symbolism; for each institution constitutes a particular symbolic network. A given economic organization, a system of law, an instituted power structure, a religion—all exist socially as sanctioned symbolic systems. These systems consist in relating symbols (signifiers) to signifieds (representations, orders, commands or inducements to do or not to do something, consequences for actions—significations in the loosest sense of the term)[1] and in validating them as such, that is to say in making this relation more or less obligatory for the society or the group concerned. A property title, a bill of sale is a symbol of the socially approved 'right' of the owner to undertake an unlimited number of operations with respect to the object of his ownership. A paycheque is the symbol of the wage earner's right to demand a given number of banknotes, which, in turn, are the symbol of their possessor's right to perform a variety of acts of purchasing, each of which will be symbolic in its turn. The work itself which is the basis for the paycheque, although it is eminently real both for its subject and in its results, is, of course, constantly bound up with symbolic operations (in the mind of the person working, in the instructions he receives, etc.). And it becomes a symbol itself when, after being reduced to hours and minutes multiplied by given coefficients, it enters into the accounting office's calculations of the paycheque or the company's 'operations account', or when, in the event of disputes, it fills the empty squares in the premises and conclusions of the legal syllogism that will settle matters. The decisions of economic planners are symbolic (both ironically and not). Court decisions are symbolic and their consequences are almost entirely so, including the hangman's act which, although eminently real, is also immediately symbolic at another level.

Any functionalist view is aware of and has to acknowledge the role of symbolism in social life.

Only rarely, however, does it acknowledge the importance of this—and then it tends to limit this importance. Either symbolism is seen as merely a neutral, surface covering, as an instrument that is perfectly adequate for expressing a pre-existing content, the 'true substance' of social relations, neither adding anything nor taking anything away. Or else a 'special logic' of symbolism is acknowledged, but this logic is viewed wholly as the insertion of the symbolic within the rational order, which imposes its own consequences whether these be intended or not.[2] Ultimately, in this view form is always dependent on substance, and the substance is 'real—rational'. But in reality this is not so, and this destroys the interpretive claims of functionalism.

Consider the institution that is so important in all societies, religion. It always contains (we shall not discuss here the limiting cases) a ritual. For

---

[1] 'Signifier' and 'signified' are taken here and in what follows *latissimo sensu*.

[2] 'In a modern State, the law must not only correspond to the general economic situation and be its expression, it must also be a systematic expression of it so that it does not inflict a denial upon itself due to its internal contradictions. And, to succeed in this, it reflects less and less faithfully the economic realities.' Engels, in a letter to Conrad Schmidt, 27 Oct. 1890; repr. in Marx and Engels, *Selected Works in One Volume* (International Publishers, New York, 1968), 697.

example, the Mosaic religion. The definition of its cultic (in the broadest sense of the term) ritual contains an endless proliferation of details; this ritual, established with much greater detail and precision than the Law properly speaking,[1] stems directly from divine commandments, and because of this fact all its details are set on the same plane. What is it that determines the specificity of these details? Why are they all set on the same plane?

To the first question we can give only a series of partial replies. The details are determined in part by a reference to reality or to a given content (in a closed temple you need candelabra; a particular wood or metal is more precious in the culture considered and so worthy of being used—but even here the symbol and its entire problem of designation through direct metaphor or opposition is apparent: no diamond is precious enough for the Pope's tiara, yet Christ himself washed the feet of his Apostles). These details have a relation to content that is not functional but symbolic (whether in reality or in the religious imagination: the menorah has seven branches). Finally, details can be determined by the logical–rational implications or consequences of the preceding considerations.

These considerations, however, do not allow us to interpret a given ritual in a satisfactory, overall way. First of all, they always leave residuals; in the fourfold, intersecting network of the functional, the symbolical and their consequences, the gaps are more numerous than the points covered. Next, they assume that the symbolic relation is self-evident, whereas it poses immense problems: to begin with, the fact that the 'choice' of a symbol is never either absolutely inevitable, or merely haphazard. A symbol never imposes itself with a natural necessity, but neither does it ever lack *all* reference to reality (only in some branches of mathematics can we hope to find entirely 'conventional' symbols—and even here, a convention that has held over a period of time ceases to be a pure convention). Finally, nothing allows us to determine the *boundaries* of the symbolic in this matter. Sometimes, from the point of view of the ritual, the matter is indifferent, sometimes it is the form, and sometimes neither one: the matter of a particular object may be decided upon, but not that of all objects; it is the same in the case of form. A certain type of Byzantine church is in the form of a cross; we think we understand why (but we have to ask ourselves then why all Christian churches are not similar). The pattern of the cross, however, which could have been reproduced in the other segments and sub-segments of the architecture and in the decoration of the church, is not reproduced in this way. It is taken up again at certain levels but at other levels we find other patterns, and there are other entirely neutral

[1] In Exodus, the Law is formulated in four chapters (20–3) but the ritual and the instructions concerning the construction of the Temple take up eleven chapters (25–30 and 36–40). Injunctions concerning the ritual, moreover, return repeatedly; cf. Leviticus, 1–7; Numbers, 4, 7–8, 10, 19, 28–9, etc. The construction of the Temple is also described with a wealth of details on several occasions in the historical books.

levels, elements that simply serve as supports or for filling in. The choice of points that symbolism grabs hold of to give shape to and to 'sanctify' in the second degree the matter related to the sacred seems to a large extent (but not entirely) arbitrary. The boundary can lie almost anywhere: there is the bareness of Protestant churches and the jungle-like lushness of certain Hindu temples; and suddenly, just where symbolism seems to have invaded every square inch of matter, as in some Siamese pagodas, one sees that it has all at once lost its content and has become essentially mere decoration.[1]

In short, a ritual is not a rational affair—and this allows us to reply to the second question we were asking: why are all the details placed on the same plane? If a ritual were a rational matter, we could find the distinction between the essential and the secondary, the hierarchization characteristic of every rational network. But in a ritual there is no way of distinguishing, in accordance with any criteria based on content, between what counts more and what counts less. The fact that all the elements comprising a ritual are placed on the same plane with respect to their importance is precisely the indication of the non-rational character of its content. To say that sacredness does not contain different degrees is another way of stating the same thing: everything the sacred has taken hold of is equally sacred (and this is also true for the rituals of obsessional neuroses or perversions). [. . .]

We have tried to indicate the reasons why the idea that institutional symbolism is a 'neutral' or 'adequate' expression of functionality, of the 'substance' of underlying social relations is unacceptable. Actually, though, this idea is meaningless. It effectively postulates a substance which would be preconstituted in relation to institutions; it holds that social life has 'something to express' which is already completely real prior to the language in which it is to be expressed. It is impossible, however, to grasp a 'content' of social life that would be primary and that would then 'provide itself with' an expression in institutions independently of the latter. This 'content' (except as a partial and abstract moment, separated only after the fact) is definable only within a structure and this structure always contains the institution. The 'real social relations' concerned here are always *instituted*, not because they wear legal garb (in certain cases, they may very well not do so), but because they have been posited as universal, symbolized and sanctioned ways of doing things. This is also true, of course, and perhaps even more so, for 'infrastructures', the relations of production. The master–slave, serf–lord, proletariat–capitalist, wage-earner–bureaucracy relation is *already* an institution and cannot arise as a *social* relation without immediately becoming an institution. [. . .]

---

[1] This is a consequence of the basic law that all symbolism is *diacritical* or acts 'by means of difference': a sign can emerge as a sign only against the background of something that is not a sign or that is a sign of something else. However, this does not permit us concretely to determine where the dividing line should pass in every instance.

We shall therefore posit that there are significations that are relatively independent of the signifiers that carry them and that they play a role in the choice and in the organization of these signifiers. These significations can correspond to the *perceived*, to the *rational* or to the *imaginary*. The close relations that practically always exist between these three poles must not make us lose sight of their specificity.

Consider God. Whatever points of support his representation may take in perceived reality, whatever his rational effectiveness may be as an organizing principle of the environing world for certain cultures, God is neither a signification of something real, nor a signification of something rational; nor is he a symbol of something else again. What is God—not as a theological concept and not as a philosopher's idea—but for us who are thinking about what he is for those who believe in God? They can evoke him, refer to him only with the help of symbols, even if this be simply the 'Name'—but for them and for us, too, when we are considering this historical phenomenon constituted by God and those who believe in God, he infinitely surpasses this 'Name'; he *is* something other. God is neither the name of God nor the images a people may give of him, nor anything of the sort. Carried by, pointed at by all these symbols, he is, in every religion, that which makes these symbols religious symbols—a central *signification*, the organization of signifiers and signifieds into a system, that which supports the intersecting unity of both those components and which also permits the extension, multiplication and modification of this signification. And this signification, which is neither something perceived (real) nor something thought (rational), is an imaginary signification. [. . .]

What compounds the problem, and what probably explains why it was seen for so long from a partial perspective and why, even today, in anthropology as well as in psychoanalysis we observe such great difficulty in distinguishing the various registers of the action of the symbolic and of the imaginary, are not simply the 'realist' and 'rationalist' prejudices (a curious mixture of these can be found in the most extreme tendencies of contemporary 'structuralism') which prevent investigators from recognizing the role of the imaginary. The main reason is that, in the case of the imaginary, the signified to which the signifier refers is almost impossible to grasp as such, and, by definition, its 'mode of being' is a mode of non-being. On the register of the 'external' or 'internal' perceived (real), the distinct physical existence of the signifier and the signified is immediate: no one would confuse the word 'tree' with a real tree, the words 'anger' or 'sadness' with the corresponding effects. On the level of the rational, the distinction is no less clear: we know that the word (the 'term') that designates a concept is one thing and the concept itself is something else again. But in the case of the imaginary things are not so simple. To be sure, on an initial level, we can also distinguish here the words and what they designate, the signifiers and the signifieds. 'Centaur' is a word that refers to an imaginary being distinct from this word, a being that can be 'defined' by words (by this trait it resembles a pseudo-concept) or represented by images (by this trait it resembles a pseudo-object of perception).[1] But even this easy and superficial example (the imaginary Centaur is only a recombination of pieces taken from real beings) is not exhausted by these considerations, because, for the culture that experienced the mythological reality of the Centaurs, their being was something other than the verbal description or the sculpted representation that could be given of them. But how are we to get a hold of this final a-reality? In a certain sense, like the 'thing-in-itself', it offers itself only on the basis of its consequences, its results, its derivatives. How can we grasp God, as an imaginary signification, except on the basis of the shadows (*Abschattungen*) projected onto the effective social action of a people—but, at the same time, how could we overlook that, just like the thing perceived, he is the condition for the possibility of an inexhaustible series of such shadows, but, unlike the thing perceived, he is never given 'in person'?

Consider a subject who lives a scene in the imaginary, abandons himself to a daydream or accompanies with phantasies an actually experienced scene. The scene consists of 'images' in the broadest sense of the term. These images are made of the very material out of which symbols can be made; are they symbols? In the explicit consciousness of the subject, no; they do not stand for something else, they are 'lived' for themselves. But this does not exhaust the question. They can represent something else, an unconscious fantasy—and this is how they are generally seen by psychoanalysts. The image is therefore a symbol here—but of what? In order to know, one must enter the labyrinths of the symbolic elaboration of the imaginary in the unconscious. What is at the end of it? Something that is not there to *represent* something else; something that is instead the operative condition for every subsequent representation, but that already itself exists in the mode of representation: the fundamental phantasy of the subject, his or her nuclear (and not 'primitive') scene, where that which constitutes the subject in his or her singularity exists; the organizing–organized schema that provides its own image and exists not in symbolization but in the imaginary presentification that is already for the subject an embodied and operative signification, the initial grasp and the first, overall constitution of an articulated, relational system positing, separating and uniting the 'inside' and the 'outside', the sketch of gesture and the sketch of perception, the division into archetypal roles and the originary ascription of a role to the subject as such, positive and negative valuation, the source of subsequent symbolic significance, the origin of privileged and specific investments of the subject, something at once structuring and structured. On the level of the individual, the production of this fundamental phantasy stems from what we

---

[1] There is an 'essence' of the Centaur: two definite sets of possibilities and impossibilities. This 'essence' is 'representable': there is nothing imprecise about the 'generic' physical appearance of the Centaur.

have termed the radical imaginary (or the radical imagination); this phantasy itself exists both in the mode of the actual imaginary (of the imagined) and is a first signification and core of subsequent significations.

It is doubtful that this fundamental phantasy can be grasped directly; at the most, it can be reconstructed on the basis of its manifestations because it does appear as the ground of the possibility and the unity of everything that makes up the singularity of the subject other than as a purely combinatory singularity, as the sum of all that which, in the life of the subject, goes beyond his or her reality and history, the final condition for the fact that a reality and a history *do happen to* the subject.

When we are concerned with society—which, obviously, is not to be transformed into a 'subject' in either the literal or metaphorical sense—we encounter the same difficulty, but compounded. For here we do have indeed, starting with the imaginary that abounds immediately on the surface of social life, the possibility of penetrating the labyrinth of the symbolization of the imaginary. And by pursuing the analysis further, we do arrive at significations that are not there *in order to* represent something else, that are like the final articulations the society in question has imposed on the world, on itself, and on its needs, the organizing patterns that are the conditions for the representability of everything that the society can give to itself. Of their very nature, however, these patterns do not themselves exist in the form of a representation one could, as a result of analyses, put one's finger on. One cannot talk in this case of 'images', however vague and indefinite the sense ascribed to this term. God is perhaps, for each of the faithful, an 'image'—which can even be a 'precise' representation—but God, as an imaginary social signification, is neither the 'sum', nor the 'common part', nor the 'average' of these images; it is rather their condition of possibility and what makes these images images 'of God'. And the imaginary core of the phenomenon of reification is not an 'image' for anyone. The imaginary social significations do not exist strictly speaking in the mode of representation; they are of another nature, for which it is of no use to seek an analogy in the other spheres of our experience. Compared to individual imaginary significations, they are infinitely larger than a phantasy (the pattern underlying what is designated as the Jewish, Greek or Western 'image of the world' is of infinite extension) and they have no precise place of existence (if indeed the individual unconscious can be called a precise place of existence). They can be grasped only indirectly and obliquely: as the gap, at once obvious and impossible to delimit precisely, between a first term—the life and the actual organization of a society—and a second term, likewise impossible to define—this same life and organization conceived of in a strictly 'functional-rational' manner; as a 'coherent deformation' of the system of subjects, objects and their relations; as the curvature specific to every social space; as the invisible cement holding together this endless collection of real, rational and symbolic odds and ends that constitute every society, and as the principle that selects and shapes the bits and pieces that will be accepted there. Imaginary social significations—at any rate, those that are truly primary—*denote* nothing at all, and they *connote* just about everything. It is for this reason that they are so often confused with their symbols, not just by the peoples that use them but also by the scientists who analyse them, and who, as a result, come to consider that their signifiers only signify themselves (since they refer to nothing real, nothing rational that one could *point to*), and to ascribe to these signifiers as such, to symbolism considered in itself, a role and an effectiveness infinitely superior to those they certainly possess.

[*The Imaginary Institution of Society* (Polity Press, Cambridge, 1987), 3, 117–19, 124, 139–40, 141–3.]

Class and the Historians

E. P. Thompson's seminal contribution to the literature on class is represented in the first two selections. Despite the emphasis on struggle, and on class as a relationship, the familiar explanatory framework of historical materialism is clearly evident in Thompson's theoretical formulations (even if his practice did not always match his theory): productive relations give rise to 'experience', which then gives rise to 'consciousness'. There is a clear hierarchy of cause and effect, and this is apparent in both pieces. The analysis of eighteenth-century social relations in Britain brilliantly and suggestively describes the nature of these relations and of popular culture, especially the role of custom (it could be argued that custom, not class, is the central element in Thompson's history, and the one which he most illuminatingly explores). However, whether the social relationship he describes is a class one remains a matter of debate: as Thompson argues, class defines itself as it eventuates in struggle; classes do not struggle because they exist, but exist because they struggle. However, simply because groups of people struggle does that make their struggle a 'class' struggle, especially when the groups involved do not use the terms of class, as was the case in the eighteenth century? Why not use the term 'social struggle' instead of 'class struggle'?

This does not mean that for a consciousness of class divisions in society to arise the explicit terms of class must be available. It does mean, however, that a relatively clear awareness of identity and purpose be present, and, if we wish to define class in economic terms, that this awareness involves economic relationships. In both respects it is unclear whether what E. P. Thompson describes for the eighteenth century is class: economic relations do not seem primary in the terms of the identities described for the eighteenth century, 'gentry', 'plebs', and 'the crowd'. The terms are decidely open-ended: it is difficult to see where the 'plebeity', for example, stopped and started in terms of the many other social markers of the time. The terms are in another sense too restrictive, in that they tend to preclude attention to other, perhaps competing, systems of social classification.

Katznelson attempts to relate cultural and structural models of class in terms of a model of different 'levels' of class formation. These 'levels' are not viewed as unilinear in their effect, but, rather as in Thompson, a clear pattern of development is apparent, one in which economic factors have a 'necessary' if not a 'sufficient' cause. Though the links between the different levels is viewed in sophisticated terms, 'consciousness' and politics fairly clearly lie at the end of the process not at its beginning. The 'motor' of the process of change Katznelson describes is proletarianization. It is this process that connects and unifies the different levels of 'class formation'. However, as was seen in the

Introduction above, it is unwise to rely on proletarianization as an explanation of class formation. Without the idea, however, the very notion of a developmental view of class, of 'class formation' through its various 'levels', comes into question. The points of view of Thompson and Katznelson, in their juxtaposition of notions of 'culture' and 'structure', can between them be said to represent the orthodoxy of Anglo-American social history.

The rest of this part is given over to recent critiques of this position, the central issue of such critiques involving the ways in which class becomes available as a basis for people's cognition and their action. The existing arguments of social history—as outlined here—are seen to give an inadequate account of this process. Stedman Jones dwells on the notions of 'experience' and 'consciousness' as the link between evidence for discontent and evidence for a language of class antagonism, in historians' accounts of nineteenth-century Chartism. The one was seen as the expression of the other, Chartist discourse expressing the 'experience' of discontent, an 'experience' conceived of as giving evidence for discontent a direct human expression and subjectivity. Language was simply seen as the neutral medium of this experience, bringing the 'unconscious' into 'consciousness', and individual experience into general experience. What these terms conceal is that language actively structures experience. Stedman Jones employs a 'non-referential' conception of language to reveal how Chartism created a political language that was not about economic but political concerns. It was a 'class' language that articulated political, not economic relationships.

This in turn raises all sorts of questions about the nature of language and the identities it can bring into play. Joan W. Scott argues for a deepened understanding of 'language' as denoting the means by which meaning is created, in particular the articulation of cultural codes informed by the operation of systems of difference. Despite his claims, she regards Stedman Jones as dealing still in a traditional, referential conception of language. She also argues for an expanded sense of the political, embracing the content and play of the systems of difference she describes. While Stedman Jones's prescription is right, his result is wrong: a constitutive understanding of language in fact reveals its capacity, as a political language, to articulate economic class concerns as well as political ones. But it reveals much more as well, namely gender, with which class is indissolubly linked. Language is therefore seen to articulate several sorts of identity (to which gender is always related).

Joyce takes up the matter of multiple identities, in arguing for the importance of 'the people' and 'people' beside class, as a means of understanding the development of British history. What is apparent is the interplay of identities, and their frequent ambiguity and plasticity. Indeed, it may be misleading to employ the term identity in the singular, for instance in the cases of 'class', 'gender', or 'people', as unified categories of description. Identity is itself multiplex, as well as identities multiple. None the less, Joyce is concerned to delineate the reality of *differences* between categories, while seeing that such categories are not unitary. The idea of singular identities serves a heuristic purpose in pointing to differences, something especially necessary in the light of the tendency in much social analysis to collapse these differences into so many differing versions of the same reality of class. If identity is multiplex, and identities multiple, in the ways suggested, then understanding the principles around which this diversity is organized and given coherence becomes an important question. As in the question of class, the problem is one of knowing how identity becomes available as a principle of cognition and action. The second contribution of Joyce, in Part F, addresses the organization of identity in terms of the concept of narrative. As regards the concept of 'language' itself, Joyce is concerned to expand it beyond the political sphere alone, as well as beyond purely verbal communication.

Rancière and Sewell indicate how the 'linguistic turn' owes much to the labour and social history of France. This historiography has been nearest to the French intellectual currents that have been so important in recent decades, especially post-structuralism. Rancière employs post-structuralist notions of language, and the techniques of 'deconstruction', to explore the repressions of difference constantly at play in discourses of and about workers, differences between intellectuals and workers, and between worker-intellectuals and the mass of labour. The former relationship involves the historian too, as s/he confronts the worker in history: these levels of textualization are eloquently explored in Rancière's own writing, a brief extract of which is given here. His work has been quietly influential, though Sewell's pessimistic estimation of existing labour history is probably not inaccurate: 'a broad and complacent materialist perspective dominates the field'. Sewell therefore sets out to contest the materialist common sense of labour history by questioning the materiality of economies.

He also traces the historical lineage of 'materialism', seeing how in the Enlightenment and in the nineteenth century the 'material' became the stuff of social science and political economy, something amenable to 'laws' and hence 'scientific' understanding. 'Society' became describable in terms of materialist sciences: for instance, the 'laws' of political economy, the ordering principles of human life themselves, were found to be in the domain of the material, particularly of production and exchange. Sewell here serves as a bridge to Part D, 'The History of the Social': the labour history he inveighs against, complete with its materialist understanding of classes, is ironically the unwitting heir of Enlightenment, and pre-Enlightenment discourse. As he says, 'Marxists proudly proclaim their radicalism by employing an arbitrary identification of the economic as material, never realizing that they have inherited this idea intact and uncriticized from traditional Christian and aristocratic discourse. Would-be friends of the proletariat hence believe they are being progressive when they denounce as "idealists" those who actually take seriously what past proletarians thought. The claim that the economy is uniquely 'material' always was arbitrary, misleading and tendentious; that it continues to be clung to by purportedly leftist scholars is an embarrassing anachronism.' Therefore, while pointing to the next part, Sewell also addresses the concerns of the previous one: dualisms, in this case 'idealism' and 'materialism', are, indeed, arbitrary and misleading.

(a) Culture and Structure: Social History Orthodoxy

E. P. THOMPSON

18 **The Making of Class**

This book has a clumsy title, but it is one which meets its purpose. *Making* because it is a study in an active process, which owes as much to agency as to conditioning. The working class did not rise like the sun at an appointed time. It was present at its own making.

Class, rather than classes, for reasons which it is one purpose of this book to examine. There is, of course, a difference. 'Working classes' is a descriptive term, which evades as much as it defines. It ties loosely together a bundle of discrete phenomena. There were tailors here and weavers there, and together they make up the working classes.

By class I understand a historical phenomenon, unifying a number of disparate and seemingly unconnected events, both in the raw material of experience and in consciousness. I emphasize that it is a *historical* phenomenon. I do not see class as a 'structure', nor even as a 'category', but as something which in fact happens (and can be shown to have happened) in human relationships.

More than this, the notion of class entails the notion of historical relationship. Like any other relationship, it is a fluency which evades analysis if we attempt to stop it dead at any given moment and anatomize its structure. The finest-meshed sociological net cannot give us a pure specimen of class, any more than it can give us one of deference or of love. The relationship must always be embodied in real people and in a real context. Moreover, we cannot have two distinct classes, each with an independent being, and then bring them *into* relationship with each other. We cannot have love without lovers, nor deference without squires and labourers. And class happens when some men, as a result of common experiences (inherited or shared), feel and articulate the identity of their interests as between themselves, and as against other men whose interests are different from (and usually opposed to) theirs. The class experience is largely determined by the productive relations into which men are born—or enter involuntarily. Class-consciousness is the way in which these experiences are handled in cultural terms: embodied in traditions, value-systems, ideas, and institutional forms. If the experience appears as determined, class-consciousness does not. We can see a *logic* in the responses of similar occupational groups undergoing similar experiences, but we cannot predicate any *law*. Consciousness of class arises in the same way in different times and places, but never in just the same way.

There is today an ever-present temptation to suppose that class is a thing. This was not Marx's meaning, in his own historical writing, yet the error vitiates much latter-day 'Marxist' writing. 'It', the working class, is assumed to have a real existence, which can be defined almost mathematically—so many men who stand in a certain relation to the means of production. Once this is assumed it becomes possible to deduce the class-consciousness which 'it' ought to have (but seldom does have) if 'it' was properly aware of its own position and real interests. There is a cultural superstructure, through which this recognition dawns in inefficient ways. These cultural 'lags' and distortions are a nuisance, so that it is easy to pass from this to some theory of substitution: the party, sect or theorist, who disclose class-consciousness, not as it is, but as it ought to be.

But a similar error is committed daily on the other side of the ideological divide. In one form, this is a plain negative. Since the crude notion of class attributed to Marx can be faulted without difficulty, it is assumed that any notion of class is a pejorative theoretical construct, imposed upon the evidence. It is denied that class has happened at all. In another form, and by a curious inversion, it is possible to pass from a dynamic to a static view of class. 'It'—the working class—exists, and can be defined with some accuracy as a component of the social structure. Class-consciousness, however, is a bad thing, invented by displaced intellectuals, since everything which disturbs the harmonious coexistence of groups performing different 'social rôles' (and which thereby retards economic growth) is to be deplored as an 'unjustified disturbance-symptom'.[1] The problem is to determine how best 'it' can be conditioned to accept its social rôle, and how its grievances may best be 'handled and channelled'.

If we remember that class is a relationship, and not a thing, we cannot think in this way. 'It' does not exist, either to have an ideal interest or consciousness, or to lie as a patient on the Adjustor's table. Nor can we turn matters upon their heads, as has been done by one authority who (in a study of class obsessively concerned with methodology, to the exclusion of the examination of a single real class situation in a real historical context) has informed us:

Classes are based on the differences in legitimate power associated with certain positions, i.e. on the structure of social rôles with respect to their authority expectations. . . . An individual becomes a member of a class by playing a social rôle relevant from the point of view of authority. . . . He belongs to a class because he occupies a position in a social organization; i.e. class membership is derived from the incumbency of a social rôle.[2]

---

[1]   An example of this approach, covering the period of this book, is to be found in the work of a colleague of Professor Talcott Parsons: N. J. Smelser, *Social Change in the Industrial Revolution* (London, 1959).

[2]   R. Dahrendorf, *Class and Class Conflict in Industrial Society* (London, 1959), 148–9.

The question, of course, is how the individual got to be in this 'social rôle', and how the particular social organization (with its property-rights and structure of authority) got to be there. And these are historical questions. If we stop history at a given point, then there are no classes but simply a multitude of individuals with a multitude of experiences. But if we watch these men over an adequate period of social change, we observe patterns in their relationships, their ideas, and their institutions. Class is defined by men as they live their own history, and, in the end, this is its only definition.

[*The Making of the English Working Class* (Penguin, London, 1968), 9–11.]

E. P. THOMPSON

19 Class and Class Struggle

IV

It seems that, once again, it is necessary to explain how a historian—or how *this* historian—understands the term 'class'. Some fifteen years ago I concluded a rather protracted work of analysis into a particular moment of class formation. In the Preface I offered some comments on class which concluded: 'Class is defined by men as they live their own history, and, in the end, this is its only definition.'[1]

It is generally supposed today, among a new generation of Marxist theorists, that such a statement must either be 'innocent' or (far worse) 'not innocent': i.e. evidence of an ulterior surrender to empiricism, historicism, etc. These people have very much better ways of defining class: definitions moreover which can be swiftly reached within theoretical practice and without the fatigue of historical investigation.

That Preface was, however, a considered one, arising out of both historical and theoretical practice. (I did not start out from the conclusions in the Preface: the Preface expressed my conclusions.) In general, after fifteen more years of practice, I would uphold the same conclusions. But perhaps these should be re-stated and qualified.

1. Class, in my own usage, is a *historical* category: that is, it is derived from the observation of the social process over time. We know about class because people have repeatedly behaved in class ways; these historical events disclose regularities of response to analogous situations, and at a certain stage (the 'mature' formations of class) we observe the creation of institutions, and of a culture with class notations, which admits of trans-national comparisons. We

[1] *The Making of the English Working Class* (Pelican edn.), 11.

theorize this evidence as a general theory of class and of class formation: we expect to find certain regularities, 'stages' of development, etc.

2. But at this stage it is only too often the case that the theory takes precedence over the historical evidence which it is intended to theorize. It is easy to suppose that class takes place, not as historical process, but inside our own heads. Of course we do not admit that it goes on only in our heads, although a great deal of argument about class is in fact only an argument in the head. Instead, models or structures are theorized that are supposed to give us objective determinants of class: for example, as expressions of differential productive relations.[1]

3. From this (false) reasoning there arises the alternative notion of class as a *static*, either sociological or heuristic, category. The two are different, but both employ categories of stasis. In one very popular (usually positivistic) sociological tradition, class can then be reduced to literal quantitative measurement: so many people in this or that relation to the means of production, or, in more vulgar terms, so many wage-earners, white-collar workers, etc. Or class is what class people say they *think* they belong to in response to a questionnaire; once again, class as a historical category—the observation of behaviour over time— has been expelled.

4. I would like to say that class as a historical category is the proper or mainstream Marxist usage. I think that I could show that this is Marx's own usage, in his more historical writings, but this is not the place to argue scriptural authority. It is certainly the usage of many (but not all) in the British tradition of Marxist historiography, especially of the older generation.[2] However, it has become very clear in recent years that class as a static category has taken up occupation within very influential sectors of Marxist thought as well. In vulgar economistic terms this is simply the twin to positivistic sociological theory. From a static model of capitalist productive relations there are derived the classes that ought to correspond to this, and the consciousness that ought to correspond to the classes and their relative positions. In one common (usually Leninist) form this provides a ready justification for the politics of 'substitution': i.e. the 'vanguard' which knows better than the class itself what its true interests (and consciousness) ought to be. If 'it' does not happen to have that consciousness, then whatever it has is 'false consciousness'. In an alternative (very much more sophisticated) form—for example, with Althusser—we still have a profoundly static category; a category which finds its definition only

[1] I do not mean to suggest that such static structural analysis is not both valuable and essential. But what it gives us is a determining logic (in the sense of both 'setting limits' and 'exerting pressures': see the critically important discussion of determinism in Raymond Williams, *Marxism and Literature* (Oxford, 1977)), and not the historical conclusion or equation— that these productive relations = these class formations. See also para. 7 below, and p. 136 n. 2 below.

[2] It appears to me to be the usage generally found in the historical practice of Rodney Hilton, E. J. Hobsbawm, Christopher Hill, and many others.

within a highly theorized static structural totality, which disallows the real *experiential* historical process of class formation. Despite this theory's sophistication, the results are very similar to the vulgar economistic version. Both have a similar notion of 'false consciousness', or 'ideology' although Althusserian theory tends to have a larger theoretical arsenal to explain ideological domination and the mystification of consciousness.

5. If we return to class as a historical category, we can see that historians can employ the concept in two different senses: (a) with reference to real, empirically observable correspondent historical content; (b) as a heuristic or analytic category to organize historical evidence which has a very much less direct correspondence.[1] In my view the concept may properly be employed in both ways; nevertheless, confusion often arises when we move from one sense to the other.

(a) It is true that class in its modern usage arises within nineteenth-century industrial capitalist society. That is, class in its modern usage only became available to the cognitive system of the people then living at that time. Hence the concept not only enables us to organize and analyse the evidence; it is also, in a new sense, *present in the evidence itself*. We can observe, in industrial Britain or France or Germany, class institutions, class parties, class cultures, etc. This historical evidence has in its turn given rise to the mature concept of class and has, to some degree, marked it with its own historical specificity.

(b) This (anachronistic) historical specificity must be guarded against when we employ the term in the second sense in the analysis of societies prior to the industrial revolution. For the correspondence of the category to the historical evidence then becomes very much less direct. If class was not available within people's own cognitive system, if they saw themselves and fought out their own historical battles in terms of 'estates' or 'ranks' or 'orders', etc., then if we describe these struggles in class terms we must exert caution against any tendency to read back subsequent notations of class.

That we choose to continue to employ the heuristic category of class (despite this ever-present difficulty) arises not from its perfection as a concept but from the fact that no alternative category is available to analyse a manifest and universal historical process. Thus we cannot (in the English language) talk of 'estate-struggle' or 'order-struggle', whereas 'class-struggle' has been employed, not without difficulty but with signal success, by historians of ancient, feudal and early modern societies; and these historians have, in the course of their employment, imposed their own refinements and qualifications on the concept within their own historical fields.

---

[1] Cf. E. J. Hobsbawm, 'Class Consciousness in History', in Istvan Meszaros (ed.), *Aspects of History and Class Consciousness* (London, 1971), 8: 'Under capitalism class is an immediate and in some sense a directly *experienced* historical reality, whereas in pre-capitalist epochs it may merely be an analytical construct which makes sense of a complex of facts otherwise inexplicable.' See also ibid., 5–6.

6. This emphasizes, however, that class, in its heuristic usage, is inseparable from the notion of 'class-struggle'. In my view, far too much theoretical attention (much of it plainly a-historical) has been paid to 'class', and far too little to 'class-struggle'. Indeed, class-struggle is the prior, as well as the more universal, concept. To put it bluntly: classes do not exist as separate entities, look around, find an enemy class, and then start to struggle. On the contrary, people find themselves in a society structured in determined ways (crucially, but not exclusively, in productive relations), they experience exploitation (or the need to maintain power over those whom they exploit), they identify points of antagonistic interest, they commence to struggle around these issues and in the process of struggling they discover themselves as classes, they come to know this discovery as class-consciousness. Class and class-consciousness are always the last, not the first, stage in the real historical process.[1] But if we employ a static category of class, or if we derive our concept from a prior theoretical model of a structural totality, we will not suppose so: we will suppose that class is instantaneously present (derivative, like a geometric projection, from productive relations) and that *hence* classes struggle.[2] We are launched, then, upon the endless stupidities of quantitative measurement of classes, or of sophisticated Newtonian Marxism in which classes and class fractions perform their planetary or molecular evolutions. All this squalid mess around us (whether sociological positivism or Marxist-structuralist idealism) is the consequence of the prior error: that classes exist, independent of historical relationship and struggle, and that they struggle *because* they exist, rather than coming into existence out of that struggle.

7. I hope that nothing I have written above has given rise to the notion that I suppose that the formation of class is independent of objective determinations, that class can be defined simply as a cultural formation, etc. This has, I hope, been disproved by my own historical practice, as well as in the practice of many other historians. Certainly, these objective determinations require the most scrupulous examination.[3] But no examination of objective determinations (and certainly no model theorized from it) can give one class and class-consciousness in a simple equation. Class eventuates as men and women *live*

---

[1] Cf. Hobsbawm, 'Class Consciousness', 6: 'For the purposes of the historian . . . class and the problem of class consciousness are inseparable. Class in the full sense only comes into existence at the historical moment when classes begin to acquire consciousness of themselves as such.'

[2] Marxist Political Economy, in a necessary analytical procedure, constructs a totality within which productive relations *are posited already* as classes. But when we return from this abstracted structure to the full historical process, we find that (economic, military) exploitation are *experienced* in class ways and only thence give rise to class formations: see my 'An Orrery of Errors' in *Reasoning, One* (Merlin Press, Sept. 1978).

[3] For the determinants of class structure (and of the property or 'surplus extraction' relations which impose limits, possibilities, and 'long-term patterns' in societies in pre-industrial Europe) see Robert Brenner, 'Agrarian Class Structure and Economic Development in Pre-Industrial Europe', *Past and Present*, 70 (Feb. 1976), esp. 31–2.

their productive relations, and as they *experience* their determinate situations, within 'the *ensemble* of the social relations', with their inherited culture and expectations, and as they handle these experiences in cultural ways. So that, in the end, no model can give us what ought to be the 'true' class formation for a certain 'stage' of process. No actual class formation in history is any truer or more real than any other, and class defines itself as, in fact, it eventuates.

Class, as it eventuated within nineteenth-century industrial capitalist societies, and as it then left its imprint upon the heuristic category of class, has in fact no claim to universality. Class in that sense is no more than a special case of the historical formations which arise out of class struggle.

V

Let us return, then, to the special case of the eighteenth century. We shall expect to find class struggle but we need not expect to find nineteenth-century cases of class. Class is a historical formation, and it does not occur only in ways prescribed as theoretically proper. Because in other places and periods we can observe 'mature' (i.e. self-conscious and historically developed) class formations, with ideological and institutional expression, this does not mean that whatever happens less decisively is not class.

In my own practice I find the notion of gentry–crowd reciprocity, of the 'paternalism–deference equilibrium' in which both parties to the equation were, in some degree, the prisoners of each other, more helpful than notions of a 'one-class society' or of consensus. What must concern us is the polarization of antagonistic interests and the corresponding dialectic of culture. There is very articulate resistance to the ruling ideas and institutions of society in the seventeenth and nineteenth centuries: hence historians expect to analyse these societies in some terms of social conflict. In the eighteenth century resistance is less articulate, although often very specific, direct and turbulent. One must therefore supply the articulation, in part by de-coding the evidence of behaviour, and in part by turning over the bland concepts of the ruling authorities and looking at their undersides. If we do not do this we are in danger of becoming prisoners of the assumptions and self-image of the rulers: free labourers are seen as the 'loose and disorderly sort', riot is seen as spontaneous and 'blind'; and important kinds of social protest become lost in the category of 'crime'. But there are few social phenomena which do not reveal a new significance when exposed to this dialectical examination. The ostentatious display, the powdered wigs and the dress of the great must be seen also—*as they were intended to be seen*—from below, in the auditorium of the theatre of class hegemony and control. Even 'liberality' and 'charity' may be seen as calculated acts of class appeasement in times of dearth and calculated extortions (under threat of riot) by the crowd: what is (from above) an 'act of giving' is (from below) an 'act of getting'. So simple a category as 'theft' may turn out to be, in certain circumstances, evidence of protracted attempts by villagers to defend ancient common-right usages, or by labourers to defend customary perquisites. And following each of these clues to the point where they intersect, it becomes possible to reconstruct a customary popular culture, nurtured by experiences quite distinct from those of the polite culture, conveyed by oral traditions, reproduced by example (perhaps, as the century goes on, increasingly by literate means), expressed in symbolism and in ritual, and at a very great distance from the culture of England's rulers.

I would hesitate before I described this as a *class* culture, in the sense that one can speak of a working-class culture, within which children were socialized into a value-system with distinct class notations, in the nineteenth century. But one cannot understand this culture, in its experiential ground, in its resistance to religious homily, in its picaresque flouting of the provident bourgeois virtues, in its ready recourse to disorder, and in its ironic attitudes towards the Law, unless one employs the concept of the dialectical antagonisms, adjustments, and (sometimes) reconciliations, of class.

When analysing gentry–plebs relations one finds not so much an uncompromising ding-dong battle between irreconcilable antagonists as a societal 'field-of-force'. I am thinking of a school experiment (which no doubt I have got wrong) in which an electrical current magnetized a plate covered with iron filings. The filings, which were evenly distributed, arranged themselves at one pole or the other, while in between those filings which remained in place aligned themselves sketchily as if directed towards opposing attractive poles. This is very much how I see eighteenth-century society, with, for many purposes, the crowd at one pole, the aristocracy and gentry at the other, and until late in the century, the professional and merchant groups bound down by lines of magnetic dependency to the rulers, or on occasion hiding their faces in common action with the crowd. This metaphor allows one to understand not only the very frequent riot situation (and its management) but also much of what was possible and also the limits of the possible beyond which power did not dare to go. It is said that Queen Caroline once took such a fancy to St James's Park that she asked Walpole how much it would cost to enclose it as private property. 'Only a *crown*, Madam,' was Walpole's reply.[1] [. . .]

Hence one characteristic paradox of the century: we have a *rebellious* traditional culture. The conservative culture of the plebs as often as not resists, in the name of 'custom', those economic innovations and rationalizations (as enclosure, work-discipline, free market relations in grain) which the rulers or employers seek to impose. Innovation is more evident at the top of society than below, but, since this innovation is not some normless and neuter technological/sociological process ('modernization', 'rationalizing') but is the innovation of capitalist process, it is most often experienced by the plebs in the

---

[1] Horace Walpole, *Memoirs of the Reign of King George the Second* (1847), ii. 220–1.

form of exploitation, or the expropriation of customary use-rights, or the violent disruption of valued patterns of work and leisure. Hence the plebeian culture is rebellious, but rebellious in defence of custom. The customs defended are the people's own, and some of them are in fact based upon rather recent assertions in practice. But when the people search for legitimations for protest, they often turn back to the paternalist regulations of a more authoritarian society, and select from among these those parts most calculated to defend their present interests; food rioters appeal back to the Book of Orders and to legislation against forestallers, etc., artisans appeal back to certain parts (e.g. apprenticeship regulation) of the Tudor regulatory labour code.[1] [. . .]

The eighteenth-century evidence appears to me to gesture towards a rather more coherent mental universe of symbolism informing practice than Thomas allows for the seventeenth.[2] But the coherence (and here I would expect some anthropologists to lay this paper down in disgust) arises less from any inherent cognitive structure than from the particular field of force and sociological oppositions peculiar to eighteenth-century society; to be blunt, the discrete and fragmented elements of older patterns of thought become integrated by class. [. . .]

For this plebeian culture is, in the end, constrained within the parameters of gentry hegemony: the plebs are ever-conscious of this constraint, aware of the reciprocity of gentry–crowd relations,[3] watchful for points to exert their own advantage. The plebs also take over to their own use some of the gentry's rhetoric. For, once again, this is the century of the advance of 'free' labour. The custom that was 'good' and 'old' was often of relatively recent assertion. And the distinctive feature of the manufacturing system was that, in many kinds of work, labourers (taking petty masters, journeymen and their families together) still controlled in some degree their own immediate relations and modes of work, while having very little control over the market for their products or over the prices of raw materials or food. This explains something of the

---

[1] As late as 1811 sophisticated London trade unionists, in appealing to the apprenticeship clauses of the Statute of Artificers ('Mechanics! Protect your Liberties from Lawless Invaders!!!'), commenced with an 'Ode to the Memory of Queen Elizabeth':

> Her memory still is dear to journeymen,
> For shelter'd by her laws, now they resist
> Infringements, which would else persist.
> Tyrannic masters, innovating fools
> Are check'd, and bounded by her glorious rules.
> Of workmen's rights, she's still a guarantee . . .

Report of the Trial of Alexander Wadsworth against Peter Laurie, 28 May 1811: Columbia University Library, Seligman Collection, Place pamphlets, vol. xii.

[2] See the exchange between Hildred Geertz and Keith Thomas in Journal of Interdisciplinary History, 6/1 (1975), and Keith Thomas, Religion and the Decline of Magic (London, 1971).

[3] Cf. Genovese, Roll, Jordan, Roll (New York, 1974), 91: 'The slaves accepted the doctrine of reciprocity, but with a profound difference. To the idea of reciprocal duties they added the doctrine of reciprocal rights.'

structure of industrial relations and of protest, as well as something of the culture's artefacts and of its cohesiveness and independence of control.[1] It also explains much of the consciousness of the 'free-born Englishman', who took to himself some part of the constitutionalist rhetoric of his rulers, and defended stubbornly his rights at law and his rights to protest turbulently against military, press-gang or police, alongside his rights to white bread and cheap ale. The plebs were aware that a ruling class that rested its claim to legitimacy upon prescription and law had little authority to over-rule their own customs and rights. [. . .]

This symbolic contest acquires its significance only within a particular equilibrium of social relations. The plebeian culture cannot be analysed independently of this equilibrium; its definitions are, in some part, antagonisms to the definitions of the polite culture. What I have been attempting to show, perhaps repetitiously, is that each element of this society, taken separately, may have precedents and successors, but that when all are taken together they add up to a sum which is more than the sum of the parts: it is a structured set of relations, in which the State, the Law, the libertarian ideology, the ebullitions and direct actions of the crowd, all perform roles intrinsic to that system, and within limits assigned by that system, which limits are at the same time the limits of what is politically 'possible'; and, to a remarkable degree, the limits of what is intellectually and culturally 'possible' also. The crowd, at its most advanced, can rarely transcend the libertarian rhetoric of the radical Whig tradition; the poets cannot transcend the sensibility of the humane and generous paternalist.[2] The furious anonymous letters which spring up from society's lower depths blaspheme against the gentry's hegemony but offer no strategy to replace it.

In one sense this is a rather conservative conclusion, for I am endorsing eighteenth-century society's rhetorical self-image—that the Settlement of 1688 defined its form and its characteristic relations. Given that that Settlement established the form of rule for an agrarian bourgeoisie,[3] it seems that it was as

---

[1] I am supporting here the argument of Gerald M. Sider, 'Christmas mumming and the New Year in Outport Newfoundland', *Past and Present* (May 1976).

[2] I do not doubt that there was a genuine and significant paternalist tradition among the gentry and professional groups. But that is a different theme. My theme here is to define the limits of paternalism, and to present objections to the notion that 18th-cent. social (or class) relations were mediated by paternalism, on paternalism's own terms.

[3] Professor J. H. Hexter was astonished when I uttered this improper copulation ('agrarian bourgeoisie') at the Davis Centre seminar in Princeton in 1976. Perry Anderson was also astonished ten years earlier: 'Socialism and Pseudo-Empiricism', *New Left Review*, 35 (Jan.–Feb. 1966), 8, 'A bourgeoisie, if the term is to mean anything, is a class based on *towns*; that is what the word means.' See also (on my side of the argument), Genovese, *The World the Slaveholders Made*, 249; and a judicious commentary on the argument by Richard Johnson, *Working Papers in Cultural Studies*, 9 (Birmingham, Spring 1976). My re-statement of this (somewhat conventional) Marxist argument was made in 'The Peculiarities of the English', *Socialist Register* (1965), esp. 318. Here I emphasize not only the economic logic of agrarian capitalism, but the specific

much that form of State power as it was that mode of production and productive relations which determined the political and cultural expressions of the
next hundred years. Indeed that State, weak as it was in its bureaucratic and
rationalizing functions, was immensely strong and effective as an auxiliary
instrument of production in its own right: in breaking open the paths for
commercial imperialism, in imposing enclosure upon the countryside, and in
facilitating the accumulation and movement of capital, both through its bank-
ing and funding functions and, more bluntly, through the parasitic extractions
of its own officers. It is this specific combination of weakness and of strength
which provides the 'general illumination' in which all colours of that century
are plunged; which assigned to the judges and the magistracy their roles;
which made necessary the theatre of cultural hegemony and which wrote its
paternalist and libertarian script; which afforded to the crowd its opportunity
for protest and for pressures; which laid down the terms of negotiation between authority and plebs, and which established the limits beyond which
negotiation might not go. [. . .]

Eventually an independent plebeian culture as robust as this might even
have nurtured alternative expectations, challenging this hegemony. This is not
my reading of what took place, for when the ideological break with paternalism came, in the 1790s, it came in the first place less from the plebeian culture
than from the intellectual culture of the dissenting middle class, and from
thence it was carried to the urban artisans.[1] But Painite ideas, carried through
by such artisans to an even wider plebeian culture, instantly struck root there;
and perhaps the shelter provided by this robust and independent culture
enabled them to flourish and propagate themselves, until they gave rise to the
great and undeferential popular agitations at the end of the French Wars.

Theoretically I am saying this. The concept of hegemony is immensely
valuable, and without it we would be at a loss to understand how eighteenth-
century social relations were structured. But while such cultural hegemony
may define the limits of what is possible, and inhibit the growth of alternative
horizons and expectations, there is nothing determined or automatic about

amalgam of urban and rural attributes in the life-style of the 18th-cent. gentry; the watering-
places; the London or town season; the periodic urban passage-rites, in education or in the
various marriage markets; and other specific attributes of a mixed agrarian–urban culture. The
economic arguments (already ably presented by Dobb) have been reinforced by Brenner,
'Agrarian Class Structure', esp. 62–8. Additional evidence as to the urban facilities available to
the gentry is in Peter Borsay, 'The English Urban Renaissance: The Development of Provincial
Urban Culture, c.1680–c.1760', Social History, 5 (May 1977).

[1] The question as to whether a subordinate class can or cannot develop a coherent intellectual critique of the dominant ideology—and a strategy reaching beyond the limits of its
hegemony—seems to me to be a historical question (that is, one to which historical evidence
offers many different answers, some of them highly nuanced), and not one which can be solved
by pronouncements within 'theoretical practice'. The number of 'organic intellectuals' (in
Gramsci's sense) among the artisans and workers of Britain between 1790 and 1850 should never
be understated.

this process. Such hegemony can be sustained by the rulers only by the constant exercise of skill, of theatre and of concession. Second, such hegemony, even when imposed successfully, does not impose an all-embracing view of life; rather, it imposes blinkers, which inhibit vision in certain directions while leaving it clear in others. It can co-exist (as it did co-exist in eighteenth-century England) with a very vigorous self-activating culture of the people, derived from their own experience and resources. This culture, which may be resistant at many points to any form of exterior domination, constitutes an ever-present threat to official descriptions of reality; given the sharp jostle of experience, the intrusion of 'seditious' propagandists, the Church-and-King crowd can become Jacobin or Luddite, the loyal Tsarist navy can become an insurrectionary Bolshevik fleet.

['Eighteenth-Century English Society: Class Struggle without Class?'
Social History, 3/2 (May 1978), 146–51, 154, 156, 158, 161–2, 163–4.]

IRA KATZNELSON
....
20 **Levels of Class Formation**

As a concept, class has soaked up so much meaning that it has become bulky to use. Because it is often employed without a clearly specified definition, debates about class often become conversations in which people talk past each other because they are talking about different dimensions of class. Without clear analytical distinctions between levels or layers of class, it is hard to improve on the 'class in itself–for itself' model. With the specification of different levels it becomes possible to construct the various cases of class formation in their own terms and to explore the competing capacities of various macrohypotheses about linkages between the levels. Above all, the distinctions that follow are meant to be aids to concrete description and explanation.

The *first* level is the structure of capitalist economic development, whose main elements include an economy based on privately owned autonomous firms that seek to make profit-maximizing decisions. These enterprises employ labor for a wage and sell what they produce in the market. This process of economic development contains some elements shared by all capitalist societies and others that are distinctive to each. As Karl Polanyi pointed out, this 'great transformation' entailed the commodification of money, land, and labor. Capitalism is unthinkable without proletarianization; and, as Marx observed as the centerpiece of his political economy, capitalism is impossible without a quite specific mechanism of exploitation.

Because these key properties are shared by all capitalisms, it is appropriate at this first level of class analysis to propose such distinctions as collective capital and collective labor, and productive and unproductive labor. And it is at this level that the heuristic model building Marx did in his mature works of political economy must test its mettle against other competing accounts.

Structural analyses of capitalism at this level use class analytically as a construct that is 'experience-distant' (that is, as a concept employed by specialists to further scientific, philosophical, or practical aims). Used in this way as a tool to analyze the 'motion' of capitalist development, class has no direct or unmediated phenomenological referents.

But economic development, of course, occurs not just in theory or in capitalism in general, but in real places at actual times. If capitalism is structured everywhere in coherent ways, it is also structured in different particular manners. Each specific national history of capitalist development is shaped by the shared impulses and boundaries of all capitalisms; but each national economy is shaped not only by these tendencies. Family patterns, demography, cultural traditions, inherited practices, state organization and policies, geopolitics, and other factors help determine the specific empirical contours of macroscopic economic development at this first level of class.

Even as we pay attention to these variations, however (as, for example, Aristide Zolberg does in the concluding essay of this book), at this level of economic structure class remains an experience-distant analytical concept, needed to describe and explain what happened because class is a constitutive element of any capitalist structure. Distinctive national histories of capitalist economic development perforce are structural histories of class formation in the sense of Charles Tilly's 'thin' definition in his treatment of the demographic origins of the European proletariat: 'people who work for wages, using means of production over whose disposition they have little or no control'.[1] Proletarianization at this level provides a necessary, indeed the necessary condition for class formation in the more thickly textured senses of ways of life, dispositions, or patterns of collective action. But even when we take variations in macrolevel economic development into account it is not a sufficient condition. It is impossible to infer ways of life, dispositions, or collective action directly from analyses of class at the first level.

Nevertheless, broad patterns of economic development are of central importance in shaping patterns of life and social relations in specific capitalist societies. This *second* level, determined in part by the structure of capitalist development, refers to the social organization of society lived by actual people in real social formations. For this reason, theories that deal with this level of class must be 'experience-near'.

Because this second level includes such economic phenomena as workplace social relations and labor markets, it is tempting to collapse the first two levels

---

[1] Charles Tilly, 'Demographic Origins of the European Proletariat', in David Levine (ed.), *Proletarianization and Family Life* (Academic Press, New York, 1984), 1.

of class into the single category of the 'economy'. Such a conflation, however, eliminates in one stroke a series of important questions about the connections between key aspects of capitalist accumulation and national economic histories on one side and the organization of labor markets and workplaces on the other. As any student of capitalist industrialization knows, the growth and expansion of capitalism has proved capable of fostering many different kinds of workplaces and work. This is a theme to which the essays below return as they search for the implications of variations in capitalist development and in the social organization of work for the content and forms of class formation in different societies.

Although the second level of class includes work settings and labor markets (here classes can be stacked up and counted according to criteria that distinguish between various active members of the labor force),[1] it is not coextensive with these social relationships. The level of ways of life refers to how actual capitalist societies develop at work *and* away from it.

One of the hallmarks of industrial capitalist societies is that they tend to foster ways of life that differentiate between the location and social organization of these two realms. Over time, this distinction is expressed in the social geography of industrial cities. Work leaves the home. Cross-class households break up. Whole regions of cities come to be defined as areas of residence or of production. Further, residential communities segregate by the class position of their residents (in both the Marxist sense of location in a system of production and the Weberian sense of capacity to consume goods and services in the marketplace). With these separations between work and home and between the social classes in space, class relations are lived and experienced not only at work but also off work in residence communities.

The first two levels of class are closely related, of course, in that it is something of a conceit to separate too starkly the structure of capitalist accumulation and the self-sustaining development of the economy at the first level from how such broad patterns of economic development exist for working people where they labor and where they live at the second level. Moreover, if we understand that neither level of social relations is purely economic, then it makes sense to see the second level as an attribute of the first. But however closely connected, they are separate nonetheless, and many debates, such as the one between Erik Olin Wright and Nicos Poulantzas about mappings of class, suffer from the failure to make this distinction.[2]

---

[1] For an extended theoretically informed empirical analysis along such lines, see Erik Olin Wright, *Class Structure and Income Determination* (Academic Press, New York, 1979).

[2] Theoretical discussions of the base-superstructure metaphor within Marxism also suffer from a collapse of these two levels into the 'economy'. A brilliant attempt at 'bringing workers back in' at the point of production through an analysis of the labor process, which succeeds in overcoming the theoretical problems I have alluded to—albeit a treatment rather different in emphasis than that of this essay and book—is Michael Burawoy, *The Politics of Production: Factory Regimes under Capitalism and Socialism* (Verso Books, London, 1985).

At the first two levels of class it is appropriate to construct classifications of class relations, and the literature of social science is full of them. At both levels class is defined, from an orthodox Marxist position, as G. A. Cohen writes, solely 'with reference to the position of its members in the economic structure, their effective rights and duties within it. A person's class is established by nothing but his objective place in the network of ownership relations, however difficult it may be to identify such places neatly.' Even if the criteria used in such definitions are expanded to other bases of class relations and to patterns of class embedded in residence communities, Cohen is right to stress that at these levels of analysis a person's 'consciousness, culture, and politics do not enter the *definition* of his class position. . . . Not even his behavior is an essential part of it.'[1] Yet by themselves no such schemata, however compelling, can tell us how class exists distinct from other bases of solidarity and action in specific societies at specific times. This level of analysis may tell us how workers exist and live in certain circumstances, but not how they will think or act in those experienced circumstances.

At a *third* level social classes are not heuristic or analytical constructs nor do they consist of members of this or that cell of a typology. At this level, classes are formed groups, sharing dispositions. Such cognitive constructs map the terrain of lived experience and define the boundaries between the probable and improbable. Note that I am deliberately avoiding the term 'class consciousness' in order to make clear my rejection of any notion of degrees of consciousness, with the highest corresponding to the 'real' interests of the working class. Further, the scheme of four levels of class does not imply a series of necessary stages or a natural progression (after all, ways of life are not independent of thought or action). It is, rather, a classification that aims to promote the development of theory free from developmental assumptions.

I take it that the third level of class is what Thompson means when he writes:

Class is a social and cultural formation (often finding institutional expression) which cannot be defined abstractly, or in isolation, but only in terms of relationship with other classes; and, ultimately, the definition can only be made in the medium of *time*—that is, action and reaction, change and conflict. When we speak of *a* class we are thinking of a very loosely-defined body of people who share the same congeries of interests, social experiences, traditions, and value-system, who have a *disposition* to *behave* as a class, to define themselves in their actions and in their consciousness in relation to other groups of people in class ways.[2]

This suggestive formulation condenses a number of significant issues. To say that people share dispositions can mean that they have come to share

---

[1] G. A. Cohen, *Karl Marx's Theory of History: A Defence* (Princeton University Press, Princeton, 1978), 73.

[2] E. P. Thompson, 'The Peculiarities of the English', in *Socialist Register* 1965, ed. Ralph Miliband and John Saville (Merlin Press, London, 1966), 357. Emphasis in original.

understandings of the social system or that they have come to share values of justice and goodness. These two kinds of disposition are at least partially independent. Further, whether they are class dispositions is a contingent matter. Members of a class may share dispositions of either kind, but they need not necessarily be class based analytically or normatively. Further, either knowledge- or norm-based dispositions may view the current situation as the outcome of circumstances that cannot be altered or as posing the possibility of something better.

Much of the variation between the French, American, and German cases consists of variations in the ways working people, confronting changes in the conditions of life at the second level of class, mapped and interpreted these changes at the level of dispositions. Most new social history joins the story of class formation here, studying situations from the point of view of a specific working class in a specific place at a specific time. It is at this level that a Geertzian cultural analysis of the ways people construct meaning to make their way through the experienced world is most compelling,[1] especially because shared dispositions are interactive. They are formed by the manner in which people interact with each other. Thus dispositions are transindividual, not merely opinions or views of individual actors. They constitute cultural configurations within which people act. In Bernard Cohn's terms, 'there can be no practical realities without the symbolic coding of them as *practical*. . . . People cannot act as maximizers—either out of self interest or out of deep psychological conditionings—. . . without the preexistence of meaning in cultural terms.'[2]

The third level of class, that of dispositions, is not coextensive with class structures and class-based ways of life; nor, however, do dispositions simply mirror reality. Rather, they are plausible and meaningful responses to the circumstances workers find themselves in. [. . .]

Thompson follows his discussion of class dispositions by adding, 'but class itself is not a thing, it is a happening'.[3] Here he moves much too quickly from this third level of class to a *fourth*, collective action. Groups of people sharing motivational constructs ('disposition to behave') may or may not act collectively to transform disposition to behavior. Even where workers have close

[1] H. Geertz, *The Interpretation of Cultures* (Basic Books, New York, 1973); Paul Rabinow and William M. Sullivan (eds), *Interpretive Social Science: A Reader* (University of California Press, Berkeley, 1979). In Geertz's work there is some ambiguity about whether he wishes to claim that culture is the encompassing concept or whether culture is a distinctive mapping of society.

[2] Bernard S. Cohn, 'History and Anthropology: The State of Play', *Comparative Studies in Society and History*, 22 (Apr. 1980). Emphasis in original. William Roseberry puts the point this way: 'People do not simply act in terms of objective limits or positions but also in terms of apparently subjective evaluations of limits, positions, and possibilities. As they do so, the "subjective" becomes "objective"; culture becomes material. Action is, in short, meaningful, as Weber long ago insisted' (William Roseberry, 'Why Should Marxists Take Culture Seriously?' paper presented at the Annual Meeting of the American Anthropological Society, Nov. 1984).

[3] Thompson, 'Peculiarities', 357.

contact at work and in their residential communities; even if this interaction promotes strong collective identities; and even if these workers share common systems of meaning that incline them to act in class ways, they may not necessarily act together to produce collective action. For this reason it is useful to distinguish between class at the third level and at the fourth, which refers to classes that are organized and that act through movements and organizations to affect society and the position of the class within it. This kind of behavior is self-conscious and refers to activity that is more than just the common but unself-conscious shared behavior of members of a class. After all, members of categorical classes must immanently share certain behaviors, but they do not necessarily act consciously and collectively in pursuit of common goals.

The 'class in itself–for itself' formulation makes thinking about the links between the social organization of class, class dispositions, and collective action superfluous. But in fact class conflict of any particular kind is not necessarily entailed in the class organization of patterns of social life, nor even in the development of groups of people inclined to act in class ways. The one broad exception to this general rule of contingency is the development of trade unions to fight for better wages and working conditions at the place of work. Although here too there are wide variations between the experiences of different working classes, there are no examples of national histories of class formation utterly lacking in the effort to create trade unions.

There are always impediments to collective action,[1] to those occasions when 'sets of people commit pooled resources, including their own efforts, to common ends'. A key feature of the historical study of class must consist 'of discovering which sets of people, which resources, which common ends, and which forms of commitment were involved in different places and times. Did the configurations change systematically with the advances of capitalism and large organizations?'[2] Both the content and the form of collective action are highly variable, and this variation demands explanation.

Class, Thompson suggestively points out, is a 'junction term', which lies at the intersection of structure and process, social being and social consciousness. Structural change gives rise to changed experience: that is, both to a set of subjective perceptions of objectively ordered realities and to a more active process of learning, possibly leading to action to modify the objective realities. I have already noted that Thompson, in my view, makes the movement from

---

[1] The best-known treatment of these impediments is Mancur Olson, *The Logic of Collective Action* (Harvard University Press, Cambridge, Mass., 1965). See also Russell Hardin, *Collective Action* (Johns Hopkins University Press, Baltimore, 1982). For a stunning treatment of related issues of strategy and rationality, see Jon Elster, *Ulysses and the Sirens: Studies in Rationality and Irrationality* (Cambridge University Press, New York, 1979).

[2] Charles Tilly, 'Introduction', in Louise A. Tilly and Charles Tilly (eds), *Class Conflict and Collective Action* (Sage Publications, Beverly Hills, Calif., 1981). Also see the discussion of collective action in his *From Mobilization to Revolution* (Addison-Wesley, Reading, Mass., 1978).

class structure to class action too certain a passage, but this teleological element can be extruded from his formulation.

The distinctions drawn here between the four levels of class may be read as an elaboration of Thompson's insight that class is a junction term. They allow us to specify more precisely the points of connection *between* the structure of class relations at the macroeconomic level; the lived experience of class in the workplace and in the residence community; groups of people disposed to act in class ways; and class-based collective action. These points of contact specify the possibility of alternative kinds of relationships between the levels, a problem best approached by asking what we mean by class formation after moving beyond 'class in itself–for itself' formulations.

It is possible, of course, to continue to define class formation in terms of specific outcomes, rather than to leave open the content of class formation. We might say that class formation has occurred only when class exists at all four levels of structure, patterns of life, dispositions, and action simultaneously. This would have a number of advantages. It would turn our attention to the links between class levels, and it would treat class formation as only one of a number of possible outcomes. It would dispose of the Hobson's choice between structuralist formulations that claim, at least implicitly, that experience is ideology, and culturalist stances fashionable in much current linguistic and semiotic theory in which class society is said to exist only when it is signified.

But despite these advantages, such a definition would be unsatisfactory. An outcome approach hinging on the appearance of class at each of the four levels without specifying the components of class and the range of both class and nonclass possibilities at each of the levels too starkly posits a dichotomous outcome (and in this way resembles the tradition of 'revolutionary consciousness'): class either exists or does not as the basis of social solidarity and action. This distinction does not appear to be terribly helpful in explicating the puzzles posed by our three cases. Further, such an approach fails to answer the question, class formation with respect to what content?

Class formation may be thought of more fully and more variably as concerned with the conditional (but not random) process of connection between the four levels of class. The specification of four levels of class allows us to keep the advantages of defining class formation in terms of outcomes while providing a more elaborated and variable object of comparative historical analysis. The content of each of the four levels of necessity will vary from society to society; no level need be understood or analyzed exclusively in class terms; and the connections between the levels are problematical and conditional.

Questions about the content of each level and about the connections between the levels of class constitute the very heart of the analysis of class formation. A precise (but not too narrow) charting of class formation, based on a contingent but not undetermined approach to the relationship between these levels, and the attempt to develop macrocausal hypotheses about variations in class formation are the interrelated tasks that follow from this approach.

Although their analytical emphases differ and the range of questions they ask is very broad, the essays that make up the main part of this book are constructed to permit such systematic comparisons. The essays treat comparable periods. They use the typology of levels of class in the double sense of identifying the aspects of each case that need to be constructed and identifying the relevant theoretical issues at each level. And they try to account for variations in patterns of class formation by looking at common sources for the construction of hypotheses and explanation. In short, read alone or together, the essays respect the distinctiveness of each case while recognizing that, together, they compose a family.

[*Working-Class Formation: Nineteenth-Century Patterns in Western Europe and the United States* (Princeton University Press, London, 1986), 14–19, 19–23.]

(b) The 'Linguistic Turn'

GARETH STEDMAN JONES

21 Class, 'Experience', and Politics

The latest essays in this book indicate a shift in my thinking not only about these particular topics but also about the social historical approach as such.[1] Most important in this respect was the process of rethinking that lay behind my essay on Chartism.

I wanted to make a study of Chartism both because my work on a projected biography of Engels suggested the need to find a critical yardstick by which to judge his picture of the movement, and because no overview of English working class development was possible without an adequate interpretation of that crucial episode. The weakness of my critique of Foster's book had derived from the vagueness of its treatment of Chartism as a political phenomenon.[2] The decline of Chartism had there been described only from a most stratospheric angle of vision in terms of a failure of the social Weltanschauung supposedly represented by the Chartists in the face of the advance and stabilization of the national and international economy. Similarly, in accounting for its beginnings, although I had felt a long-standing unease at the theoretical level about Edward Thompson's picture of the formation of working-class consciousness, it was impossible to provide a more satisfactory alternative without independent engagement with the primary sources.

In my initial attempt to find a way into the problem, I mistook Thompson's strength for his weakness. By situating and tying down more precisely, as an ideology, what Thompson portrayed as working-class consciousness around 1830, I thought it might be possible to account both for the strengths and the limits of the social movements in the first half of the nineteenth century. Given this hypothesis, two questions then presented themselves. Firstly, why did this type of consciousness apparently reach a peak in Chartism and then decline? Thompson's book provided no obvious answer to that question. Secondly, whose consciousness precisely was it? Was it really that of the 'working class'? Or was it that of a historically more specific group of wage earners—journeymen and outworkers faced with the proletarianization of their trades, rather than a proletariat in a more familiar Marxist sense? Thompson's book largely sidestepped that question, while the attempt by Foster to identify the most revolutionary form of class consciousness with a *factory* proletariat

---

[1] 'Rethinking Chartism' (1981) and 'Why is the Labour Party in a Mess?' (1982).

[2] John Foster, *Class Struggle and the Industrial Revolution* (London, 1974).

squarely posed a question which any Marx-based approach would have to confront.

In an article not reproduced here, I attempted some form of answer to both these questions.[1] Briefly, my solution was that the movement which had come into existence by the 1830s, while not confined to artisans, was nevertheless premissed upon a particular set of assumptions espoused by artisans about work, class relations and the role of the state. Such an outlook could also be identified in the use of labour theories of property derived from natural right, in the preoccupation with the land, in the focus upon the 'capitalist' as trader rather than employer, and in the location of exploitation in politically sustained forms of unequal exchange rather than in the productive process itself. Thompson's book could end on a peak because in the radical and co-operative movements of 1829–34, these peculiarities were not apparent. In Chartism, on the other hand, a much broader movement incorporating the new factory districts as well as the workshop and outwork trades, such problems came to the fore. Thus the decline of Chartism could partly be attributed to the limitations inherent in an ideology, which was dominant within it, that was incapable of articulating the new pattern of class relations in the factory districts of the North.

Further research and reflection, however, revealed the radical inadequacy of this approach. The attempt to arrive at a new understanding of Chartism through the use of the concept of ideology proved a blind alley. As a category it turned out to be inert and unilluminatingly reductive. The term 'ideology' tends to be used to link a certain set of beliefs or preoccupations with the material situation of a precisely specified social group. Yet a comparison of Chartist argument with eighteenth century radicalism made it less and less clear what was distinctively artisanal about the Chartist platform. The basic assumptions upon which the radical case was based predated the entry of artisans and other workers into politics and were not fundamentally reshaped as a result. More generally, a preoccupation with ideology simply missed what was most urgent to explain about Chartism—its political character, the specific reasons for its rise and fall, its focus upon representation and its lack of interest in the demarcation of socio-economic status within the unrepresented. The difficulty of an explanation in terms of the limitations of an artisanal consciousness or ideology, like most social approaches to the decline of Chartism, was that it did not identify with any precision what it was that declined.

Having arrived at this point, I decided to reverse my initial assumption: given the existence of good material grounds for discontent, it was not consciousness (or ideology) that produced politics, but politics that produced

---

[1] G. Stedman Jones, 'The Limits of a Proletarian Theory in England before 1850', unpublished paper presented to a conference of social historians at Bielefeld, 1977. For an important study of the politics of artisans in this period, see Iorwerth Prothero, *Artisans and Politics in Early Nineteenth Century London* (Folkestone, 1979).

consciousness. This meant opening up an unfamiliar line of enquiry into Chartism—an approach which would drop all the social presuppositions which had encrusted the literature on Chartism since the beginning and would isolate the politics of Chartism as an object of study in its own right. To do this, however, was more difficult than at first appeared. For it involved not only an empirical programme of research—finding out the reasons for discontent stated by the Chartists, and the political solutions they envisaged. It also meant knowing what weight to give to these utterances in the interpretation of Chartism as a whole and the reasons why most commentators on Chartism had implicitly or explicitly discounted their significance. This problem was theoretical. It concerned the place of language, consciousness and experience.

Early observers of Chartism like Engels, and most historians of Chartism since, have worked with two sorts of evidence: on the one hand, evidence of reasons for discontent—unemployment, machine breaking, catastrophic depressions, overwork, child labour, overcrowding, extreme poverty and so on; on the other hand, evidence of the widespread employment of a language of class antagonism in the radical political movements of the period. What has been problematic has been the way in which these two types of evidence have been connected. Part of the problem is precisely that it has not been seen as a problem. Philosophical assumption—explicit or unwitting—has supplied the missing links by interjecting terms like 'experience' or 'consciousness', tying the two poles together in a way which seems intuitively obvious. What these terms suggest is that the relationship between the two sorts of evidence is one of simple expression. The stronger term 'consciousness', in its usage by social historians, is Hegelian in origin. It assumes an objective and necessary process in which what is latent will be made manifest, and it provides criteria by which the adequacy of the manifestation may be judged. 'Experience' on the other hand is compatible with a seemingly more empiricist approach to history.[1] It puts to one side the question of the necessity or objectivity of the process and presents such a process more as a matter of fact registered through the subjectivities of those engaged within it. In practice, however, the difference between the two terms is not as great as it might appear. For tacit assumptions are made about what is to count as experience, about its meaningfulness, and about its cumulative and collective character.

What both 'experience' and 'consciousness' conceal—at least as their usage has evolved among historians—is the problematic character of language itself. Both concepts imply that language is a simple medium through which 'experi-

---

[1] This is not to imply that 'experience' cannot also be conceived in Hegelian fashion. See, e.g., G. W. F. Hegel, *Phenomenology of Spirit*, trans. A. V. Miller (Oxford, 1977), 55–7. Nor, of course, do I mean to imply that the philosophical problem of 'consciousness' in its broadest sense begins with Hegel. For an illuminating discussion of the philosophical construction of 'consciousness' in the 17th cent., see Richard Rorty, *Philosophy and the Mirror of Nature* (Oxford, 1980), 45–69.

ence' finds expression—a romantic conception of language in which what is at the beginning inner and particular struggles to outward expression and, having done so, finds itself recognized in the answering experience of others, and hence sees itself to be part of a shared experience. It is in some such way that 'experience' can be conceived cumulatively to result in class consciousness. What this approach cannot acknowledge is all the criticism which has been levelled at it since the broader significance of Saussure's work was understood—the materiality of language itself, the impossibility of simply referring it back to some primal anterior reality, 'social being', the impossibility of abstracting experience from the language which structures its articulation. In areas other than history, such criticisms are by now well known and do not need elaboration. But historians—and social historians in particular—have either been unaware or, when aware, extremely resistant to the implications of this approach for their own practice, and this has been so most of all perhaps when it touches such a central topic as class.

In order, therefore, to bring to the fore the politics of Chartism, freed from the a priori assumptions of historians about its social meaning, I applied a non-referential conception of language to the study of Chartist speeches and writings. Concretely, this meant exploring the systematic relationship between terms and propositions within the language rather than setting particular propositions into direct relation to a putative experiential reality of which they were assumed to be the expression. How well I succeeded in utilizing the insight to be derived from such an approach in the resulting essay, readers may judge. But provisionally it seems to me that such an approach allows a way round the otherwise insoluble riddles raised in the age-old debates about continuity/discontinuity in nineteenth and twentieth century social history by restoring politics to its proper importance.

In general, whether steeped in the older traditions of labour history or the newer conventions of social history, historians have looked everywhere except at changes in political discourse itself to explain changes in political behaviour. Starting implicitly or explicitly from an essentialist conception of class, in which all the different languages of class are measured against Marxist or sociological conceptions of class position, they have taken as their task the demonstration of concordance with, or the explanation of deviation from, positions which socio-economic logic ascribes. The implicit assumption is of civil society as a field of conflicting social groups or classes whose opposing interests will find rational expression in the political arena. Such interests, it is assumed, pre-exist their expression. Languages of politics are evanescent forms, mere coverings of an adequate, inadequate or anachronistic kind, through which essential interests may be decoded.

In order to rewrite the political history of the 'working class' or 'working classes', we should start out from the other end of the chain. Language disrupts any simple notion of the determination of consciousness by social being because it is itself part of social being. We cannot therefore decode political language to reach a primal and material expression of interest since it is the discursive structure of political language which conceives and defines interest in the first place. What we must therefore do is to study the production of interest, identification, grievance and aspiration within political languages themselves. We need to map out these successive languages of radicalism, liberalism, socialism etc., both in relation to the political languages they replace and laterally in relation to rival political languages with which they are in conflict. Only then can we begin to assess their reasons for success or failure at specific points in time. It is clear that particular political languages do become inapposite in new situations. How and why this occurs involves the discovery of the precise point at which shifts occur as well as an investigation of the specific political circumstances in which they shift. To peer straight through these languages into the structural changes to which they may be notionally referred is no substitute for such an investigation, not because there is not a relationship of some kind, but because such connections can never be established with any satisfying degree of finality.

[*Languages of Class: Studies in English Working-Class History,
1832–1982* (Cambridge University Press, 1983), 16–22.]

JOAN W. SCOTT

22 | Language, Gender, and Working-Class History

This essay is an attempt to address a problem that seems to me increasingly evident and stubbornly resistant to easy solution. That problem is the one faced by feminist historians in their attempts to bring women as a subject and gender as an analytic category into the practice of labor history. If women as subjects have increased in visibility, the questions raised by women's history remain awkwardly connected to the central concerns of the field. And gender has not been seriously considered for what it could provide in the way of a major reconceptualization of labor history. Some feminist historians (myself included) have therefore viewed with cautious optimism their colleagues' increasing interest in theories of language. Those theories (contained in the

This essay is based on an article that was originally published in *International Labor and Working Class History*, 31 (1987), 1–13. It has been revised and expanded to address critiques, published also in that issue, by Brian Palmer, Anson Rabinbach, and Christine Stansell. It includes as well portions of my reply to these critiques, published in 32 (1987), 39–45. It is printed here with permission from the University of Illinois Press, which holds the copyright. I am grateful to Palmer, Rabinbach, and Stansell for comments that pointed up problems in the original essay, all of which will not have been corrected here to their satisfaction. I am appreciative, as well, of suggestions from Denise Riley and Elliott Shore, which substantially improved the argument.

writings of post-structuralists and cultural anthropologists), and better referred to as epistemological theories, offer a way of thinking about how people construct meaning, about how difference (and therefore sexual difference) operates in the construction of meaning, and about how the complexities of contextual usages open the way for changes in meaning.

These theories are potentially of great use for the conceptualization of gender and the reconceptualization of historical practice. And yet, for the most part, they have not been used that way. Instead they have been superficially applied, giving feminist historians some cause for frustration, if not pessimism about the kinds of changes we can expect from labor history. The recent spate of articles by labor historians on 'language' demonstrates my point, for they reduce this important concept to the study of 'words'.[1] Words taken at their face value as literal utterances become one more datum to collect and the notion of how meaning is constructed—as a complex way of interpreting and understanding the world—is lost. With the loss of an understanding of meaning, the importance and usefulness of thinking about labor history in terms of gender also disappears. We are left with separate studies of women and of words and those may add new material, but they will never alone transform the way we think about the history we write. [. . .]

My purpose in this essay is to argue that there is a connection between the study of 'language' and the study of gender, when both are carefully defined; that certain epistemological theories, by providing historians with a way to analyze how gender figures in the construction of social and political meaning, thereby provide us with a way to recast our understanding of the place of gender in history, of the operations of sexual difference in the 'making' of the working class. By 'language' I mean not simply words in their literal usage but the creation of meaning through differentiation. By gender I mean not simply social roles for women and men but the articulation in specific contexts of social understandings of sexual difference. If meaning is constructed in terms of difference (by distinguishing explicitly or implicitly what something is from what it is not); then sexual difference (which is culturally and historically variable, but which always seems fixed and indisputable because of its reference to natural, physical bodies) is an important way of specifying or establishing meaning. My argument, then, is that if we attend to the ways in which 'language' constructs meaning we will also be in a position to find gender. Especially in Western Europe and North America in the nineteenth and twentieth centuries—the places and periods with which I am most familiar and

---

[1] See the editors' introduction to the special issue of the *Radical History Review* on 'Language, Work and Ideology', 34 (1986), 3: 'As radicals, we are concerned about the languages of power and inequality: how words express and help to construct dominance and subordination.' The conflation of 'language' and 'words' is exactly the problem that needs to be avoided and that I will address throughout this essay. See also Christine Stansell's critique of this essay in *International Labor and Working Class History*, 31 (1987), 24–9.

in which most labor historians work—the connections are unavoidable. The connections are unavoidable as well because it was precisely in this period that gender was articulated as a problematic issue.

How then have historians managed to avoid the connections for so long? A look at Gareth Stedman Jones's *Languages of Class*, especially his 'Introduction' and the long essay called 'Rethinking Chartism', may provide something of an answer.[1] [. . .]

I

The theoretical claim of 'Rethinking Chartism' (one I agree with) is that the backgrounds, interests, and structural positions of members of the movement cannot explain its emergence or decline. We get nowhere, Stedman Jones tells us, pursuing lines of inquiry that assume social causation because there is no social reality outside or prior to language. Hence class is not a thing whose existence predetermines or is reflected in class consciousness; rather it is 'constructed and inscribed within a complex rhetoric of metaphorical associations, causal inferences and imaginative constructions' (p. 102). Class and class consciousness are the same thing—they are political articulations that provide an analysis of, a coherent pattern to impose upon, the events and activities of daily life. Although the rhetoric of class appeals to the objective 'experience' of workers, in fact such experience only exists through its conceptual organization; what counts as experience cannot be established by collecting empirical data but by analyzing the terms of definition offered in political discourse (by the state, employers, discrete political movements, etc.). The categories within which empirical data are placed, after all, are not objective entities but ways of perceiving or understanding, of assigning importance or significance to phenomena or events. The origins of class must be sought then not in objective material conditions, nor in the consciousness said to reflect those conditions, but in the language of political struggle. '[I]t was not consciousness (or ideology) that produced politics, but politics that produced consciousness' (p. 19). [. . .]

Stedman Jones's essay conflates two different definitions of politics: one labels as politics any contest for power within which identities such as class are created; the other characterizes as politics (or political) those goals of a collective movement aimed at formal participation in government or the state. The first definition is by far the more radical for it contains the nonreferential conception Stedman Jones endorses in his Introduction. It suggests that there is always a politics—in the sense of a power relationship—in the operations of discourse. The second is essentially descriptive, employing the approach of conventional

[1] G. S. Jones, *Languages of Class: Studies in English Working Class History, 1832–1982* (Cambridge University Press, Cambridge, 1983).

intellectual history—establishing continuities of thought, pointing out underlying assumptions, and organizing into a coherent outlook the diverse ideas of
various proponents. Stedman Jones means to use the first definition, but in his
essay on Chartism he uses the second. He cannot put into practice the theory he
espouses in his Introduction because of the methods he employs to analyze
history. First, he reads 'language' only literally, with no sense of how texts are
constructed. Second, he slips back to the notion that 'language' reflects a
'reality' external to it, rather than being constitutive of that reality.

By treating meaning as 'language' and reading only literally, Stedman Jones
finds Chartism to be a political movement because it was interested in formal
political representation as a solution to social problems. The key to Chartism,
he says, was its use of radical 'vocabulary', the importation of older words and
ideas into an early nineteenth-century context. He spends much of the essay
showing that the message of Chartism was similar to that of Owenism, trade
unionism, and the 'Ricardian socialism' of the period—all understood the state
as the ultimate source of oppression. Chartism was a heterogeneous movement, including all the unenfranchised in its notion of class; the contents of the
message, in other words, was political in a formal and literal sense. This
procedure shows class to be a political concept not so much because it was
formulated in a particular kind of (discursive) conflict but because it contained
or referred to political ideas (the vestiges of English radicalism). [. . .]

[. . .] Stedman Jones uses theories of language, which have a far more radical
potential, in an essentially conservative manner, to correct certain conclusions
that historians have made, but not to make us rethink entire questions. His
analysis is less informed by a notion of the 'materiality of language itself' (p. 20)
than it is by an idea that attention to the words people used (rather than how
words acquire and construct meaning) provides a way to determine which
reality mattered most in a particular historical context. His reinterpretation of
Chartism argues for a closer fit between the 'vocabulary' of the movement
and our description of it; rather than reversing the direction of our causal
thinking he merely shifts the causality from the economic to the political sphere.
Stedman Jones does not entertain the possibility that economic grievances
are about power and politics, that Chartists might have sought economic
change by political means, that their visions of power intertwined economics
and politics. He wants to argue that Chartist politics were not immanent
in productive relations and that Chartism drew on many different socio-
economic groups in the population. Its political appeal, in other words, created
the identity of individuals in the movement. But Stedman Jones's literalism
leads him to deny the possibility that 'class' was part of the political identity that
was created. He rejects economic causality and class when, in fact, it would
have been more useful for his argument to acknowledge 'class' but locate its
origins in political rhetoric. Stedman Jones stops short of opening up a reconceptualization of Chartist history because he treats 'language' simply as a vehicle

for communicating ideas rather than as a system of meaning or a process of signification.

For Stedman Jones to achieve the radical promise of the theory he espouses, he would have to attend to certain aspects he ignores. These are, first, the notion that 'language' reveals entire systems of meaning or knowledge—not only ideas people have about particular issues but their representations and organizations of life and the world. To say, as Stedman Jones does, that Chartism was not a class movement because it sought participation in government is to miss the opportunity to see a larger politics at work, to see, that is, how an identity of class constructed (and contained) social practice, through which people established, interpreted, and acted on their place in relation to others. These relations to others—of subordination or dominance, equality or hierarchy—constituted social organization. The problem comes, in part, from using the word 'language' itself, for it somehow reduces the idea of meaning to instrumental utterances—words people say to one another—rather than conveying the idea of meaning as the patterns and relationships that constitute understanding or a 'cultural system'. Stedman Jones's confusion also stems from his use of 'class' as an objective category of social analysis, instead of as an identity historically and contextually created.

The second related aspect of this theory that Stedman Jones overlooks is the way meaning is constructed through differentiation. He assumes a kind of one-dimensional quality for 'language'—that words have a shared and stable definition in all contexts (a 'vocabulary') through which communication occurs. Yet the theorists by whom he is inspired (he cites Saussure) maintained that words acquired meaning by implicit or explicit contrasts established in specific contexts (or discourses). One cannot read Foucault (another presence—albeit implicit—in Stedman Jones's work) without understanding that meaning is multidimensional, established relationally, directed at more than one auditor, framed in an already existing (discursive) field, establishing new fields at the same time. Positive definitions depend on negatives, indeed imply their existence in order to rule them out. This kind of interdependence has ramifications well beyond literal definitions, for it involves other concepts, other relationships in any particular usage. (Thus, for example, seventeenth-century political theorists made analogies between marriage contracts and social contracts that affected how people understood both; and nineteenth-century socialists depicted capitalist exploitation of workers as prostitution, thereby intertwining economic and sexual spheres.) Meaning is developed relationally and differentially and so constitutes relationships. Thus, to apply this to Stedman Jones's subject, one would expect that the category of the working class rested not only on antitheses (capitalists, aristocrats) but on inclusions (wage-earners, the unrepresented) and exclusions (those who held no property in their labor, women and children). The universal category of class, like the universal category of worker, secured its universality through a series of oppositions. The goal of a reading of Chartism from this perspective, it seems to me, is not to reduce it neatly to a formal political struggle or a particular strategy offered by an organized group but to examine the process through which Chartist politics constructed class identity.

It is in analyzing the process of making meaning that gender becomes important. Concepts such as class are created through differentiation. Historically, gender has provided a way of articulating and naturalizing difference. If we look closely at the 'languages of class' of the nineteenth century we find they are built with, in terms of, references to sexual difference. In these references, sexual difference is invoked as a 'natural' phenomenon; as such it enjoys a privileged status, seemingly outside question or criticism. Those who do criticize it (and there were those who did) have a difficult time challenging its authority for they seem to be disputing nature instead of social construction. Gender becomes so implicated in concepts of class that there is no way to analyze one without the other. One cannot analyze politics separately from gender, sexuality, the family. These are not compartments of life but discursively related systems; 'language' makes possible the study of their interrelationships. As Chartists set forth their program they offered the terms of political collective identity. This identity rested on a set of differentiations—inclusions and exclusions, comparisons and contrasts—that relied on sexual difference for their meaning. Had Stedman Jones attended to the way meaning was constructed he would have seen *how* the particular category of class developed by this group relied on gender. By failing to attend to how meanings rest on differentiation he missed both class and gender in their specific manifestation in Chartism.

II

How might Stedman Jones have 'read' Chartism and better captured the process by which the working class was conceived? [. . .]

[. . .] Stedman Jones underestimates the importance and complexity of the definition of class that was elaborated by Chartists. For they did develop a notion of 'class'. In the material he cites, there is clearly evident a conception of the particular position, the identity, of 'working men' whether antagonistic to or in cooperation with masters, the middle classes, shopkeepers, or aristocrats. What is striking is how various orators grapple with the lines of distinction contrasting producers and idlers, laborers and profiteers, workers/middle classes/aristocrats, wage slaves and tyrants, honest democrats and usurious monopolists. The blame for inequality and injustice was placed, for the most part, on the government system, but there is no doubt that 'class' was being signified—developed as a way of organizing collective identity through an appeal to shared economic, political, and social 'experience'. The interesting questions to ask, it seems to me, are how all these contrasts created a place in social and political discourse for a working class identity, and what that vision was. [. . .]

Not only was the Chartist language setting out the terms of political coalition, but it worked to establish the similarity or comparability of different social groups. The point was to organize working men to demand entry into the political realm by insisting on a common denominator despite certain differences. That common denominator was property, albeit of different types. Chartists developed one aspect of Lockean theory that associated property with the enjoyment of individual political rights, by claiming that the fruit of one's labor or labor power was itself property.[1] As they did so they acknowledged another similarity to those already represented—the fact that all were men. The Chartist demand for universal manhood suffrage acknowledged (what was already in effect in franchise requirements) that only men concluded and entered the social contract; indeed, the identity Chartists claimed with those already represented was that all were male property holders.[2]

At the same time, Chartism used references to gender to position itself within debates of the popular movement and differentiated itself from certain of its threads, notably those that were expressive, associational, and religious. It did so by casting those utopian movements as 'feminine', itself as 'masculine'. (That the Utopians played with gender quite differently is surely significant in this conflict; they projected a future harmonious world in terms of the complementarity of the sexes or of androgyny, positively valuing both feminine and masculine principles.)[3] This gendered differentiation served not only to clarify Chartism's goals but to underscore its argument about the eligibility of workingmen for the vote.

Those who contest the notion that the working class (and sometimes, in this rhetoric, 'the people') was embodied in masculine form usually point to the fact that women participated in and supported the movement. This is undoubtedly true, but it does not contradict the argument. Rather, it confuses masculine/feminine with male/female; the former are a set of symbolic references, the latter physical persons, and though there is a relationship between them, they are not the same. Masculine/feminine serves to define abstract qualities and characteristics through an opposition perceived as natural: strong/weak, public/private, rational/expressive, material/spiritual are some examples of gender coding in Western culture since the Enlightenment. There is nothing in such usage to prevent individuals of either sex from accepting

---

[1] William Sewell, Jnr has shown a similar logic at work among French laborers in the same period. See his *Work and Revolution in France: The Language of Labor from the Old Regime to 1848* (Cambridge University Press, New York, 1980).

[2] The political theorist Carole Pateman argues that what was at stake in liberal theory and in concepts of fraternity was not only male property generally but men's (sexual) property in women's bodies. See *The Sexual Contract* (Polity Press, Cambridge, 1988).

[3] Barbara Taylor, *Eve and the New Jerusalem: Socialism and Feminism in the Nineteenth Century* (Pantheon, New York, 1983).

these definitions, nor from reinterpreting them to explain their own situations. That women supported a 'masculine' movement was not a contradiction, it was rather an affirmation of Chartism's particular interpretation.[1]

The gendered representation of class that Chartism offered, however, *was* a factor in the ways women participated in that movement and in the ways general programs and policies addressed them. And it probably contributed in the long run to firming up a concept of class that endured long after Chartism's decline. For one, no matter how much later struggles stressed the need for a reorganization of the economy and a redistribution of wealth, the invocation of universal human rights was carried on within the masculine construction of property and rationalist politics. One result of this was to push alternative conceptions of class such as those offered by utopian socialists to the periphery. Another effect was to render sexual difference itself invisible. Class, after all, was offered as a universal category even though it depended on a masculine construction. As a result, it was almost inevitable that men represented the working class. Women then had two possible representations. They were either a specific example of the general experience of class and then it was unnecessary to single them out for separate treatment; for they were assumed to be included in any discussion of the working class as a whole. Or, women were a troubling exception, asserting particular needs and interests detrimental to class politics, objecting to husbands using household money for union dues, demanding different kinds of strategies in strikes, insisting on continuing religious affiliations in an age of secular socialism. Both representations are evident in the history of labor movements and in the writing of their histories and they help us locate reasons for the invisibility of women in the making of the working class.

[*Gender and the Politics of History* (Princeton University Press, London, 1988), 53–4, 55–6, 56–7, 57–8, 58–61, 62–4.]

23   A People and a Class

The icons of popular art suggest the force and longevity of populist notions over this period. They also indicate that rather than a single populism, it is a variety or 'family' of populisms that should be considered, a variety in which the capacity for change and adaptation was marked. In the northern, industrial districts there was, however, a decided continuity amidst this variety and

---

[1] On women in Chartism, see Dorothy Thompson, 'Women and Nineteenth Century Radical Politics: A Lost Dimension', in Juliet Mitchell and Ann Oakley (eds.), *The Rights and Wrongs of Women* (Pelican, London, 1976), 112–38.

change. This was evident in a radical populism conceiving of the true England as the industrial north in struggle with Privilege. The conception of a 'family' of populisms was invoked in the first part of this book, on politics. There the roots of social identity were in important measure seen to lie in ideas and associations taken from politics, in particular the populist traditions of popular radicalism and the many tranformations these went through up to 1914. The controlling narrative of popular politics appears to have concerned a righteous and dispossessed 'people' rather than a 'working class'. The political sphere paralleled the sphere of art here: the idea of the true, unadorned England of the north was a variant of the broader mythology of the true political nation of the excluded English.

The excluded English could be seen as the labouring English, and in this sense 'class' appropriations occurred, even though this was in practice rather limited. It was in the sphere of work and the operations of the trade union that class became more decidedly evident, particularly in the sense of class taken in this book to have most theoretical and empirical utility: conceptions of social relations as turning centrally upon the relationship of labour and capital, of this relationship as tending to conflict, and of society as more exclusive than inclusive in character; all these were evident increasingly from the 1860s and 70s, though they developed most markedly in the early twentieth century, especially post-1914. The late and gradual 'making' of the English working class in this sense should be noted. This sense of class in the English regions was highly particularistic, in respect both of its rootedness in particular locales, and its view of capitalism and the nature of industry, the 'trade' and employers. These aspects meant that the view of class that developed could be perfectly compatible with 'populist' appeals of a political and social sort. Class in England was largely built up out of the often ill-fitting bricks of these distinctive local and regional experiences, in which the parochial and the sectional were often finely balanced with the catholic and the solidaristic. It is amply evident from the consideration of politics and work that rather different conceptions of the social order were evident in different spheres of people's lives.

The section on culture enabled a closer consideration of these conceptions, and suggested that populist views were probably dominant. The importance of territorial aspects of 'community', such as nation, region, town and neighbourhood, was pursued more systematically here, and in chapter 6 it became evident how conceptions of the social order were related to attempts to bring order and decency to the experience of poverty, insecurity and labour. This attempt was a matter of investing the everyday *milieu* of people's lives with symbolic significance. This process produced a multiplicity of outcomes, class being only one of the ways in which people patterned and gave meaning to the social order. The major tension in the culture of the labouring poor between fatalism and utopia became evident in this study of the semiology of the social order, but it was indeed present in all areas of popular life. In the chapter on

history a populist sense of the past was apparent, both in 'Protestant liberta-
rianism' and in the expression of 'liberal culture' that succeeded this—the view
of history as the unfolding of reason and progress. The close connection
between political and historical views is also apparent here, politics being one
expression of an historical sense widely disseminated in popular society. The
populist dimensions of ideas about language and culture were also marked and
these ideas were reproduced in popular life through the schoolroom and other
agencies of cultural dissemination. Language use itself expressed something of
the tensions evident in social conceptions, 'class' differences of a broad sort
emerging (between educated and uneducated, or rich and poor), yet language
was also the shared experience of different social levels in a broadly populist
way, particularly in the industrial north.

The family of populisms makes itself known through the representations of
popular art; the ballads showing a marked kinship with what was earlier
termed a 'classical' populism, and the music hall evincing both a 'liberal' and a
'conservative' populism. Given this variety, the search for what was earlier
called a dominant English popular tradition in these matters may be illusory.[1]
Nonetheless, and assuming from the evidence so far presented that the possibilities here concern the range of populist outlooks more than they concern
class, it seems to me that it is possible to identify what was earlier termed
radical populism as the dominant strain. The evidence of dialect literature in
particular points to this, and it does so in two senses of the word radical: the
more clear-cut sense of provincial England, indeed, northern Britain as well as
northern England as the seat of the crusade against privilege; and a more
diffuse sense apparent in terms of the notions of popular justice, equality and
fraternity tapped in the literature. This sense was exploited in other kinds of
popular art, but in the development in dialect of a populist discourse about
'ordinary people', 'folk', (especially 'decent folk'), one sees it taking its most
sustained and elaborate form. These senses of radical leave out of the account
the assumed, but usually unstated, radical political sympathies of so many
authors.

Dialect was obviously only one place where this radical populism was to be
found. It was there in religious notions, especially in notions of both the past
and the liberties of a Protestant people. Conceptions of religious identity were
often fused with conceptions of the English national past. It was of course in
politics itself that this sense was most developed, taking its most characteristic
form in radical Liberalism. Looking again at politics in the light of the subsequent parts of this book, it is evident just how significant were notions of
dispossession and exclusion in the broader popular culture beyond Liberalism,
notions taking explicit political form in the idea of lost rights and liberties. The
utopian impulse was also very widely evident, and with it the claim to the

---

[1] See Joyce, *Visions of the People*, 220.

restitution both of rights and of a commonality of human feeling, a legacy lost
with the waning of a golden age. In looking at politics one also becomes aware
that what was earlier called its 'controlling narrative' applied far beyond
politics alone. This narrative is one key to understanding what is here termed
a dominant English tradition of radical populism. Another is the concrete
experiences and feelings of those who embodied this tradition. The question of
narrative can be addressed first.

Perhaps, in line with the emphasis on discourse evident in this book, it is
better to talk of a 'master narrative' rather than of a 'master identity', though
it does in fact seem the case that the labouring poor of the industrial England
of the time interpreted this narrative in a remarkably uniform way, making out
of it what is here called a dominant tradition. In respect of narrative, the
work of American historians and scholars on the significance of such 'master
plots' or narratives in American history is very revealing.[1] Perhaps in the
English (and to some degree the British) case there was a single tale tying
together a diversity of representations. In the American case there was, and is,
the narrative of the Republic and its mission, a narrative closely tied to the
religious sense through the identification with Providence.[2] But it is variation
and conflict within bodies of national myth and narrative that also need
emphasis. In nineteenth-century America there developed a particular craft or
artisan appropriation of this central myth, the idea of the 'artisan Republic' as
it were, seen in the fusion of the emblems and political language of the
Republic with the social traditions and labour relations of the crafts.[3]

For the English case the notion of a master narrative is more difficult. So
indeed is that of a dominant popular tradition, especially when one bears in
mind the weight of fatalism and quiescence so often felt in the culture of the
labouring poor. Nonetheless, a story emerges. The subject of this is the destiny
of the nation, a destiny as in the American case often firmly tied to providential
religion. The appropriation of this subject concerned the 'true people' of
England, those who have been excluded from their birthright. England and
Providence became identified with the history, character and fate of 'the
people', and in many respects 'the people' itself becomes the subject of the
narrative, its travail forming the stuff of legend. The principal player in
the master plot became the subject of the drama, an excluded and virtuous
people doing battle in its pilgrim's progress against the forces of privilege,
faction, darkness and ignorance. 'The people' itself, as has been seen, could
variously be seen as 'the poor', 'the labouring poor', even 'the working classes'.
They might be the unenfranchised. But for the most part they were 'ordinary

[1] See the interesting discussion in M. Denning, *Mechanic Accents: Dime Novels and Working-Class Culture in America* (London, 1987), ch. 5, esp. pp. 72–4.
[2] S. Bercovitch, *The American Jeremiad* (Madison, Wis., 1978).
[3] S. Wilentz, *Chants Democratic: New York City and the Rise of the American Working Class* (London, 1984).

people' or 'decent folk', in short everyone who showed respect and was respected, but who were yet refused their proper place in the scheme of things.

This appropriation of a dominant myth, or myths, can be termed 'class'. This returns us to a sense of class noted in the introduction: in the words of Jameson, 'the dialogue of class struggle is (normally) one in which two opposed discourses fight it out within the general unity of a shared code'. In this sense of conflicting versions of the same body of narrative one can therefore see the 'making' of the English working class as this process of re-worked myth: utilisations of the myth of 'the English people' became the means by which a sense of common social identity developed. However, the same objections as were raised earlier still apply. The deployment of notions of 'the people' is indeed the means by which a common social identity was created, but when that identity seems, as in the English case, to have had more to do with broad terms of people at large than the narrow ones of class, then the value of applying the class label is open to doubt. The consciousness of *a class* need not, and has not, been the consciousness of *class*.

Of course, describing it as the consciousness of a class also has its own problems, not unlike those raised by the labelling of artisan traditions as class traditions in the American case. The marked heterogeneity of the social and economic condition of English workers in this period will be called to mind. And, even when looking at so decidedly a proletarian group as textile workers, and at the dialect literature that expressed so many of their concerns, we find that what seems at first glance to be the possession of a particular group could be pressed into service not only by many sorts of workers, but also by many who were not manual workers. Even more with other appropriations of 'the people'; the likes of shopkeepers, teachers, employers and so on would have defined themselves, and been accepted, as part of the people (not to mention people higher up the social scale who were often taken as part of the body of the people). Nor does it do to imagine that the terms in which groups are represented are ultimately redundant: the discourse of 'the people' did not express some higher 'class' identity or unity. It mattered in its own right. Language mattered in its own right. The notion of 'languages of class' carries great dangers.

Once these dangers are recognised, however, the idea that classes developed by inflecting shared discourses with their own meaning does have value. The problem is to decide on what their 'own meaning' amounts to: it still seems to me that for the term class to have much currency terms such as 'the people' must be understood in a way in which the attributes of manual labour have prominence. In short, there must be elements of my 'restricted' definition of class present. [. . .] it is to one embodiment of 'radical populism' that I shall next turn, that of the journalist Ian Jack's Scots father, a steam mechanic by trade, born not in the Victorian but in the Edwardian years. The example is not typical, but no individual ever is typical: Jack was a skilled man, a self-educated and politically articulate Edwardian Scot. Ian Jack's account of his father tells us a great deal about values that I have attempted to explore in this book, values that clearly had a northern British as well as an English aspect, and an influence that extended far into the present century. Ian Jack talks first about his own childhood;[1]

I suppose that what all this amounts to is a working-class childhood. I hesitate, not to fight shy of a cliché, but because I still can't be sure; whenever I read phrases such as a 'working class culture' or 'middle class values' I feel dizzy from sociological abstraction and the need to be steadied by a fact or two.

His father (a man who felt a kinship with Yorkshire's Wilfred Pickles!), he describes in the following terms:[2]

For all his socialist convictions, I don't think my father ever saw social division in purely political or economic terms. He would make ritual attacks on the big local landlords, the Earl of Elgin and the Marquis of Linlithgow, and on people who showed how they 'fancied themselves' by sending their children to piano and elocution lessons ('Aye, but do they have books in the house?'), but it was an older moral force which generated the most heat in him, and the class conflict as I most often heard it expressed was not so much between classes as internal to each of them: it was 'decent folk' versus the rest . . . A strict application of socialist theory would mean that our natural allies were the Davidsons (crash, thump; 'Where's ma fuckin' tea?') and that we would be bound to them for life. And bound not only to the Davidsons but also to another heart of darkness in our own family's past . . . the chaos and poverty which my father had caught the last whiff of as his family completed their trek through the volcanic industrialism of Victorian Scotland.

The embers of Calvinism, at heart a seemingly narrower philosophy, freed him from class-bound loyalty and gave him a much broader choice of the good and the bad. This is hindsight and may be no more than an over-elaboration of one of my father's favourite concluding statements, *There's good and bad everywhere* . . . And so I never heard my father use 'working class' or 'middle class' as terms of approval or disapproval. The categories were far too broad and he liked clearer targets. Throughout the Fifties he took steady aim at the nearest approach to a class enemy: Edinburgh Scotsmen . . . [who] 'did not get their hands dirty' and 'lived off the back of other folk' . . . My father said: 'They've sold their birthright for a mess of porridge'. Behind the joke lay a genuine grievance. Edinburgh Scotsmen did not *make anything*, other than their wills.

The elder Jack was a man who manifestly did make things and get his hands dirty. There is therefore present in this case that pride in manual labour which was so evident throughout the period of this book. [. . .] However, when the actual ways in which a class vocabulary was used are considered, one is constantly aware how behind the explicit terms of class stood larger and more powerful social identities. The examination of the use of class revealed for

---

[1] I. Jack, 'Finished with Engines', in *Before The Oil Ran Out: Britain 1977–86* (London, 1988), 32.

[2] Ibid. 33–4.

instance the importance of moral and occupational distinctions *within* groups at the time.[1] Seemingly socio-economic descriptions of the social order turned out to have basically moral meanings, as well as political use and meanings. Behind class were more potent distinctions such as Gladstone's crusade of the 'masses' against the 'classes', or of 'the people' against the ruling class, or the rich and the poor. Class was most often subsumed in these broader categories, a process deliberately engineered in what was earlier called 'the management of class'.[2] In much the same way labour was seen as one 'interest' among many, an element in the larger entities of society and of the nation. What was there to be 'managed' was in fact often a 'class' vocabulary that really had very little to do with class as we would understand it, betokening instead distinctions of morality or social status, and not carrying all the distinctions of sub- and super-ordination, of solidarity and struggle, and of the exaltation of manual labour alone which were later to accrue around class. As has been seen, even in its most aggressive form in early Victorian popular radicalism,[3] it was the universalist, socially inclusive meanings of class that were uppermost. This went together with a stigmatisation of class as a reprehensible, selfish denial of the interest of all people. It was only later, and then less perhaps in Britain than in Europe, that class came to have these more restrictive meanings.[4]

[*Visions of the People: Industrial England and the Question of Class, 1840–1914* (Cambridge University Press, 1991), 329–34, 334–5.]

DONALD REID

23 Rancière and the Worker

The Nights of Labor marks an initial summation of Rancière's intellectual career from his Althusserian youth through his Maoist years and the assertion of his own distinct voice in *Les Révoltes logiques*. In settling accounts with Althusser in the early 1970s, Rancière developed a critique of Marx's understanding of the working class. In the second half of the decade he pursued this project with respect to the images of the working class presented by both the labor movement and labor historians. Workers were valorized most, he argued, when they fitted a norm; their 'difference' made them suspect. Rancière rooted these images of the working class in past defeats within the labor movement and a contemporary self-doubt among radical intellectuals. In the years following the collapse of *gauchisme*, these intellectuals had sought a certainty in the working-class 'other'. This fostered 'the honest concern to preserve the autonomy

---

[1] See Joyce, *Visions of the People*, 57.
[2] Ibid. ch. 3.   [3] Ibid. ch. 2.   [4] Ibid. 139–40.

of working-class struggle, popular culture, and plebeian wisdom from our own uncertainties and illusions' (p. 14).

Yet, Rancière argued, there was a danger in simply ratifying a knowledge of what constituted the working class which had itself been created by workers disappointed with the moral and political failings of fellow workers and deceived in their own aspirations for another kind of life. Whether studying *L'Atelier*, syndicalists in Vichy, or workers' culture in the Third Republic, Rancière came to the same conclusion. 'The troublesome thing was that this worker discourse never functioned so well as when it was doing so in the logic of others or for their profit.'[1]

This paradox brought Rancière back to his critique of the process of representation whose doubling always hid a repressed difference. He described his enterprise in *The Nights of Labor* as 'an order of discourse that marks the nonconciliation, the difference from itself, of social "objects" '.[2] Faced with images of the worker as militant, *sublime*, or embodiment of a culture, Rancière declared, 'We are not going to scratch images to bring truth to the surface; we are going to shove them aside so that other figures may come together and decompose there' (p. 10). Such a project marked a settling of accounts with the *gauchistes*' preoccupation with their status as intellectuals (as well as the labor history tradition Thompson incarnated). 'I took the inverse of the great *gauchiste* theme: the relations of intellectual labor and manual labor. It is not a question here of reeducating intellectuals, but on the contrary of the irruption of negativity, of thought, in the social category always defined by the positivity of its "making" '.[3]

Rancière conceives of texts not as passive objects to be deciphered and categorized, but as active, constantly posing questions to the would-be interpreter. In the interpreter's quest for a working-class essence, the voices in which workers speak of their existence and aspirations are distorted, amplified, censored, and pushed aside to confirm 'the already known'. Rancière asks historians, 'What exactly is the meaning of this evasion that tends to disqualify the verbiage of every proffered message in favor of the mute eloquence of one who is not heard?' (p. 11). Yet once historians engage with this 'verbiage', they can never declare the truth revealed, the working class represented.

Rancière's method in *The Nights of Labor* shares a common strategy with the deconstructionist technique of locating points in the text that reveal contradictions engendered by the suppression of 'writing'. Rancière latches on to the 'interruptions' and 'suspensions' of working life that occur when workers try

---

[1] Rancière, 'Le Prolétaire et son double ou le philosophe inconnu', *Les Révoltes logiques* 13 (Winter, 1980–1), 6.

[2] 'Jacques Rancière', in *Entretiens avec 'Le Monde', 1: Philosophie*, ed. Christian Delacampagne (La Découverte, Paris, 1984), 165.

[3] François Ewald, 'Qu'est-ce que la classe ouvrière?', *Magazine Littéraire*, 175 (July–Aug. 1981), 64, 65.

to appropriate for themselves the power reserved for the 'other'. The element that has traditionally dominated the text—'speech' for deconstructionists; in this case the proletarian as laborer—is deconstructed to reveal the repressed 'writing', or the proletarian as thinker. The seeming conformity of workers' lives to sociological constructs gives way under a deconstructionist reading of 'interruptions' in these lives. Rancière endows neither literary nor sociological evidence with primacy. Both are unstable texts to be deconstructed; each serves as a context for rather than a reflection of the other.

Each of the three parts of *The Nights of Labor* problematizes a relationship in the conceptualization of the working class: work to the worker; the worker-*militant* to the worker; class consciousness to the worker. In Part I, Rancière reiterates his rejection of efforts to represent the working class in terms of socio-economic criteria or of a complex of gestures and actions. He describes the workers of July Monarchy Paris less in terms of sheer physical exploitation or membership in a corporate community, than as caught up in the perpetual anxiety of fighting to get and keep jobs characterized by moral degradation and mental tedium as much as corporeal hardship. It is not perhaps the working conditions per se that threaten workers with brutishness, but the never-ending need to ferret out the means to assure their sustenance. Categorization by skill, *corporation*, or workshop organization obscures the complicated, shifting world of subcontracting and de-skilling.

What defines the personnages of my book as proletarians is not their identification with a job, nor their popular roots; it is the aleatory character of a situation daily put into question, the illusory or transitory character of apparently prestigious qualifications and trades. The condition described today as that of the unstable worker [*travailleur précaire*] is perhaps the fundamental reality of the proletariat. And the modes of existence of workers in 1830 are quite close to those of our temporary workers.[1]

The central figure of Part I is the joiner/floor-layer Gabriel Gauny, who decided to make this precariousness a source of liberation—to conquer the tyranny of the animalistic need to consume through his 'cenobitic economy'. Gauny took from his experience with bourgeois Saint-Simonians not the project of making work the basis of a new moral order, but the desire to live the contradiction of a manual laborer who philosophizes.[2] Yet Gauny is more than the inversion of the GP *établi*. He is also Rancière's alter ego, the individual who can visit the prison-panopticon and see beyond Foucault's carcereal world to the lesson that work well done can lead to tyranny. It is Gauny who is able, in however incoherent, iconoclastic, and unsustainable a fashion, to preach not the rational reordering of this world, but 'the revelation of a different world and the initiation of a new kind of relationship between beings' (p. 116).

[1] *Nights of Labor*, 64–5.
[2] Rancière has assembled and edited a collection of Gauny's writings: *Le Philosophe plébéien* (La Découverte/Maspero, Paris, 1983).

Rancière works backward in *The Nights of Labor* from reflections on Gauny to reconsideration in Part II of his earlier work on the interaction of radical intellectuals and workers, itself the decisive event in Gauny's life. In the 1830s, tailors and typographers had formulated the demand to be treated as 'men', not because they were highly skilled, were in short supply, or possessed a developed, insular corporate idiom. On the contrary, they had little to protect from other workers and their trades brought them into frequent relations with the bourgeois and their language of liberty and equality. In fact it was not insularity, but contact with elements in the dominant culture that suggested to workers the possibility of a break in their seemingly preordained working lives.

No one needs to tell workers that they are exploited; this they already know. What is news to workers is the idea that they may be destined for something other than exploitation. Workers got from encounters with the 'other' not a particular doctrine, but the hint of another world, of a reason to revolt other than egotism and materialism. Such meetings of bourgeois and workers, far from anecdotal, are of central importance in the history of 'the working class':

[Workers seek] to appropriate for themselves the night of those who can stay awake, the language of those who do not have to beg, and the image of those who do not need to be flattered. . . . We must examine the mixed scene in which some workers, with the complicity of intellectuals who have gone out to meet them and perhaps wish to expropriate their role, replay and shift the old myth about who has the right to speak for others by trying their hand at words and theories from on high. (pp. 22–3)

Worker recruits and their new Saint-Simonian friends talked past one another. Each concentrated on possibilities inherent in the others' material situation while ignoring their interlocutors' dreams. Some workers saw the Saint-Simonians as a source of work; the most committed were entranced by the opportunities to philosophize—to do 'unuseful labor'—in a community of love that the Saint-Simonian students, freed from the necessity of manual labor, could inspire. They were attracted to Saint-Simonianism by the glimpse of a new world, not the improvement of their own.

The privileged Saint-Simonian youths created an image of the worker drawn from their own belief in the positive nature of work, and some—distant forerunners of GP *établis*?—even set out to live a life of manual labor. They were disappointed by workers' rejection of their efforts to organize them into an army of labor. Equally important for Rancière are the disappointed worker recruits. 'For these Saint-Simonian missionaries whom it is convenient to picture as students "in service to the people" [the Maoist credo], were in fact workers or former workers whose whole tragedy was to be sent by their apostolate toward these egotistical workers they had fled in making themselves Saint-Simonians.'[1]

---

[1] Rancière, 'Le Prolétaire et son double', 8.

The 'tragedy' of individuals who had seen another world and become forever different from and disenchanted with the untouched masses sets the stage for Part III of *The Nights of Labor*. In this section Rancière discusses the Christian Socialists of *L'Atelier* and their debates with other worker groups, the cooperatives founded with the assistance of the Second Republic after the June Days in 1848, and Icarian communities in the United States during the second half of the century. These movements sought to confirm as the essence of the working class a morality built upon labor and to guard this working class against bourgeois contamination (including the oneiric perversions and materialist fantasies instilled by Saint-Simonians and Fourierists). *L'Atelier*'s plans for association and the Communists' efforts to build Icaria were at once calls for liberation and repressive discourses of order. These ideologies of labor and the projects they inspired were characterized by irresolvable conflicts in which the virtues of sacrifice and solidarity were found to be one with the 'other's' vices of egotism and materialism. The workers' movement was born of a contradiction: 'The very same word, *emancipation*, is used to denote the advancement of the individual worker who sets up on his own and the deliverance of the oppressed proletariat' (p. 32).

Whether in Paris or in Icaria, workers refused to live up to the class mission conferred on them; they were perpetually false. This resulting deception and disappointment became enshrined in the idea of the working class that forever beckons to workers with enticing messages of rebellion and pride, discipline and order. The logic of representation is such that the 'representatives' of the workers would always be different from the workers themselves and would develop representations of workers that repressed this difference. 'The ruse of reason led dreaming workers on the true paths of the future, those of disciplines—and dictatorships—of king work.'[1]

Yet *The Night of Labor* is not a pessimistic book; Rancière's analysis admits of no such conclusiveness. He leaves the reader with a look at letters written in 1890 by an aging worker-*militante* to the Fourierist intellectual who had been her lover, in which she tells him that she has never forgotten her introduction a half-century earlier to the possibility of living another life. The politics of *The Nights of Labor* is thus not an 'allegory of despair,' Rancière explains, 'but on the contrary an invincible resoluteness to maintain, in a life devoted to the constraints of the *demande prolétarienne* and to the hazards of political repression, the initial non-consent; at once the death of utopia and the refusal of the real'.[2]

['Introduction' to Jacques Rancière, *The Nights of Labor: The Workers' Dream in Nineteenth-Century France*, trans. John Drury (Temple Press, Philadelphia), xxxi–xxxv.]

[1] 'Jacques Rancière', 165.   [2] Ibid.

What relationship is there between the Sunday extravagances of these 'arti-sans' and 'petty bourgeois' men on the one hand, and the solid realities of exploitation and class struggle on the other? As with every vertigo and every Sunday, it is one of everything and nothing. Monday they will begin again the monotony of work or the vagrancy of unemployment. The world remains unchanged when the young seamstress leaves the Saint-Simonian preaching session, to which she had gone 'to find a bit of droll amusement' and from which she returned 'filled with admiration and astonishment for the grandeur of the ideas and the unselfishness of the apostles'.[1] Nothing has changed, but nothing will ever be the same as before, either. Fifty years later, when many of the apostles will have forgotten or disavowed it, our seamstress and our joiner will still proudly bear the marks of the bite. For it is in the moments when the real world wavers and seems to reel into mere appearance, more than in the slow accumulation of day-to-day experiences, that it becomes possible to form a judgment about the world.

That is why those other worlds, which supposedly anesthetize the sufferings of the workers, can actually be the thing that sharpens their awareness of such sufferings. That is why those metaphysical problems, said to be good for bishops who find their supper ready and waiting for them, are even more essential for those who set out every morning to find the work on which their evening meal will depend. Who is better suited than those who hire out their bodies day after day to give meaning to dissertations on the distinction be-tween body and soul, time and eternity, or on the origin of humanity and its destiny? Asks L'Atelier: 'Can one explore any issue whatever without going back to first causes?'[2] Like the sham passions of poetry, the hinterworlds of metaphysics are simultaneously the supreme luxury and the supreme necessity for the common laborers. Despite his farewell to Dante, Gauny the joiner explains to a ragpicker friend of his the necessity of another world, be it the chimera of believers or that of poets, for the struggle here:

Plunge into terrible readings. That will awaken passions in your wretched existence, and the laborer needs them to stand tall in the face of that which is ready to devour him. So, from the *Imitation* to *Lélia*, explore the enigma of the mysterious and formidable chagrin at work in those with sublime concepts.[3]

So the initial relationship must be reversed. It is the secret of others that the worker needs to define the meaning of his own life and struggle. Not the

[1] Désirée Véret to Enfantin, 11 Sept. 1831, Fonds Enfantin, Bibliothèque de l'Arsenal, MS 7608.
[2] 'La Revue synthétique contre L'Atelier', *L'Atelier*, (June 1843), 88.
[3] Gauny to Ponty, 12 May 1842, Fonds Gauny, MS 168.

'secret of the commodity'—isn't every bit of that as clear as day? It is not day but night that is involved here, not the property of others but their 'chagrin', their invented sorrow that contains all real sorrows. It is not knowledge of exploitation that the worker needs in order 'to stand tall in the face of that which is ready to devour him'. What he lacks and needs is a knowledge of self that reveals to him a being dedicated to something else besides exploitation, a revelation of self that comes circuitously by way of the secret of others: that is, those intellectuals and bourgeois people with whom they will later say, and we in turn will repeat, they want to have nothing to do—and especially not with any distinction between the good ones and the bad ones.

But how can we not be struck by the gratitude shown for the love offered by the Saint-Simonian preachers, by the interest shown in the plans of all those who assured them that they had found the remedy for the ills of society in general and the poor classes in particular, by the love lavished on the great poets and popular novelists? The world of the bourgeoisie, like that of the worker, divides in two. There are those who live a vegetative existence, the rich people so persistently depicted as stretched out indolently on their sofas or feather beds, responding only to the fragrance of their own interests and incapable of experiencing the passions of those whose lives entail love, suffering, risk, and dedication. The image may not embody anger over their laziness so much as contempt for such an animal existence. But there are also those others who desert the domestic cult of Baal to set out in search of the unknown: the inventors, the poets, the lovers of the people and the Republic, the organizers of the cities of the future, and the apostles of new religions. The worker needs all of these people, not to gain scientific or scholarly knowledge of his condition, but to entertain and maintain his passions and desires for another world. Otherwise the constraints of labor will level them down to the mere instinct for survival and subsistence, turning the worker brutalized by work and sleep into the servant and accomplice of the rich people bloated with egotism and idleness.

Thus, between the smith and his image, between the image that recalls him to his place and the image that invites him to revolt, we get a slight twist: unexpected meetings and fleeting conversations between our marginal workers who want to learn the secret of noble passions and the marginal intellectuals who want to minister to the sorrows of labor. They are difficult meetings resembling the ones granted by our somber joiner Gauny to the blond preacher who calls himself Moses and dreams of new labors in Egypt: 'I am not master of my time, so I cannot go to your place tomorrow. But if you happen to be at Exchange Square between 2:00 and 2:30, we shall see each other as do the wretched shades on the margins of hell.'[1]

[*The Nights of Labor: The Workers' Dream in Nineteenth-Century France*, trans. John Drury (Temple Press, Philadelphia, 1989), 19–21.]

---

[1]   Gauny to Retouret, 12 Oct. 1833, Fonds Gauny, MS 165.

In labor studies, by comparison, a broad and complacent materialist perspective dominates the field. There have been challenges—for example, Gareth Stedman Jones's and Joan Scott's mutually hostile arguments for the primacy of language over class in the determination of labor politics or Jacques Rancière's attempts to deconstruct the myth of the artisan—but Stedman Jones, Scott, and Rancière have so far recruited few followers among labor historians, who have tended to dismiss them for lapsing into 'mere' intellectual history.[1] I believe labor history is destined to suffer from continuing intellectual doldrums unless its largely unexamined materialist common sense is more widely and vigorously contested. It would, of course, be chimerical to imagine that labor studies could, in the present situation, spawn a theoretical debate as intense and multiformed as that occurring in contemporary feminist studies. Yet the politics and the political economy of labor in the contemporary world hardly seem conducive to theoretical complacency. We are living through massive and fundamental changes in the nature, location, and meaning of work and in the fortunes of labor movements and socialist ideologies all over the globe. The world of work conjured up by labor history's materialist common sense—the production of heavy manufactured goods by unionized male laborers in large factories—is in rapid decline in the advanced capitalist democracies. The most rapidly expanding forms of work and categories of workers in advanced capitalism tend to fall through the cracks of standard labor history—clerical and service work, information, consulting, flexible specialization, design, homework, and the like, much of it performed by un-unionized women. Current developments in the world of work actually stand as an implicit theoretical challenge to labor history.

This essay does not offer concrete suggestions about new topics of empirical research that might more effectively address this challenge. Instead, it takes up the complementary and equally pressing task of theoretical critique and reformulation.

---

[1] Gareth Stedman Jones, *Languages of Class: Studies in English Working Class History, 1832–1982* (Cambridge, 1983); Joan Wallach Scott, 'On Gender, Language, and Working-Class History', in *Gender and the Politics of History* (New York, 1988), 53–67; Jacques Rancière, 'The Myth of the Artisan: Critique of a Category of Social History', *International Labor and Working-Class History*, 24 (1983), 1–16, and *La Nuit des prolétaires* (Paris, 1981). See also Donald Reid's discussion of Rancière in 'The Night of the Proletarians: Deconstruction and Social History', *Radical History Review*, 28–30 (1984), 444–63. The majority reaction of labor historians to such work is perhaps exemplified by the published comments on the Scott article by Brian Palmer and Christine Stansell, *International Labor and Working-Class History*, 31 (1987), 14–23 and 24–9, respectively. The initial version of Scott's article was published in *International Labor and Working-Class History*, 31 (1987), 1–13.

Theory and Rhetoric

What we usually call theory may be thought of as containing two complementary but distinguishable dimensions: the logical and the rhetorical. The logical task of theory is to elaborate and specify logical relations between theoretical propositions. The rhetorical task, on which I will concentrate in this essay, is to provide the figurative and linguistic frameworks or paradigms by means of which we select research problems and evaluate the relevance, appropriateness, or completeness of researchers' truth-claims.[1] I would argue that most labor historians base their judgments on an implicit or explicit reductive materialist rhetorical paradigm. What this means in practice is that those features of the historical situation regarded as material are assumed to have greater causal power than features regarded as cultural or political or ideological. In my experience, labor historians are too easily satisfied by explanations that identify a material cause—say, declining control over the process of production—but are highly skeptical about explanations that identify cultural causes—say, shifts in political or religious discourse—no matter how well-documented or tightly argued the cultural explanation may be. The normal response of labor historians to cultural explanations is to argue that the supposed cultural cause is less important than some alternative material cause or that the proposed cultural cause is itself the effect of 'deeper-lying' material factors. In this way the rhetorical common sense of labor history privileges material over cultural or political or ideological phenomena.

The extraordinary role played by the concept of proletarianization in recent labor history exemplifies the operation of this materialist common sense. Proletarianization, a preeminently material phenomenon, has tended to become a kind of omnibus, all-purpose causal force in labor history, at least for the nineteenth century. The term *proletarianization* actually combines under a single aegis a number of empirically distinct processes that have occurred in Europe and North America since the late eighteenth century: the movement of populations from agriculture to industry, the separation of producers from ownership of the means of production, a decline of producers' control over work processes, and the making obsolete of producers' skills. At least the first three of these processes underwent a global progression over the course of the nineteenth century. (The fourth, deskilling, had a more ambiguous history, since both deskilling and *re*skilling go on constantly and simultaneously in any society undergoing technological change. Labor historians have typically emphasized the deskilling and ignored the reskilling.)

The problem, as I see it, is that labor historians have tended to combine all these diverse processes under a single covering term, tending to see any

---

[1] See e.g. John S. Nelson, Allan Megill, and Donald N. McCloskey (eds.), *The Rhetoric of the Human Sciences: Language and Argument in Scholarship and Public Affairs* (Madison, Wis., 1987); and Donald N. McCloskey, *The Rhetoric of Economics* (Madison, Wis., 1985).

example of, say, declining control of production or deskilling as evidence that the underlying master process of proletarianization is at work. A few well-documented examples of deskilling or declining control in a trade or a class are thus taken as evidence that the trade or the class as a whole is experiencing the underlying process and, consequently, that workers' actions, such as strikes, insurrections, or political movements, can be explained as responses to proletarianization. Labor historians' materialist predilections, I would argue, have made them willing to accept proletarianization as a sort of universally valid material explanation. As a consequence, they have paid insufficient attention to the profoundly uneven and contradictory character of changes in production relations, not to mention the role of discourse and politics in labor history.[1]

My goal in this essay is not to criticize the concept of proletarianization but to contest the materialist rhetorical common sense on which it depends. I do so in two steps. First, I attempt a historical deconstruction of the idea that the economy is material. My object will be to demonstrate not only that the equation of the economy with the material is arbitrary and misleading but that the genealogy of this idea is suspicious as well. Second, I attempt to provide a more appropriate figuration of the object of labor history, and of social history in general, than that offered by the reductive materialist model. I do so by pushing to their logical conclusions tendencies already present in contemporary labor studies—and in the contemporary human sciences more generally.

Is the Economy Material?

The founding metaphor of the materialist paradigm is the notion that the economy is material. On close examination, however, the idea that economic life is particularly or uniformly material is quite arbitrary. Much of what goes on in the sphere of production and exchange looks awfully ideal or cultural or symbolic to me.[2] Let me offer a few examples.

We should start from the top with money. In ordinary speech the *material* is more or less equated with *money-making*. Yet money is nothing if not a symbol system—and a very complicated symbol system at that. Money is not useful in itself but is only a conventional sign of value that is used to trade for commodities. As labor specialists from Karl Marx to William Reddy have argued,

---

[1] As correctives to the homogenizing history of *proletarianization*, I would suggest Raphael Samuel, 'Workshop of the World: Steam Power and Hand Technology in Mid-Victorian Britain', *History Workshop*, 3 (1977), 6–72; Charles Sabel and Jonathan Zeitlin, 'Historical Alternatives to Mass Production: Politics, Markets, and Technology in Nineteenth-Century Industrialization', *Past and Present*, 108 (1985), 133–74; and William H. Sewell, 'Uneven Development, the Autonomy of Politics, and the Dockworkers of Nineteenth-Century Marseille', *American Historical Review*, 93 (1988), 604–37.

[2] For a particularly illuminating argument on this line, see Marshall Sahlins, *Culture and Practical Reason* (Chicago, 1976), esp. ch. 4, entitled 'La Pensée Bourgeoise', 166–204.

the fact that exchange relations are mediated by money commonly deludes people into thinking that such relations are free rather than coerced.[1] Like any symbol, in other words, money is defined by its relation to other symbols and has the power to fix the meanings, to shape the possible interpretations, of human action. Money, a symbol if ever there was one, stands at the center of and designates the very boundaries of that sphere of life that we designate as material in capitalist society.

A second aspect of economic activity that is hard to characterize as material is, of course, advertising. Since the late nineteenth century, a higher and higher proportion of the work and investment of capitalist firms has gone into advertising, that is, into symbolic representations of commodities to potential consumers. Advertising is the production of pictorial, musical, and verbal images for billboards, magazines, radio, television, and other media. These images are designed to incite potential consumers to desire specific symbolically marked commodities—to desire not bread or fountain pens but Wonder Bread and Parker pens. Moreover, the symbolic definition of commodities is not restricted to their packaging or their mediated imaging; it is also embodied in their production. Industrial designers must make sure that a Mont Blanc fountain pen is distinguishable in its actual material form from a Parker fountain pen, or a Braun electric coffee pot from a Mister Coffee. Armies of designers and advertisers, employed by major corporations and specialized agencies, engage in sculpting metal and plastic, composing tunes, and crafting evocative word sequences or photographic images. The actual work they do is not distinguishable in kind from the lofty creative activities of artists. But their activities are economic and are therefore assigned to the material sphere, while the empirically indistinguishable activities of painters, sculptors, musicians, or poets are not.

It might be objected that the seemingly immaterial aspects of economic life discussed thus far—money and advertising—concern only the circulation or exchange of commodities, not their production. In fact, the ideal or the symbolic also intrudes into production itself. The complex of machines that makes up an assembly line is not just a series of material objects but the result of an elaborately thought-out design—one that is developed on sketch-pads and blueprints, or nowadays on computers, long before it assumes a material form in the factory. Moreover, much production work is only ambiguously material. In contemporary production, workers may not actually manipulate the goods they are manufacturing; instead, they may program computerized tools and monitor their performance by means of computer-generated signals. The productivity of machines is not simply a function of their design and scientific efficiency; it also depends fundamentally on the knowledge and the morale of

---

[1] William M. Reddy, *Money and Liberty in Europe: A Critique of Historical Understanding* (Cambridge, 1987).

the labor force. Quality circles, in which workers develop means of improving the quality or efficiency of production through intensive discursive inter-change, may have contributed more to the superiority of Japanese consumer goods than has any purely mechanical technique.[1] Nor is the intrusion of the ideal into production a peculiarity of very recent and highly technologized means of producing goods. Before the introduction of assembly lines, as David Montgomery (a materialist if ever there was one) reminds us, the manager's brains were 'under the workman's cap'; it was the workers' skill and organiza-tional know-how that made possible the sustained and effective production of high-quality goods.[2] To step back even further, guild apprentices were to be taught 'the mysteries of the trade', the secret skills and formulas and the finesse and taste that would assure their ability to maintain the guild's reputation for quality and style. Aesthetic, symbolic, and organizational knowledge—all of which could be classified 'ideal' as easily as 'material'—have always been part and parcel of the production process.

When economic life is looked at closely, it turns out that a lot of what goes on in production and exchange ought to be classified as nonmaterial, according to conventional standards. Like activities that go on in other spheres—say, government, learning, religion, or warfare—production and exchange entail a complex mixture of what we would usually call the ideal and the material. The closer we look, the clearer it becomes that labeling economic activities 'materi-al' and distinguishing them from 'nonmaterial' spheres is utterly arbitrary.

A Historical Deconstruction of the 'Materiality' of the Economy

Where did the bizarre notion that production and exchange were uniquely material come from? The answer, I think, is highly paradoxical. It derives from traditional European Christian and aristocratic metaphysics, which were sub-sequently stood on their head by the Enlightenment.

The notion of a distinct material realm comes from the Christian division of the cosmos into two radically different substances: spirit, which was lofty, orderly, and powerful; and matter, which was base, disorderly, and inert. The hierarchy of spirit and matter was also used metaphorically to make distinc-tions between different categories or orders of human beings. Although all premodern European countries had analogous distinctions, we might as well take the case of Old Regime France, where the population was divided into three estates. The clergy was, of course, the First Estate because its activities—spiritual affairs—were the loftiest. The nobles were the Second Estate because

---

[1] Robert E. Cole, *Strategies for Learning: Small-Group Activities in American, Japanese, and Swedish Industry* (Berkeley, Calif., 1989); Paul Lillrank and Noriaki Kano, *Continuous Improve-ment: Quality Control Circles in Japanese Industry* (Ann Arbor, Mich., 1989).

[2] David Montgomery, *Workers' Control in America: Studies in the History of Work, Technology, and Labor Struggles* (Cambridge, 1979), 9.

they magnanimously sacrificed their lives in defense of the realm. The Third Estate, by contrast, was vile and ignoble, soiled by its labor and its base pursuit of worldly material goods. So the clichés went. On close inspection, however, it is hard to see why the actual activities of commoners should be thought of as more material than those of nobles. The nobles normally spent their time either making war or practicing for it—riding horses, handling weapons, and developing their physical prowess through exercise. Peasants' activities were quite analogous—leading teams of oxen, handling plows, axes, and pitchforks, and pursuing an endless round of physical labor. Instead of the producers of goods being classified as base because their activity was uniquely material, the production of goods was classified as material because those who produced them were regarded as base. The characterization of production and exchange as material was thus logically arbitrary. It had nothing to do with the factual extent to which the different orders' or estates' activities involved the physical manipulation of material things. Rather, the designation of production and exchange as material was a metaphor; it resulted from an effort to align the hierarchies of social status in medieval and early modern Europe with contemporary cosmological theories.

The Enlightenment challenged both the cosmology and the assumptions about social status. The Enlightenment was inspired, of course, by the astonishing advances made in natural philosophy in the seventeenth century. The discoveries of Newton and others had demonstrated that the world of matter, far from being gross and disorderly, was ordered by sublime and invariant natural laws. Simultaneously, the realm of spirit, at least as manifested in the various versions of the Christian religion, had proved in the seventeenth century to be an endless source of tumult, warfare, slaughter, and discord. Enlightenment thinkers therefore eschewed theological disputation and attempted to apply the methods of science—or, more exactly, its rhetoric—to the study of human society.

The philosophy of the Enlightenment was, broadly speaking, materialist. This materialism was manifested, for example, in Montesquieu's climatic determinism or in Lockean epistemology, which held that the mind was furnished with ideas by sense impressions taken directly from the material world. In this intellectual climate, the conventional metaphorical operation that coded production and exchange as material represented an inviting opportunity, one that was seized by the economic thinkers of the Enlightenment, both the French Physiocrats and the Scottish moralists. If production and exchange were material, they should be governed by invariant laws analogous to those that governed physical matter. Over the course of the eighteenth century the economists duly discovered such laws. It is highly significant that the first coherent school of economic thinkers actually dubbed themselves the Physiocrats. The title 'physiocracy', which of course means 'the rule of the physical', makes clear the overall thrust of the economists' project: to find the essential ordering principles of human life in the material sphere of production and exchange, the very sphere that had for so long been disdained by philosophers, theologians, and rulers as vile and lowly. That the activities they saw as determining the wealth, power, and happiness of nations could be characterized as material or physical, and therefore as analogous to the physical nature studied by the natural philosophers, subtly but powerfully fortified their claim to have discovered a genuine science of human government. The early economists, in other words, took over intact the traditional equation of production and exchange with the material, but they inverted the traditional valuation of the material, which for them implied order and reason rather than vileness and turpitude.

Both the materialist bias of the Enlightenment and the conventional coding of production and exchange as material were carried over into the nineteenth century by the political economists, and they were appropriated by Marx in his famous attempt to turn Hegel's idealism on its head. Since Marx, they have saturated the discourse of the left and have become the unquestioned conventions of labor history. Notice the irony, however: Marxists proudly proclaim their radicalism by employing an arbitrary identification of the economic as material, never realizing that they have inherited this idea intact and uncriticized from traditional Christian and aristocratic discourse. Would-be friends of the proletariat hence believe they are being progressive when they denounce as 'idealists' historians who actually take seriously what past proletarians thought. The claim that the economy is uniquely 'material' always was arbitrary, misleading, and tendentious; that it continues to be clung to by purportedly leftist scholars is an embarrassing anachronism.

['Towards a Post-Materialist Rhetoric for Labor History', in Lenard R. Barlanstein (ed.), *Rethinking Labor History: Essays on Class and Discourse Analysis* (Illinois University Press, Urbana, 1993), 16–23.]

PART D

The History of the Social